IMAGES
of America

DYER

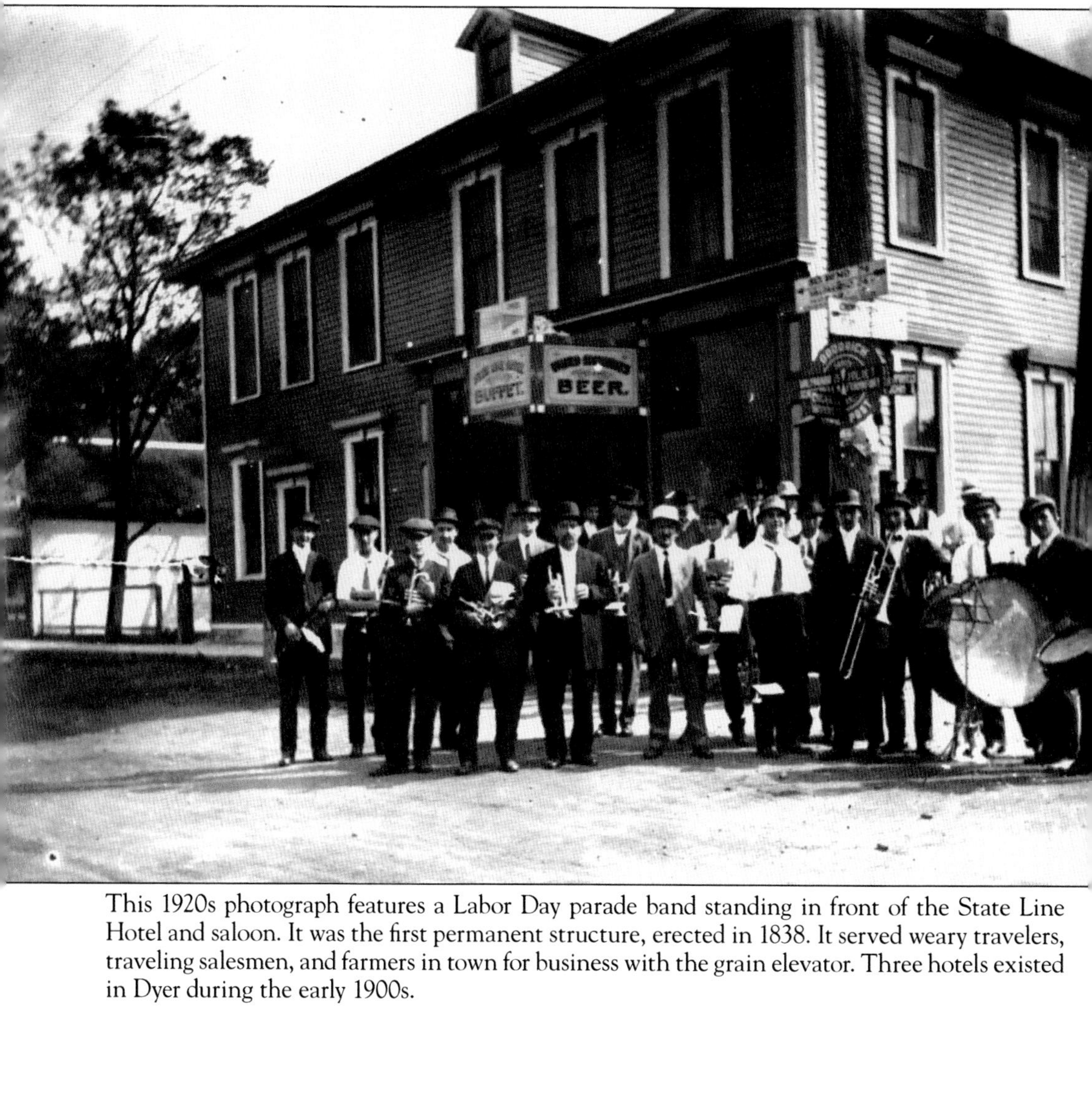

This 1920s photograph features a Labor Day parade band standing in front of the State Line Hotel and saloon. It was the first permanent structure, erected in 1838. It served weary travelers, traveling salesmen, and farmers in town for business with the grain elevator. Three hotels existed in Dyer during the early 1900s.

On the cover: Druggist Mike Burson and his wife Jean pose in the Burson Drug Store once located on the Lincoln Highway in Dyer. Mike was also known for his hobby, performing aerial feats. Often he would entertain people by parachuting from planes. This photograph was taken in the early 1930s. (Courtesy of the Dyer Historical Society.)

IMAGES
of America

DYER

Paul Anthony Benninghoff

ARCADIA
PUBLISHING

ISBN 978-0-7385-7738-8

Published by Arcadia Publishing
Charleston SC, Chicago IL, Portsmouth NH, San Francisco CA

Printed in the United States of America

Library of Congress Control Number: 2009933636

For all general information contact Arcadia Publishing at:
Telephone 843-853-2070
Fax 843-853-0044
E-mail sales@arcadiapublishing.com
For customer service and orders:
Toll-Free 1-888-313-2665

Visit us on the Internet at www.arcadiapublishing.com

To the people of Dyer: past, present, and future.

Contents

ACKNOWLEDGMENTS

First and foremost I would like to thank the Dyer Historical Society for approaching me and asking me to write this book on Dyer. The process of research and writing has been such a great experience. I have learned so much about the history of my hometown and my family. It brought about a better understanding of why I am who I am.

Of course I would like to thank my mother and father. Without them I wouldn't be the person I am today. I have my mother's kindness and compassion. I have my father's work ethic and his strength. Through both of them I have gained wisdom in knowing and doing the right thing, especially when it is unpopular with the majority.

Many thanks go to my family, immediate and extended. I would not have fared as well without their love and support. Truly there is strength in numbers.

There will always be a special place in my heart for my friends. They are another great source of love and support. Each and every one came into my life right when I needed them most. They give so much and ask so little in return. I am very blessed. Thank you.

A big thank-you goes to my best friend Sophia. She saw great things lying dormant within me, woke up the sleeping giant, and challenged it to grow. Many personal milestones have been met and passed because of her love and encouragement.

I would also like to thank my editor Anna Wilson, at Arcadia Publishing, for she was a fantastic help and a great source of positive energy. Her guidance is greatly appreciated.

Finally I would like to thank you, the reader, for choosing this book. I am glad to have you to share my passion of Dyer's history with. Best wishes to one and all!

All images appear courtesy of the Dyer Historical Society (DHS).

Foreword

I was born in Dyer, in 1973, in the midst of change. The town was mostly farmland, partly subdivisions. Dyer was a small community in the shadow of a big city, and the city was reaching out to us. The rural areas were being converted into suburbia. I grew up in the small town. I played in the farmer's fields. I knew my neighbors. The world at large seemed far away (about two miles away, but for a young child that is a distance incomprehensible).

Today, Dyer is a suburb of Chicago. The child I was would not recognize the town as it is today. Most of the old buildings, structures, and farmlands have been removed to accommodate urban sprawl. We once planted crops here. Now we build houses, gas stations, and retail centers. I am in disbelief that the changes Dyer has gone through and that I have witnessed within my lifetime happened in such a short amount of time. Some may argue that 30-odd years is not a short amount of time, but then why did those years go by so fast?

I grew up knowing only tidbits of Dyer's history. I knew that there were Native Americans in the location at one time. My family and I used to search the freshly plowed fields looking for arrowheads. Some of us were lucky to find a few. I knew that the Lucky Dragon restaurant was once an old hotel. I knew that there was a grain elevator, although I was not sure what a grain elevator was or why it seemed so important for my parents to mention it every time we passed the location where it once stood. I also knew that Kahler Middle School was once the St. John Township High School. What I did not know was how this history involved me. They were just stories from a different time.

When I got older, I learned more and more pieces of Dyer history. Soon they would string together like pearls on a necklace, and things started making sense. My family from my mother's side resided in Dyer. Distant relatives, whether by blood or by marriage, lived the history. They were, in fact, some of the ones who made the history. They were instrumental in Dyer becoming a town. Some were farmers, some business owners—my grandfather was a fire chief. People I passed and said hello to in town were in some way affiliated with my family tree, branched off long ago and now sprouting their own fruits and leaves.

When I became a member of the Dyer Historical Society, I was amazed at how much of Dyer's history had been preserved. I found such interesting information in what would seem to be unlikely places. One time I came across a ledger. It was from the 1970s, a sign-in book for the Dyer Volunteer Fire Department. It recorded who was there, when, and why. As I glanced through the pages, names very familiar to me grabbed my attention. Here an uncle, there a cousin. Then I spotted my father's name. He was a fireman when I was young, so seeing his name did not surprise me. He was there to do some maintenance work. What was amazing was that through reading about this moment scribbled in a ledger it was as if I was right there with him, looking over his shoulder, long before I was born. It was a very private and intimate moment for me to be a silent witness to what seemed like a mundane moment for him in his life. That was when I learned a very special lesson. History does not have to change the world to be important. It only needs to change you. I found a greater appreciation in and of history than I have ever known that day. I also realized the importance of these small, local historical societies. They are the guardians of personal history, each and every day history, family history, and the history of the individual.

Today, the majority of Dyer residents seem to have a history of their own. They come from other, distant places with their own stories. They are likely to be unaware that their home here in Dyer sits on some farmland from long ago. They may not be aware that Route 30 was once an old Native American trail and an ideal section of the American highway system. They may not even be aware that this town was once the site of the Lake Michigan shoreline, full of sand dunes and swamplands. There is so much history here. To those who are open to it, I would like to share.

This book comes at a perfect time. The year 2010 is Dyer's centennial. It is a wonderful tribute to the people who made Dyer what it is. This book also comes with a purpose. As stated before, many of the Dyer populace today came from other places. They do not know the town's history. I would like to share our history and heritage with them in hopes of bringing us all together, and make them aware that they too are now a part of that history.

I take pride in Dyer's history, for I am a part of it, and it is a part of me. Those who have come and made their homes here are a part of it, too. We are a community. We make history together. Each and every day, we contribute something whether we are aware of it or not. Moments turn into memories. Memories turn into stories that get passed down from one generation to the next. Stories get collected and written down in a book, much like this one.

To take an interest in history is to show an appreciation toward those who made it. Your world has a history, your country, your state, your town, your family. You have a history. Your history contributes to your family history. Your family history contributes to its community and your community to its state, country, and world history. It is all tied together. We are all tied together somewhere in our histories.

I hope you enjoy this book, appreciate it for what it is and what it means. Look at the faces of the people in the photographs, learn their names. Many are gone now, but we can all keep them alive in our memories, stories, and books. Maybe, one day, your image will be found bound in a book and people one hundred years from now will know your name. You never know if or when the future is looking over your shoulder.

Paul Anthony Benninghoff
President of the Dyer Historical Society

INTRODUCTION

Have you ever thought about what history is?

There is more to history than just names and dates, ancient civilizations and dead presidents, or long, drawn-out wars interrupted by brief periods of peace. The history in textbooks is only a small fraction of recorded history, and recorded history is only a small fraction of history, the majority being untold. Each and every one of us has a history, which in turn is part of a whole. Like the many stone bricks in the Great Wall of China, our histories are a collection that constructs a larger sculpture. But, unlike the Great Wall of China, history is not fixed to one spot. It shifts and changes as time goes on. Histories of the past shape histories of the future and present history shapes how we perceive the histories of the past. Don't believe me? Take one of your old history books and compare it to a text from today and see how much history has changed.

To fully understand an event in history one must know what preceded it, what lead up to said event. But then we must understand the leading events and what had caused them. So how far back must we go to truly understand the history that has shaped our world? The answer: Much further than man can recount. Indeed, much further than man's own history on earth. This is where the history of Dyer begins.

We need to go back about 545 million years to what is called the Cambrian period. This is the start of a long process that shapes the landscape. A small, shallow sea once resided where Dyer stands today. What life existed had perished, lined the floor, and over time produced a limestone bedding. About 510 to 445 million years ago, during the Ordovician period, plant life began to emerge. Although Dyer would still be under water at this time, it was not until after the Devonian period, approximately 410 to 356 million years ago, when fish began to populate the earth and the planet saw its first trees and forests. The sea would retreat and expose the land underneath. The significance of this is the limestone, for it will play a part when we see the ice ages come and go.

Chances are we will not be finding any traces of dinosaurs in the town of Dyer. Due to the ice ages, wind, and rain, any remains would have been erased. Any dinosaurs that did inhabit the area would have existed during the Jurassic, Cretaceous, and Triassic periods. What have been found are remains of the inhabitants that lived here during the last ice ages, which will be discussed later on.

The northern hemisphere has seen up to if not more than four ice ages. Known as the Nebraskan, Kansan, Illinoisan, and Wisconsin, these ice ages consisted of multiple glacier advancements and retreats. There were from 11 to 18 glacial advancements in the last ice age alone. The last advancements of the Wisconsin ice age are known as the Crown Point and Glenwood phases that started about 15,000 to 12,200 years ago and lasted nearly 2,400 years. Along its edge it left long curved hills and ridges called the Valparaiso Moraine.

Remember the limestone bedding mentioned before? Well, as the glaciers melted, this limestone acted like a great basin, which held the water and formed the Great Lakes. Dyer resides at what once was the southernmost shore of Lake Michigan.

Not only did the glaciers leave behind a large lake, they left much of the land under swamp and marsh. This was the time of large mammals. The American mastodon, Jefferson's mammoth, Harlan's musk ox, the saber toothed tiger, and the giant beaver roamed the area. Soon after came an invasion from the north. The Native Americans traveled from the far western continent of Asia over a land bridge at what is now the Bering Strait and started settling the Americas. It was about 10,000 years ago that they began settling the lands in and around Dyer.

To travel through this marshy and swamp-filled land, one had to take the high road in order to keep their feet dry. This is exactly what the natives did, leaving behind trails along ridges that banked the old Lake Michigan. Ridge Road in Munster, just north of Dyer, is one such location. On another highland ridge is an old Native American foot path called Sauk Trail, which cuts through Dyer where Route 30 now runs. It is speculated that deer or buffalo started this trail during migration. The tribes followed in pursuit of the game. The Sauk Trail begins in Peru, Illinois, near the Illinois River, enters Indiana at Dyer, and continues on to Valparaiso where it cuts north through LaPorte and goes all the way to Detroit, Michigan.

The first Europeans to travel this area of the country were the French explorers and fur traders. Fr. Jacques Marquette and Louis Joliet came through the Calumet region in 1673–1674 and encountered the Miami, Potawatomi, and fellow Frenchmen taking advantage of the rich wildlife that thrived in the area. The Europeans and Native Americans lived together peacefully, coexisting and trading with one another. The French who came to the area hunted and trapped, and when they had their fill left the area. The Native Americans did not see them as a threat and accepted the temporary intrusions.

All this came to a change after the French and Indian War, which had taken place from 1754 to 1763. From then until the War of 1812, the Chicago-Calumet region had been under British rule; however, the Spanish did invade for a time in 1781. They made their way up the Illinois River, cut across the Sauk Trail to Fort St. Joseph and took it over, only to retreat back to St. Louis shortly after. During this time the European-Americans came to establish a living, moving in without the intention of moving out. Now the lands and game were being taken from the Native Americans and friction began. The natives of the region sided with the British during the War of 1812, choosing the "lesser of the two evils."

The Chicago-Calumet region became part of the expanding United States after the war with the British and their Native American allies. Fort Dearborn was erected in Chicago in the year 1830 to control and protect the newly acquired land. This also marks the decade Dyer appears on the map of history. White settlers first made their homes in the area of northwest Indiana in 1834, one of which was Solon Robinson, who helped establish Lake County, Indiana. In 1838, the first permanent structure, a hotel and tavern, was built along the Sauk Trail where Dyer is today. The year 1873 marks the occasion when the Potawatomi, under Chief Pokagan, traveled the Sauk Trail for the very last time, visiting their burial grounds near Lake Station.

One

Dyer Residents and Families

Many of Dyer's first residents were German Catholic immigrants. They spoke Hoecherwelsch, a mix of low and high German. Those who spoke low German (Plotz Deutch) came from the northwestern part of Germany, near the Hanover area. Those who spoke high German (Hoech Deutch) were from the eastern part of Germany near Berlin.

These immigrants lived as farmers in the area. Some, however, chose professions such as carpenter, miller, saloonkeeper, shoemaker, doctor, and mason. Some of the families that resided in or around Dyer at this time were the Schallers, Overhages, Davises, Stommels, Beirigers, Keilmans, Gettlers, Hoffmans, Seidlers, Jaegers, Dubuerils, Kiesels, Mangolds, Kleins, Margrafs, Peschels, Scheidts, Nondorfs, Berenses, Millers, Hilbrichs, and Austgens. Today, one may find many of their descendants still living in Dyer.

The genealogy of these families is a complex, intertwining web. Many of the first families in Dyer are related by blood or by marriage. The following images are of the industrious people who plowed the fields, harvested the crops, built and ran the businesses, constructed the first churches and schools, incorporated Dyer as a town, and contributed to the town's identity and rich history.

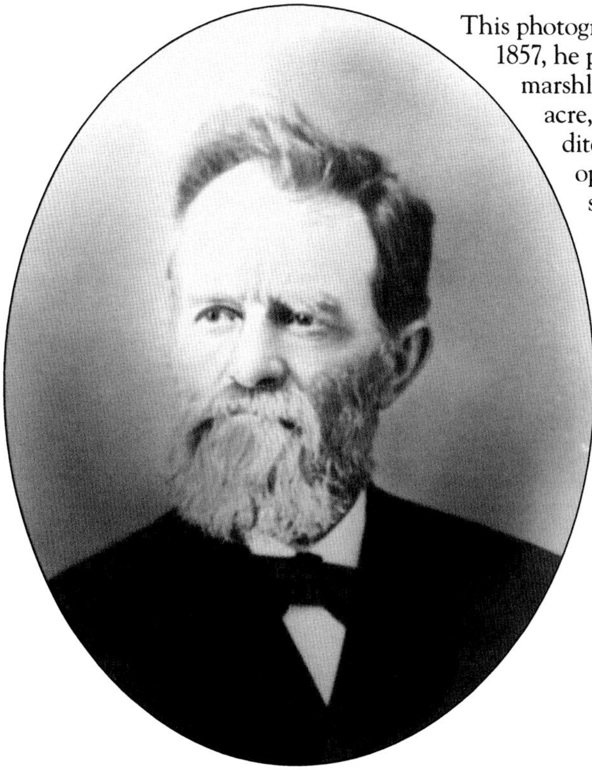

This photograph features Aaron Norton Hart. In 1857, he purchased 17,000 acres of swamp and marshlands, costing from 75¢ to $1.50 an acre, and drained it by digging a system of ditches and widening Plum Creek. This operation left the lands rich with fertile soil. This attracted many farmers to the area that became known as Dyer.

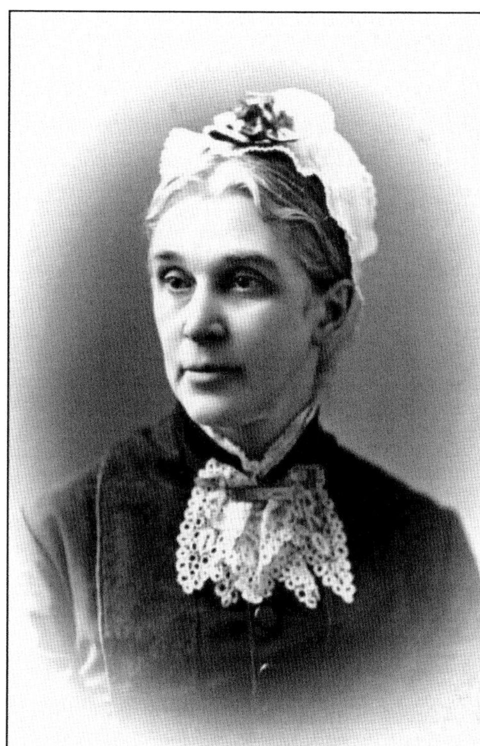

Martha Reed (Dyer) Hart was born in New Bedford, Massachusetts, on February 11, 1824. She and Aaron Hart were married on April 25, 1844. Aaron and Martha had four children, Flora Norton, James West, Milton Rhodes, and Malcolm. The family owned a home in town and on their farm in Hartsdale, located in the northeast section of Dyer.

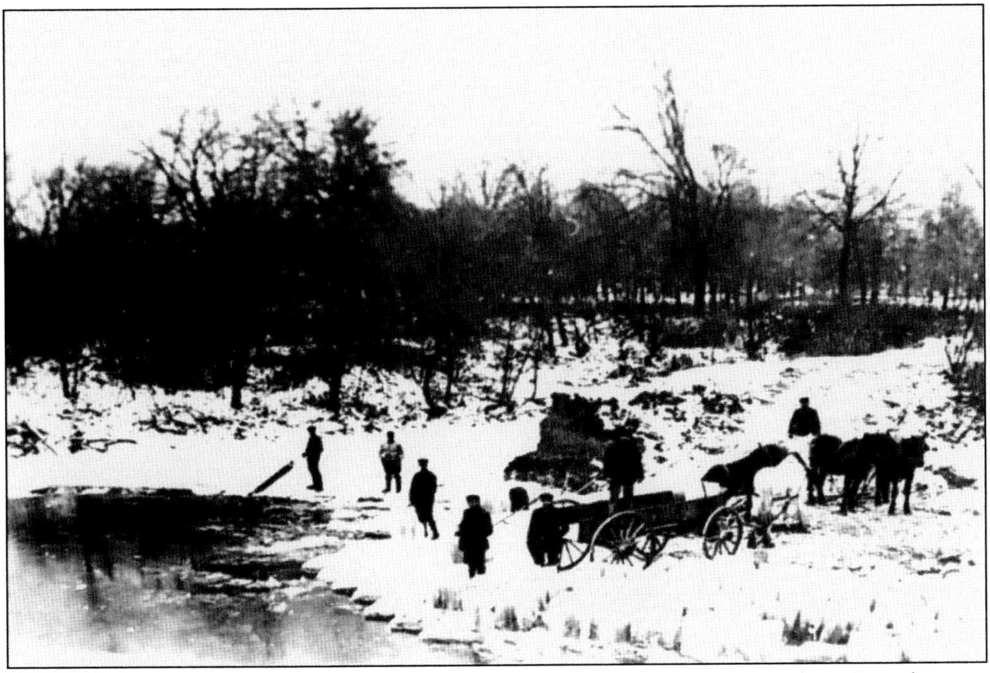

Pictured is an ice harvest on Plum Creek. The creek played an important role in Dyer history. Not only was it a source of water for cooking, cleaning, and drinking, but a water source for putting out fires, ice harvesting, and a main system for draining the swamp and marshlands.

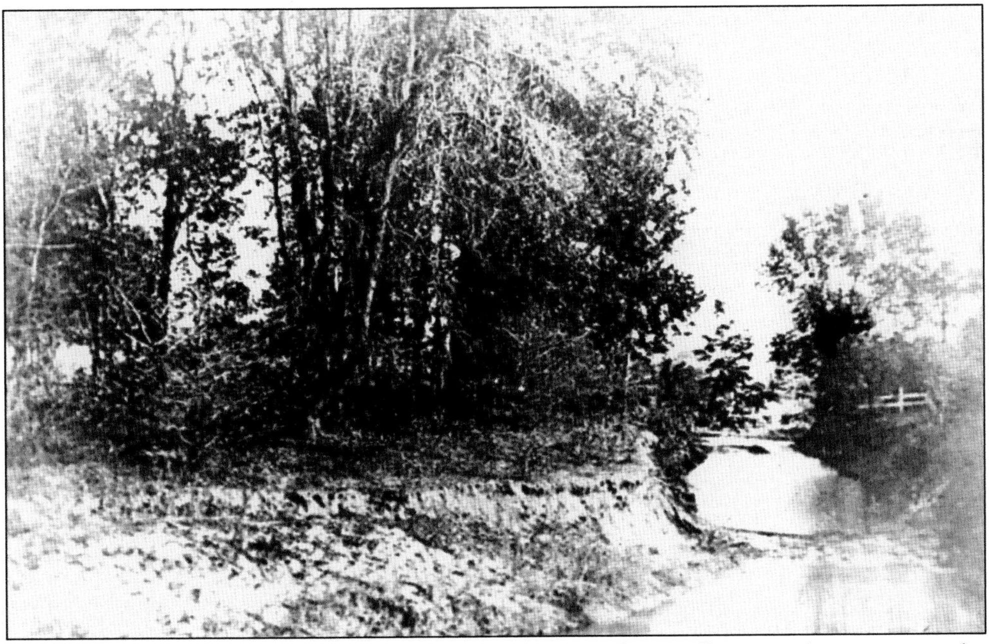

Plum Creek, also known as Hart's Ditch, originates in Goodenow, Illinois, and empties into the Little Calumet River in Munster. It was Aaron Hart's efforts at widening the creek and creating other ditch systems that drained the area of the wetlands, exposing good farming soil. This photograph was taken in 1883.

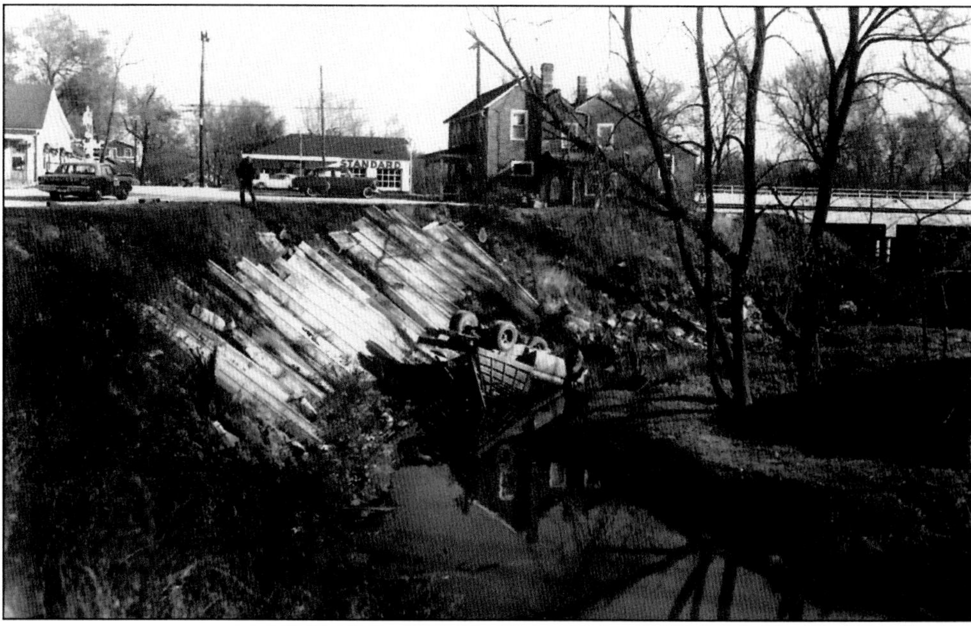

Here is another image of Plum Creek, also known as Hart's Ditch. The Lincoln Highway crosses this section just east of the Dyer business district. The drainage system runs north, emptying into the Little Calumet River in Munster. From there the water flows west into the Calumet River and east to Lake Michigan.

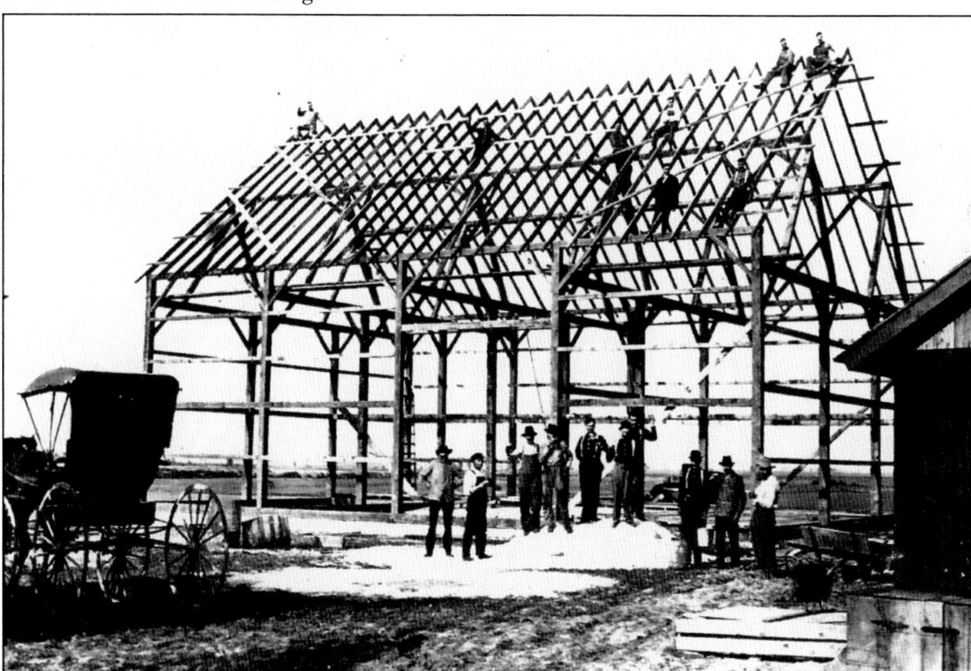

This picture features men from the community building a barn in Dyer during the early 1900s. Farming was very good in Dyer because of its fertile soil that was left behind after Aaron Hart drained the land of the standing water. Until the construction of the grain elevator in Dyer, farmers had to take their harvest by wagon to Chicago for shipping.

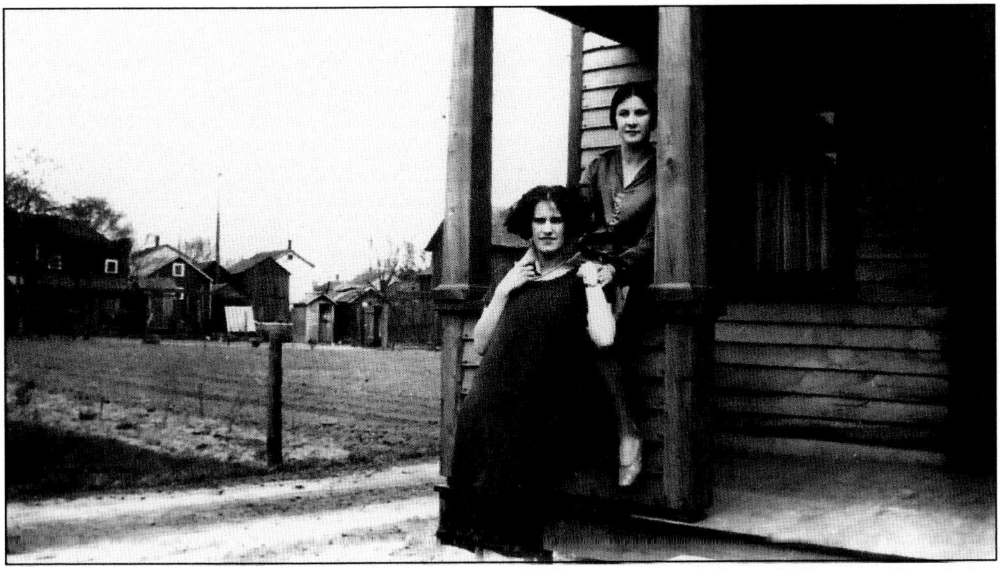

Pictured here in the early 1900s are friends Sis Keilman, lower left, and Florence Dumbsky. Friendships grew large in a small community. In Dyer, a small farming town, everyone knew everybody. A stranger stopping by a tavern or restaurant as they traveled through town stuck out. It was a close-knit community.

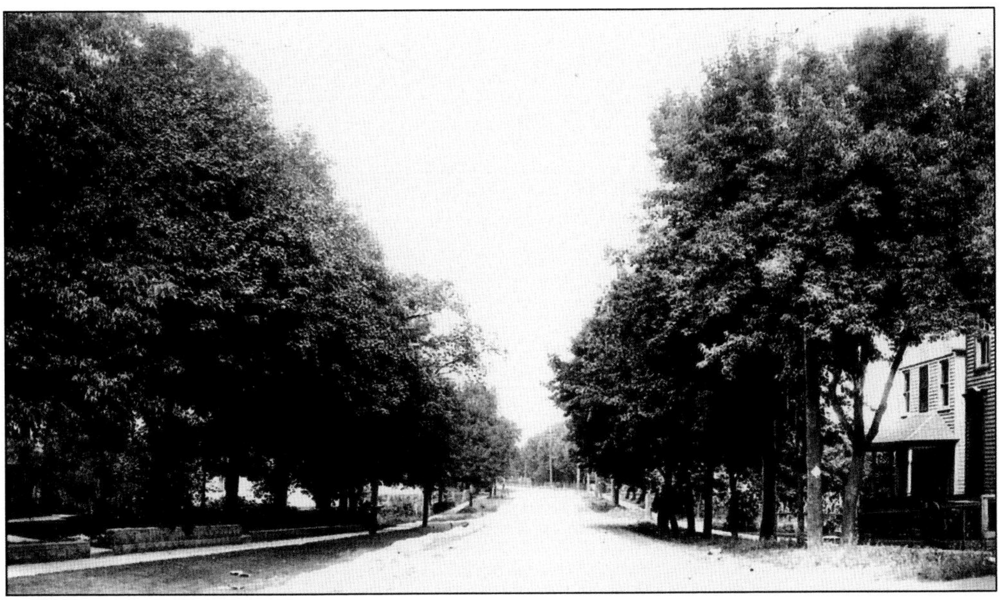

Pictured in this *c.* 1900 photograph is an old residential section of Dyer. Few homes were near the business section of town. Most residents were farmers who lived on their land in the outlying regions of Dyer. Houses were few, but the families were big.

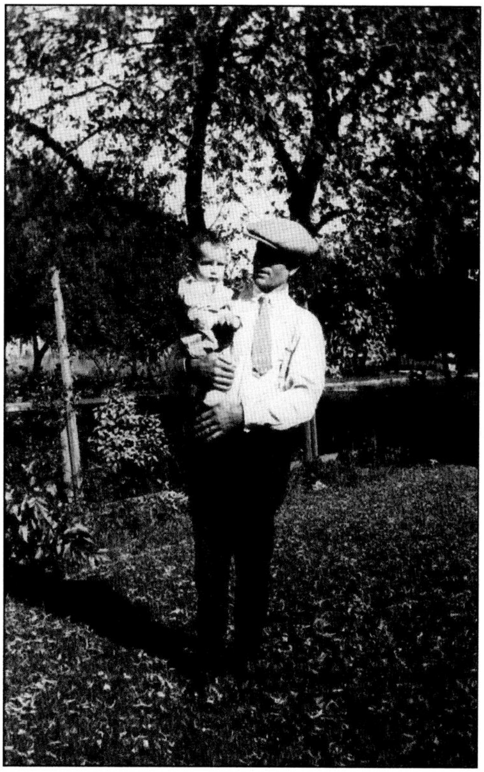

Nick Austgen purchased a tin shop from the Peschel family. Austgen turned it into a harness shop in 1902 and renamed it the N. G. Austgen Hardware and Harness store. This business was located on Hart Street, just south of the Lincoln Highway. Pictured is Austgen holding his son Donald.

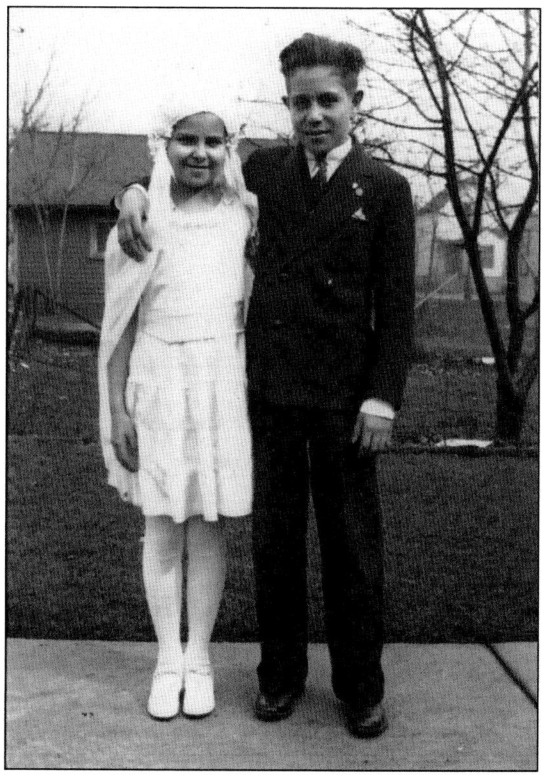

In this photograph Don and his sister Lee Austgen pose for Lee's first communion. Don and Lee were the children of Nick, proprietor of the N. G. Austgen Harness and Hardware store. Many of Dyer's citizens were parishioners of St. Joseph and received their sacraments through the church.

John Berens was well known for decorating a large tree in his yard for Christmas. After his death in 1967 the John Berens Memorial Award was instituted for holiday decorations, which then became the Citizen of the Year award. One of Dyer's first planned subdivisions was built on property purchased from John Berens.

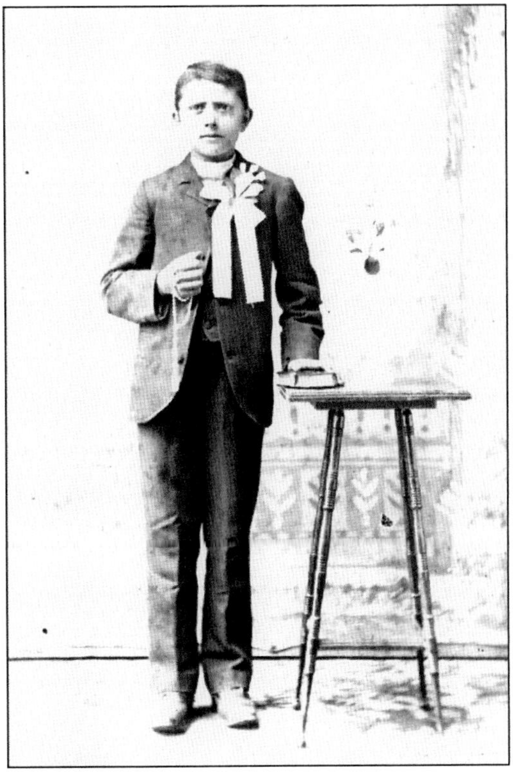

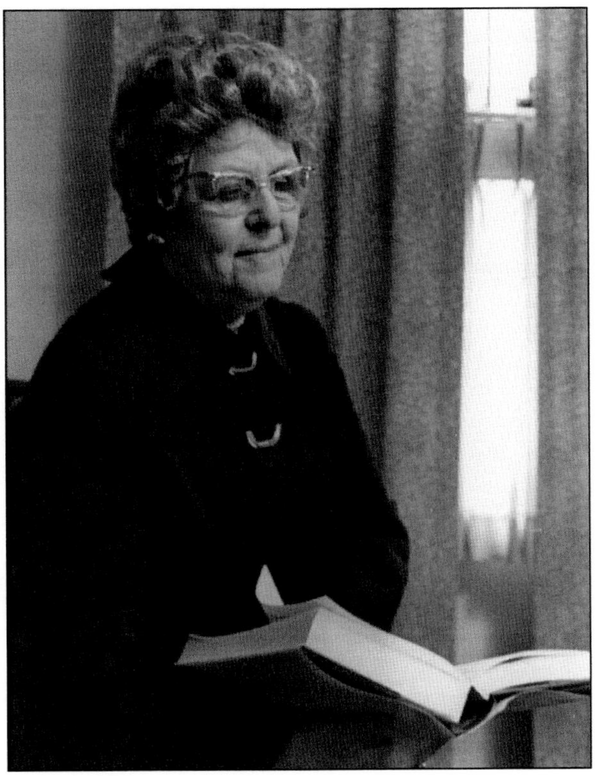

Gwendolyn Boyer, a prominent figure in the town of Dyer, has achieved much in her lifetime. She was the director of the Dyer Public Library, secretary of the Dyer Chamber of Commerce from 1957 to 1958, and was named poet laureate of Indiana in 1957.

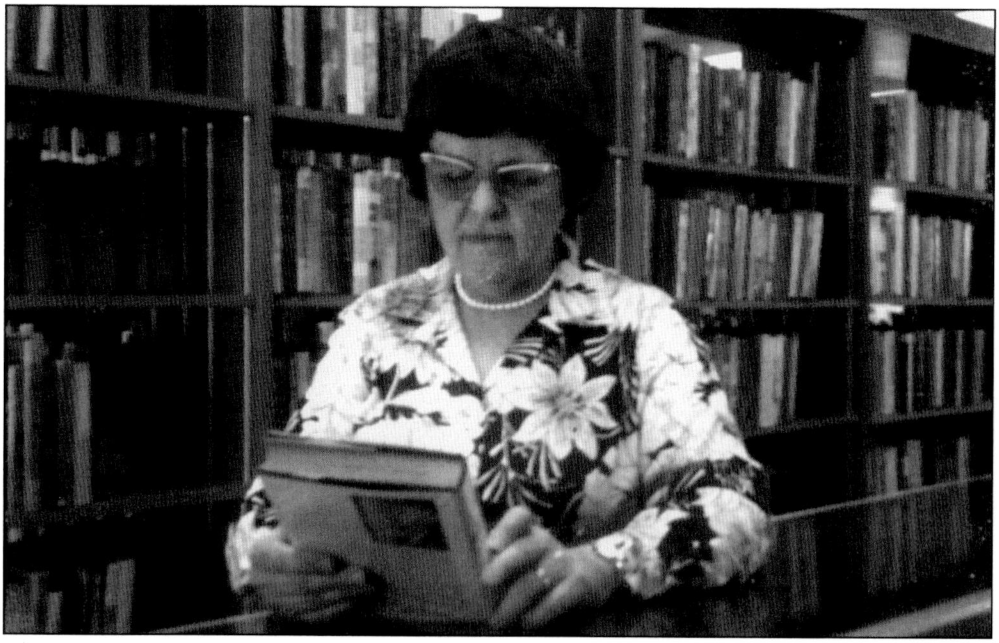

This picture, taken on June 27, 1969, features Gwen Boyer. In addition to being the town librarian and a member of the Dyer Chamber of Commerce, she was also very active in other ways. She assisted the Salvation Army and the American Cancer Society, and was a member of the Lake County Poetry Club.

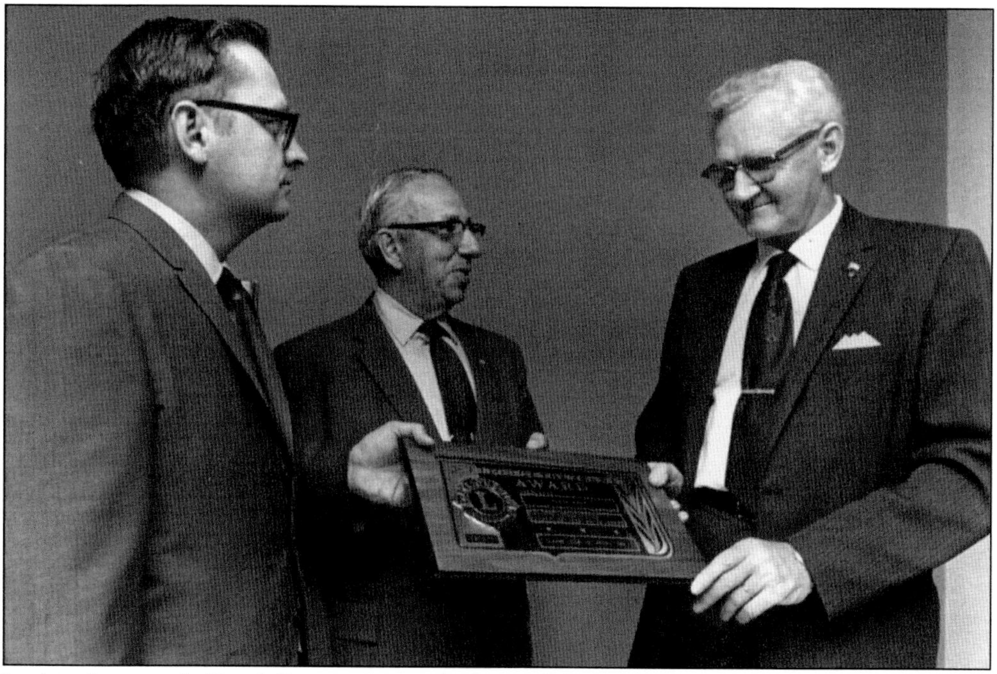

In this photograph, Frank Boyer receives the Lion of the Year Award for 1970–1971. Appearing from left to right are William Demaree, A. E. Peschel, and Frank Boyer. The Dyer Lion's Club was chartered on October 10, 1943, and continues to this day as a charitable organization in the Dyer community.

In this photograph, Frank and Gwendolyn Boyer celebrate their 25th wedding anniversary in December 1946. Both were very dedicated to their community. Frank was an avid member of the Dyer Lions Club. Gwendolyn was the director of the Dyer Public Library and the secretary of the Dyer Chamber of Commerce.

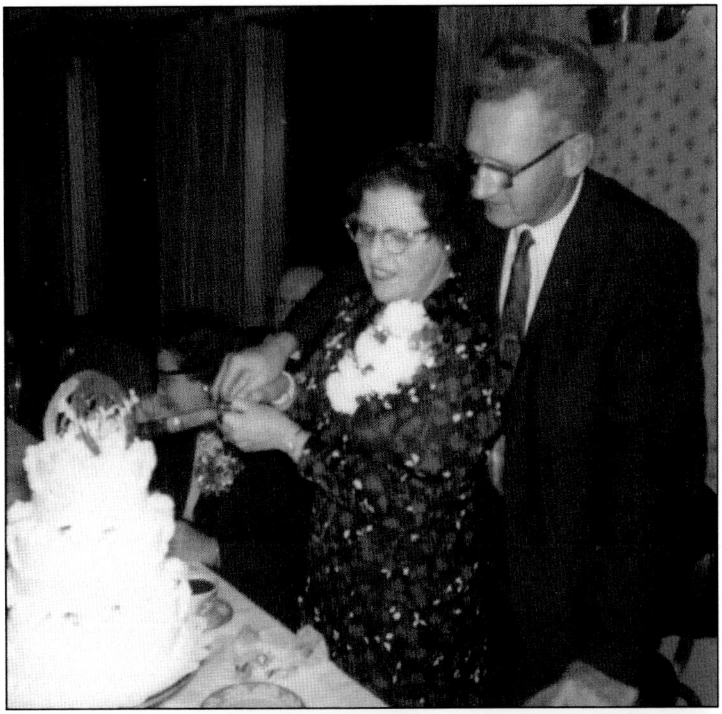

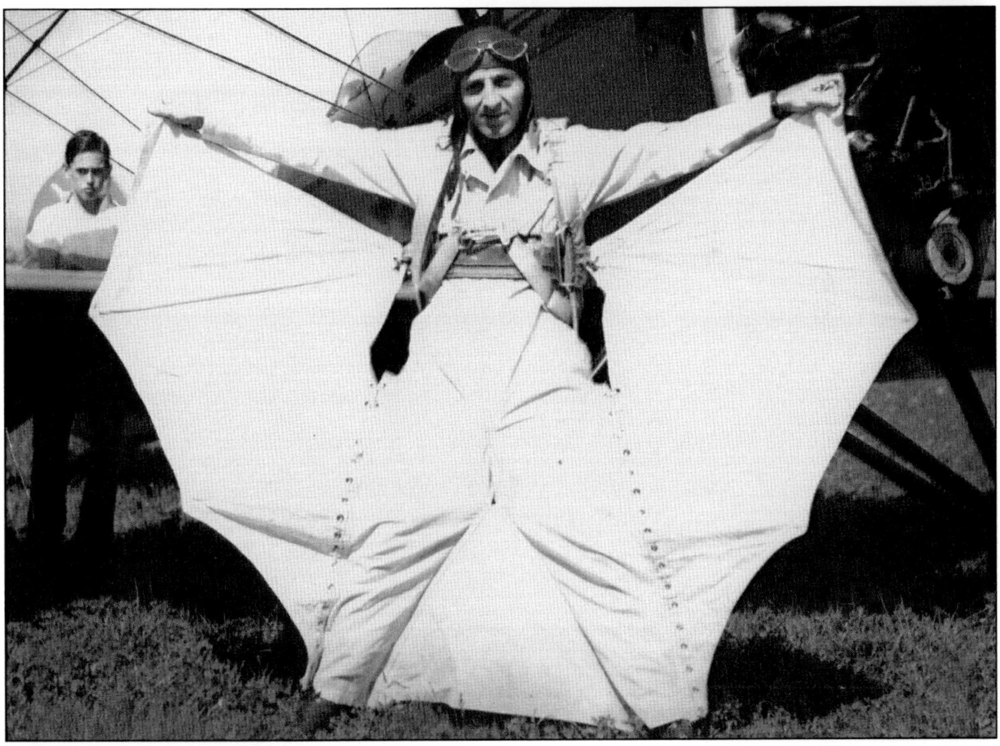

Mike Burson, local druggist, poses in his batman jump suit. Parachuting was his hobby. Many residents gathered at the Triangle Airport in Dyer just to see him parachute from a plane. Burson performed his jumps all over the country. This photograph was taken in the early 1930s.

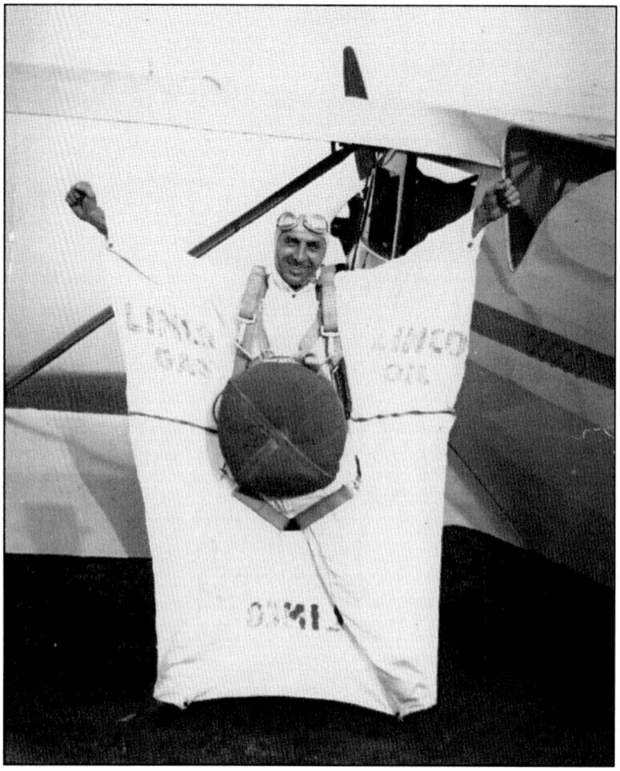

Mike Burson was a colorful character in the town of Dyer. Owner of the Burson Drug Store, Burson was also known as Ace, due to his stunts parachuting from planes. In this photograph, Burson poses in one of his jump suits. This picture was taken in the early 1930s.

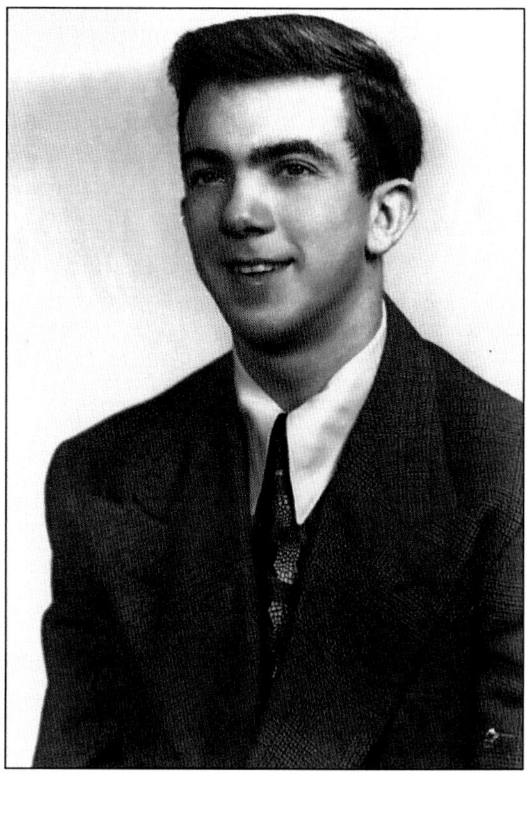

Pictured is Glen Eberly in his 1947 graduation photograph. Eberly was a teacher and principal at the Dyer High School and served on the Dyer Town Council. He also worked as a consultant for the town. In 1976, he gathered a collection of Dyer memorabilia which he put on display for the country's bicentennial.

Glen Eberly, seen here in his U.S. Army uniform, lived from 1930 to 2005. He grew up in Hammond and at the age of eight moved to Dyer. Eberly was very dedicated to preserving the history of Dyer. In 1984, with hard work from Eberly and others, the Dyer Historical Society was established.

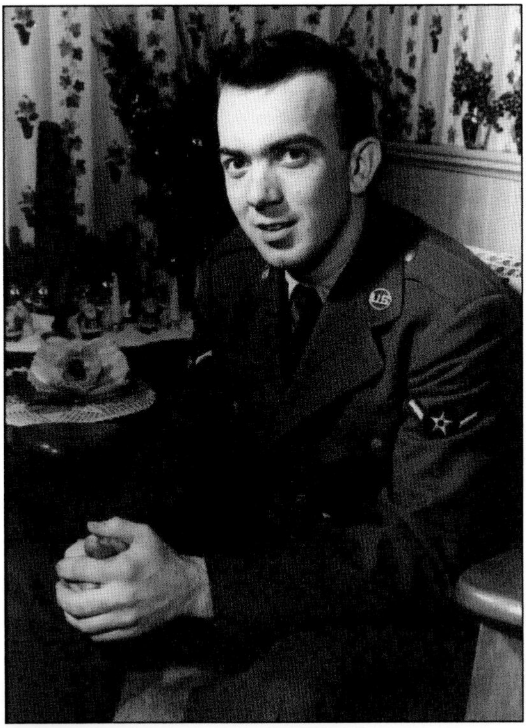

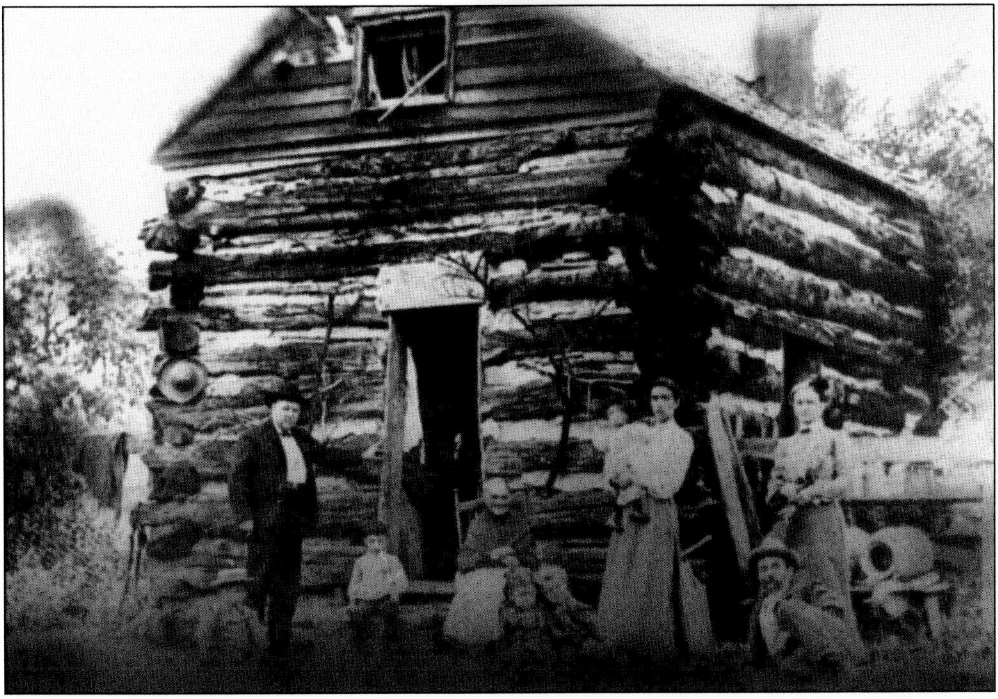

The Fagen family homestead was once located in Merillville on Sixty-first Avenue and Broadway, known then as Turkey Creek. Pictured here are Roy, Peter, Michael, Mrs. Anthony, Margaret, Catherine, Agnes in the arms of Mrs. Nickolas, Nicholas, and Hanna (wife of Peter). Michael Fagen started the Fagen Funeral Home in Dyer.

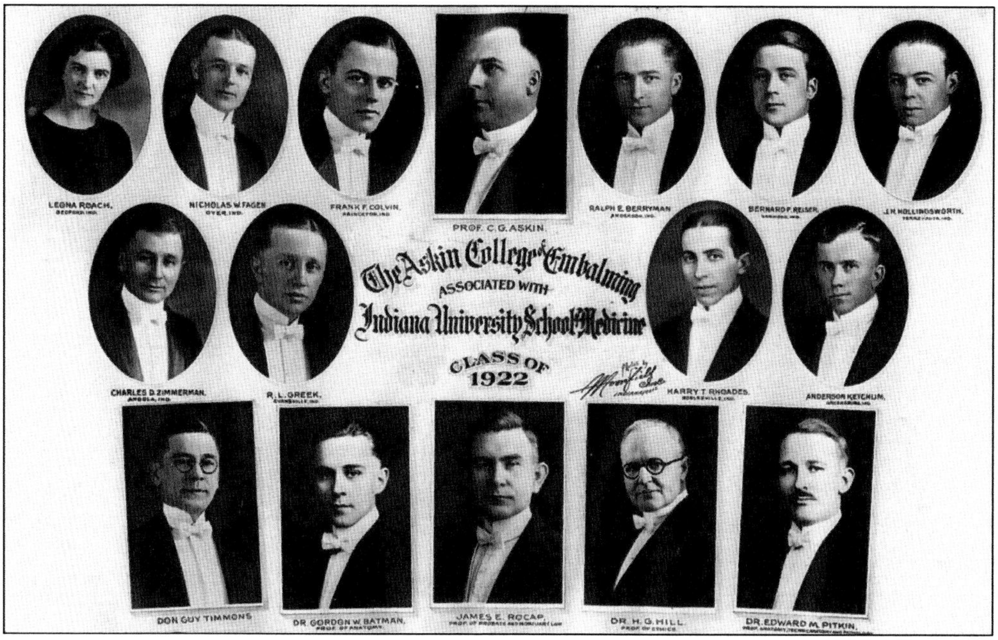

This photograph features, on the top row, second from left, Nicholas Fagen, son of Michael and Anna (Lillig) Fagen. Nick eventually took over the funeral home, served in World War I, was on the Dyer Board of Trustees, served as deputy coroner of Lake County, and was the first Boy Scout scoutmaster in the area.

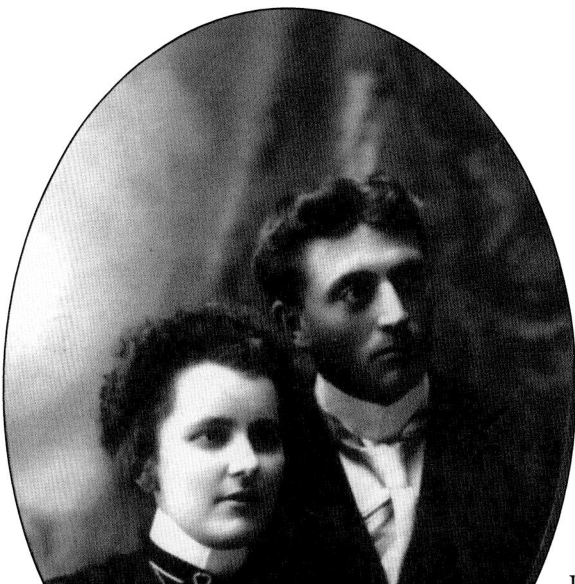

Pictured here is Eugene, also known as John, and Barbara (Eck) Geiger. Eugene was the adopted son of Michael and Anna Fagen. In addition to Eugene, Michael and Anna had three other children: Anthony, Nick, and Marie. Anthony married Louise Schaller, Marie married Roy C. Hilbrich, and Nick married Eva Turner.

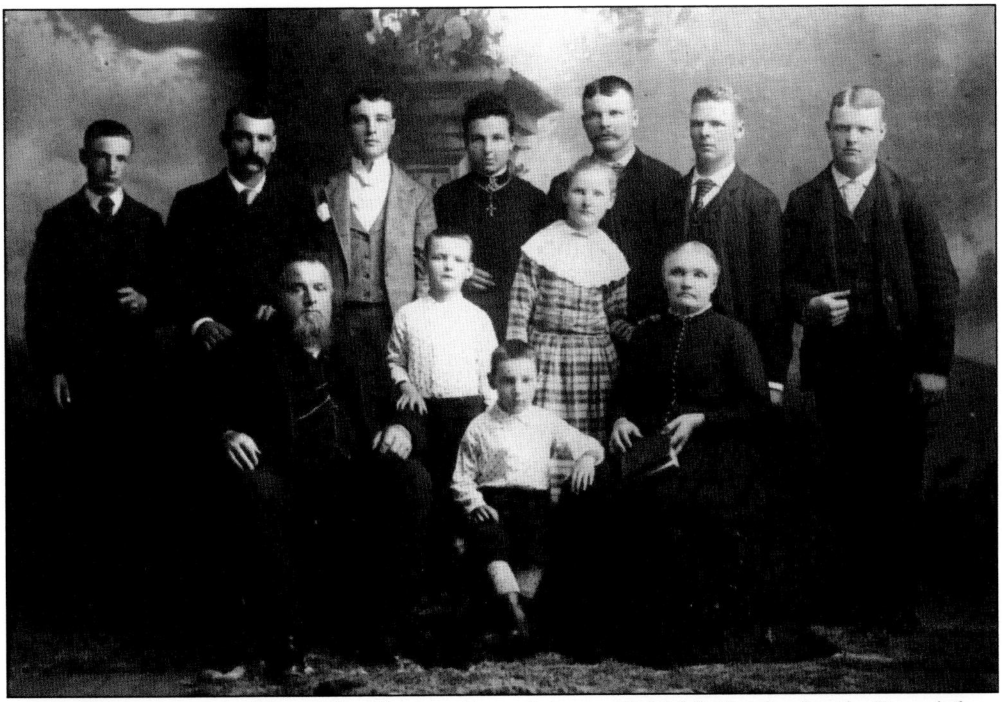

Featured here are members of the Thomas Sr. and Anna (DeVold) Gettler family. From left to right are (first row) father Thomas Sr., Nicholas, Michael, Susan, and mother Anna; (second row) Thomas Jr., Peter Paul, Mathias, Anna, John, Joseph, and William. William served as town clerk and cofounded the First National Bank.

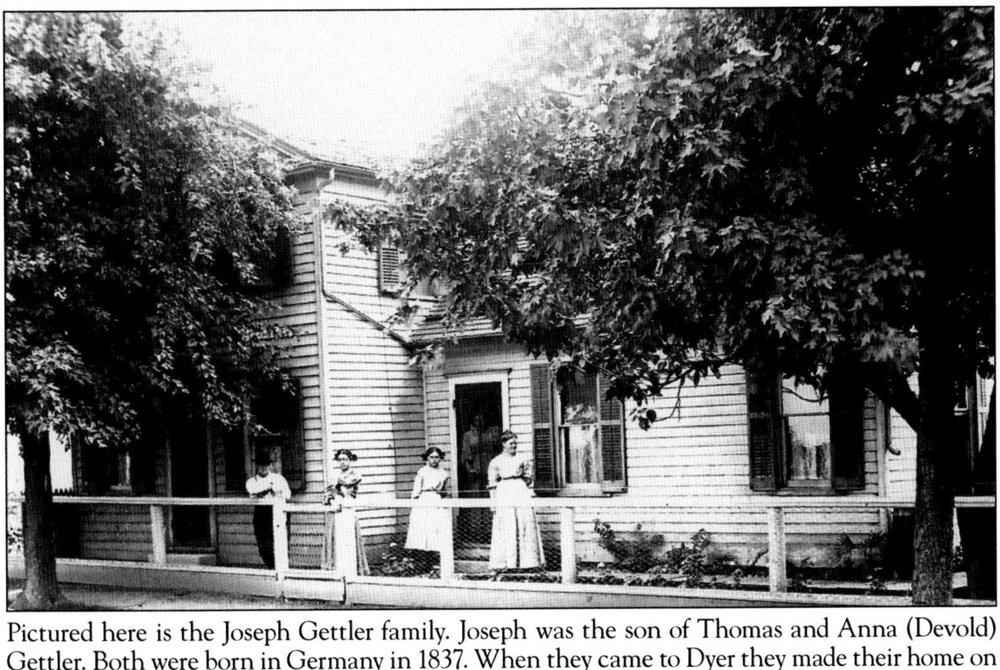

Pictured here is the Joseph Gettler family. Joseph was the son of Thomas and Anna (Devold) Gettler. Both were born in Germany in 1837. When they came to Dyer they made their home on Matteson Street where they had 10 children: Thomas Jr., Peter, Matthew, Anna, Nick, Michael, William, Susan, John, and Joseph.

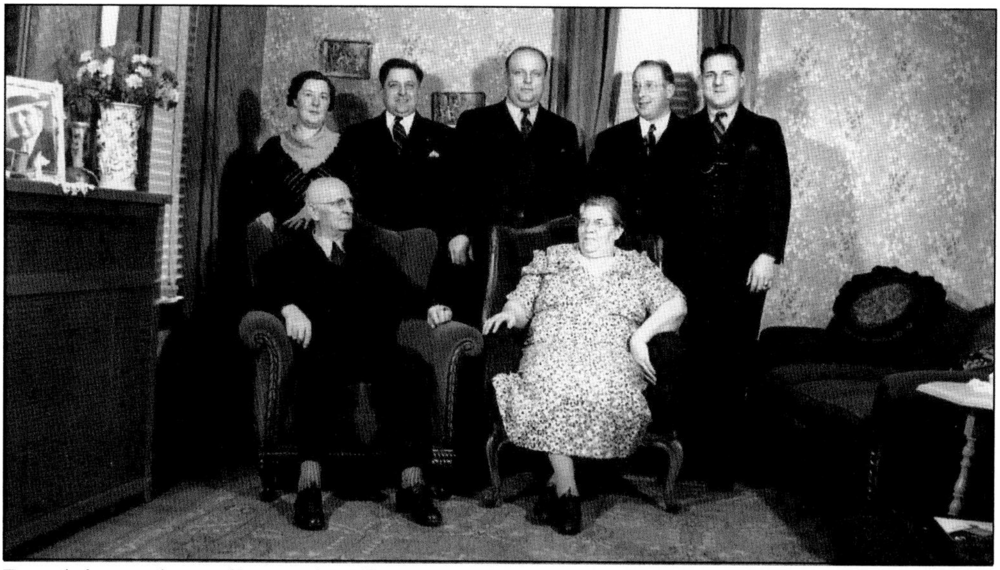

From left to right are (first row) William N. and Lizzetta H. (Wolf) Gettler; (second row) Stasia, Bill, Ed, Clem, and Ray. William was one of the founders of the First National Bank of Dyer. He was a cashier there from 1903 to 1939, became president of the bank, and served for 29 years as the town's clerk-treasurer.

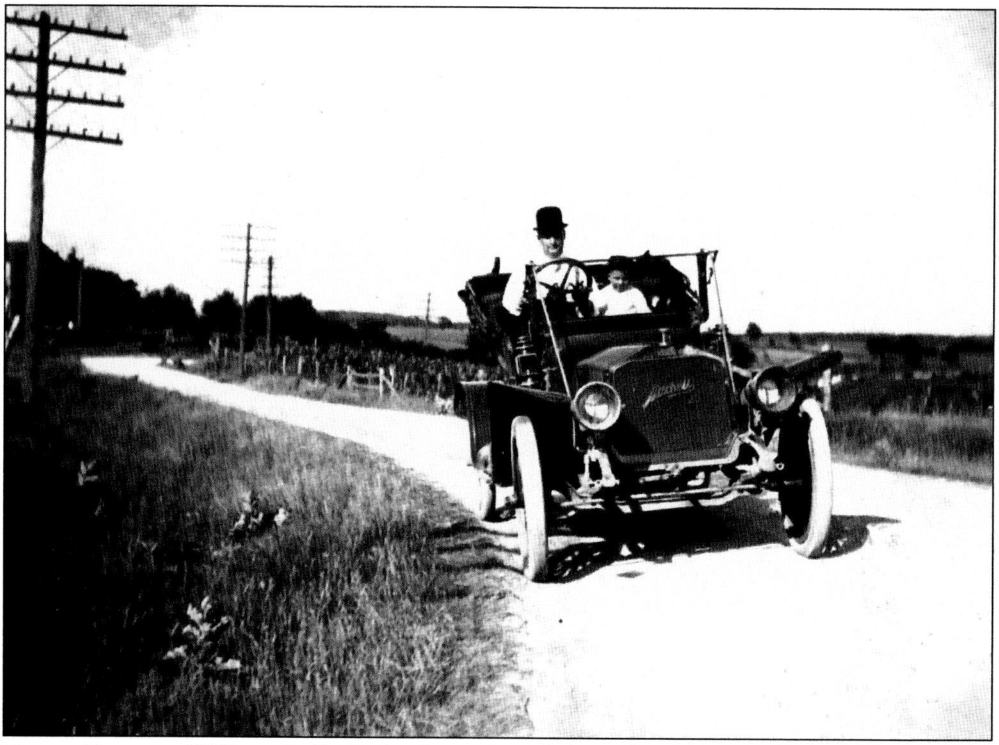

Pictured here are William (Bill) N. Gettler and son Edmond in 1910. William married Lizzetta Wolf and had five children: Stacia, Bill, Edmund, Clement, and Ray. William served as the first town clerk and cofounded the First National Bank in Dyer. He worked for the bank until his death in 1940.

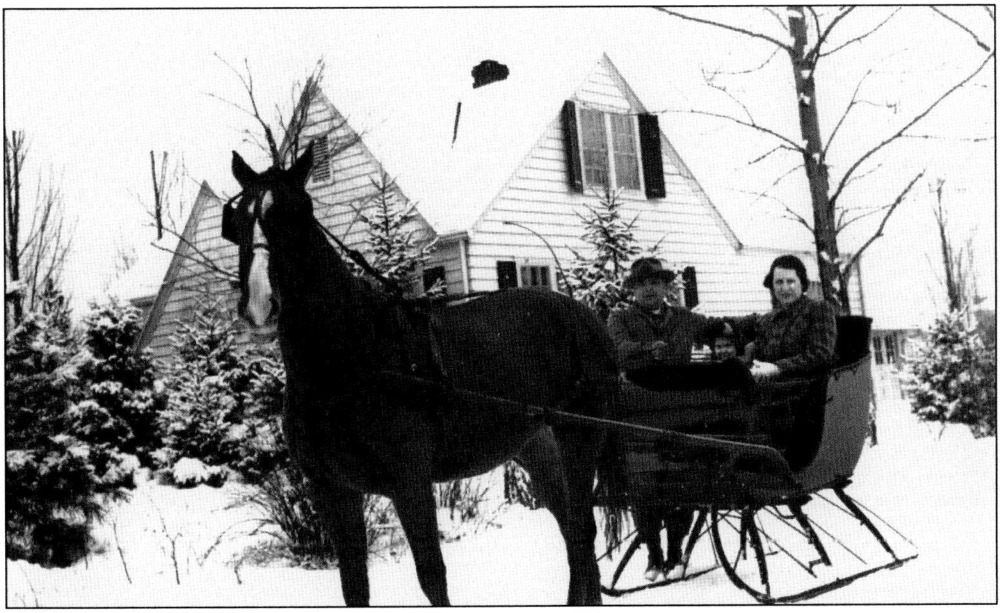

Pictured here are William J. (son of William N. Gettler) and Dorothy (Schmusser) Gettler with their child Carol on their sleigh drawn by their horse Blackie on Christmas Day 1940. William J., also known as Bill, was a cashier at the First National Bank of Dyer from 1941 to 1947, and a Dyer volunteer fireman.

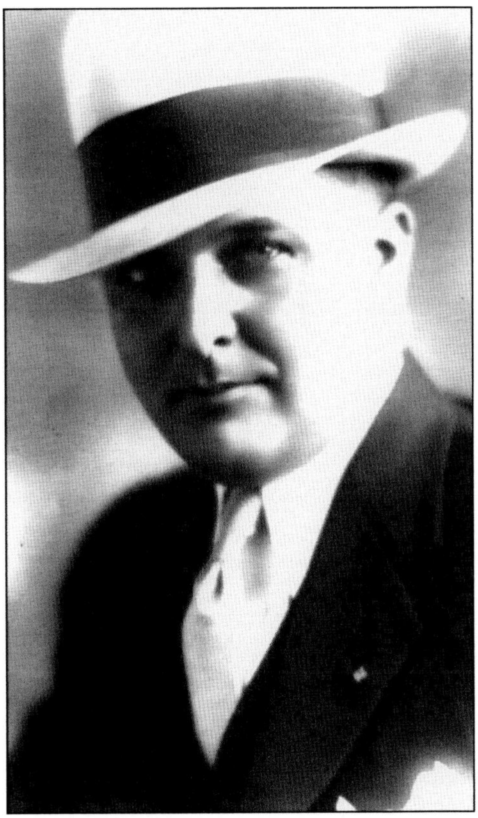

William served as the first town clerk when Dyer became incorporated as a town in 1910. He held this position until 1939. William cofounded the First National Bank in Dyer, working as a teller until taking August Stommel's position as cashier. This photograph was taken in 1929.

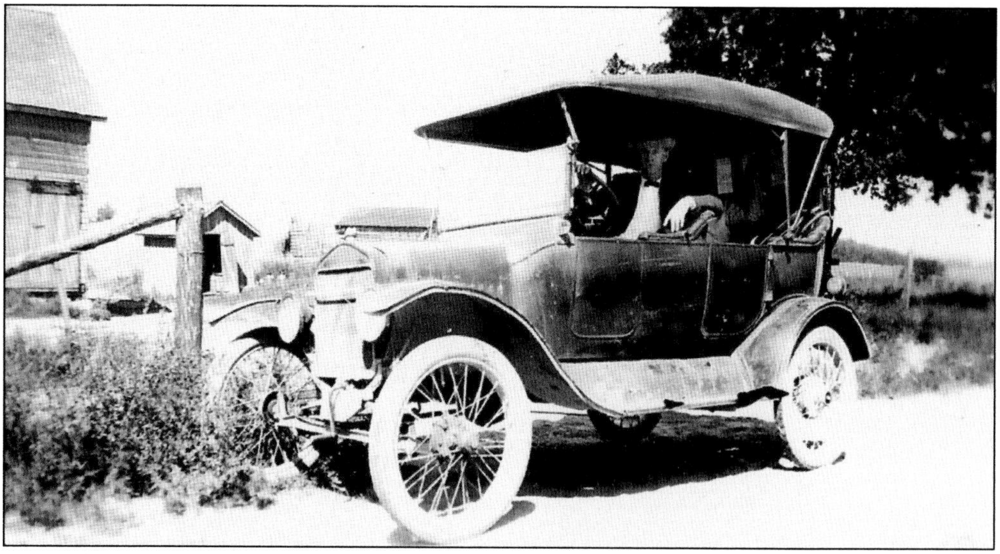

Pictured in the driver's seat is Bill Gettler, early 1900s. Bill was the son of William and Lizzeta Gettler. Bill was the town's first clerk-treasurer and a founder of the First National Bank of Dyer. Paul T. Gettler served as the town's second clerk-treasurer after William.

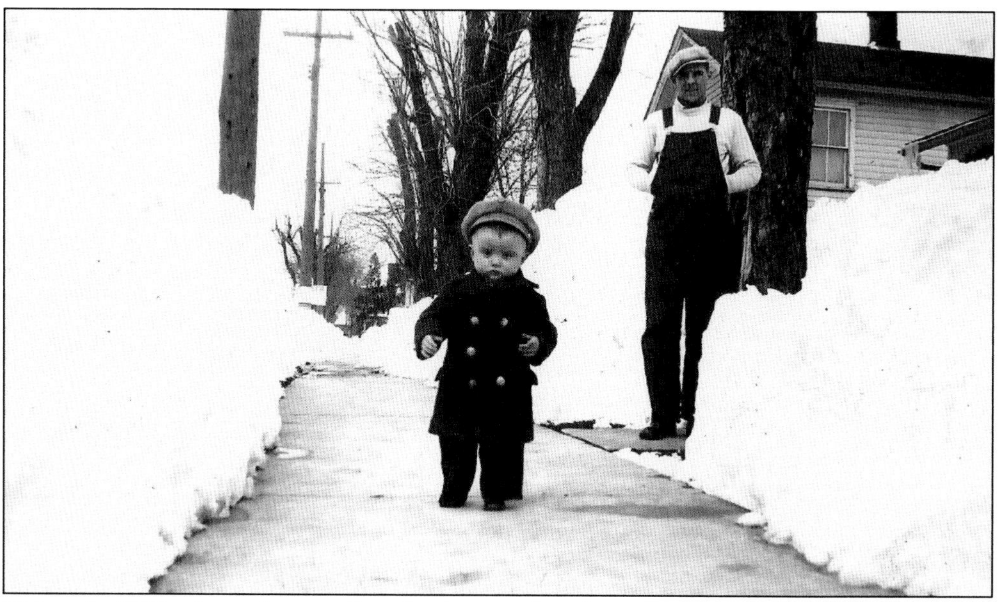

This early 1900s picture features Ray Gettler, standing far right. Though the child's first name is unknown, he is a member of the Dumbsky family. Ray was the son of William N. and Lizzetta (Wolf) Gettler. William was the first clerk-treasurer in Dyer.

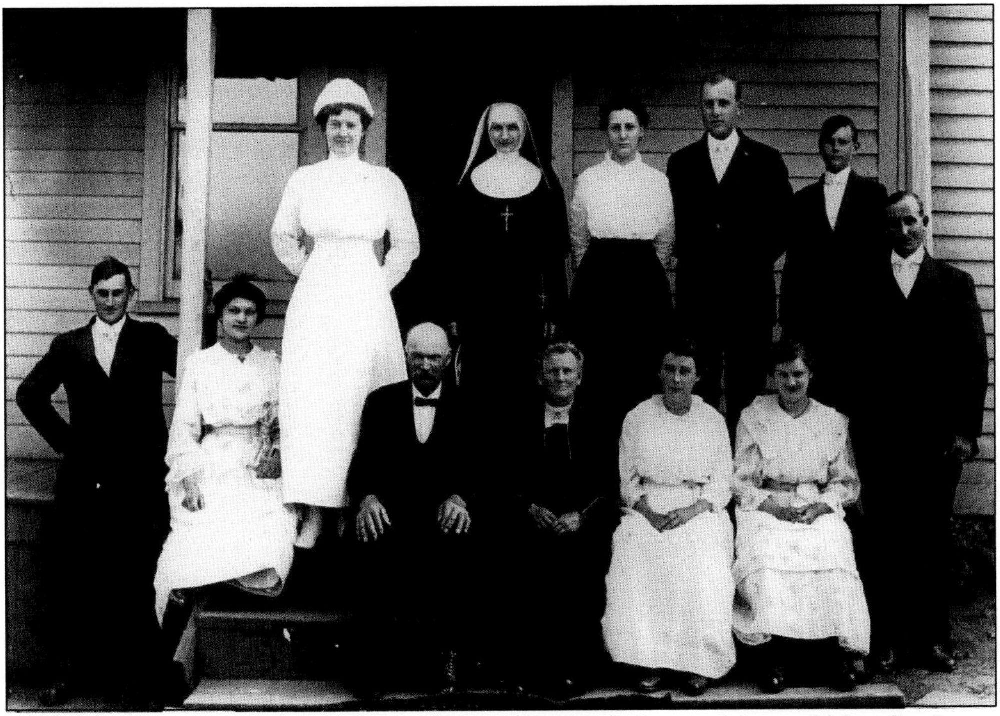

This 1910 photograph features John and Mary (Rietman) Govert. John and Mary lived on a farm south of Dyer. Their children were Alphons, Bernard, Carrie (Enzweiler), Catherine (Sr. Laurent), Julia (Held), Rosie (Held), Pauline (Sr. Philothea), and Mary (Margraf). Eventually John and Mary left the farm to live in town on Hart Street.

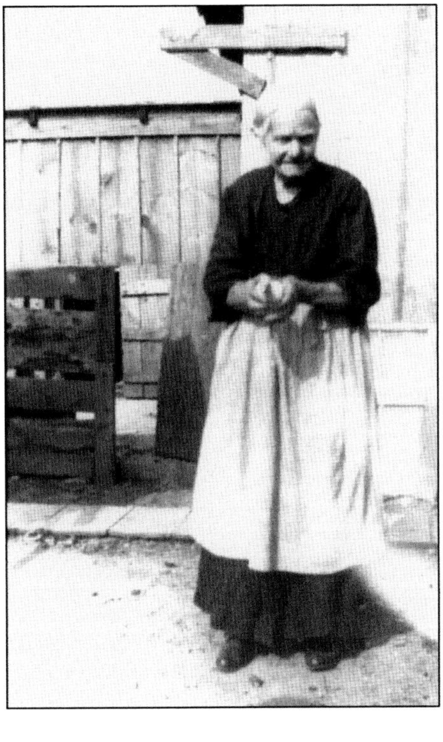

Pictured here is Catherine (Overhage) Grothaus. She married Bernard Grothaus. They came to Dyer from Germany in 1881 where they raised eight children. Catherine's brothers Henry and Arnold built her and her husband's home on Hart Street where Pheasant Hills subdivision sits today.

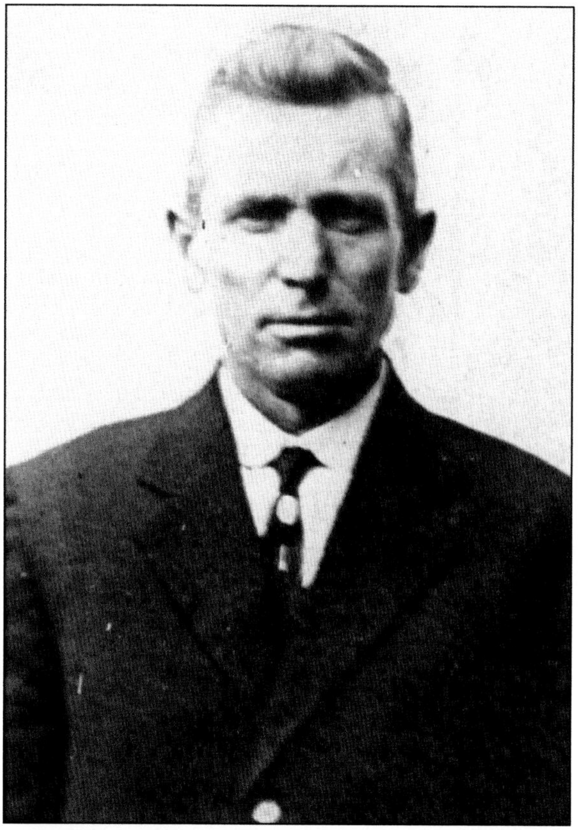

Arnold William Grothaus (1874–1940), son of Catherine and Bernard, married Theresia Victoria Klein from Chicago Heights. They produced ten children: Alphonse, Sylvester, Ludwig, Marie, Florence, Joseph, Howard, Ralph, Rose, and Francis. They too lived on Hart Street near the Pheasant Hills subdivision.

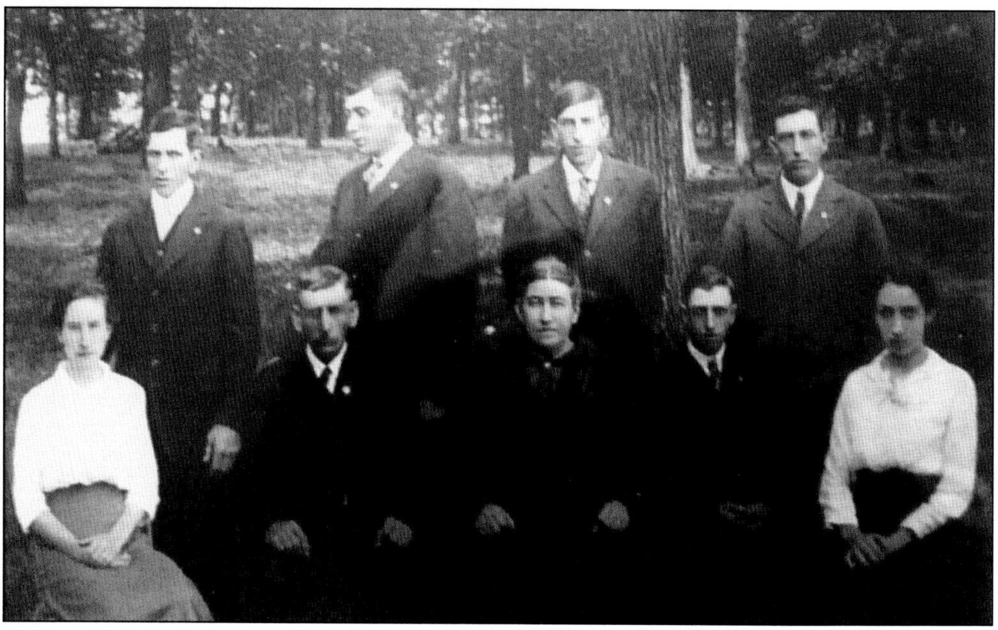

Pictured here are the Anton and Susan (Herman) Held family. From left to right are (first row) Catherine (Held) Bohney, father Anton Sr., mother Susan, Anton Jr., and Marie (Dewes); (second row) Albert, Peter, Jacob, and George.

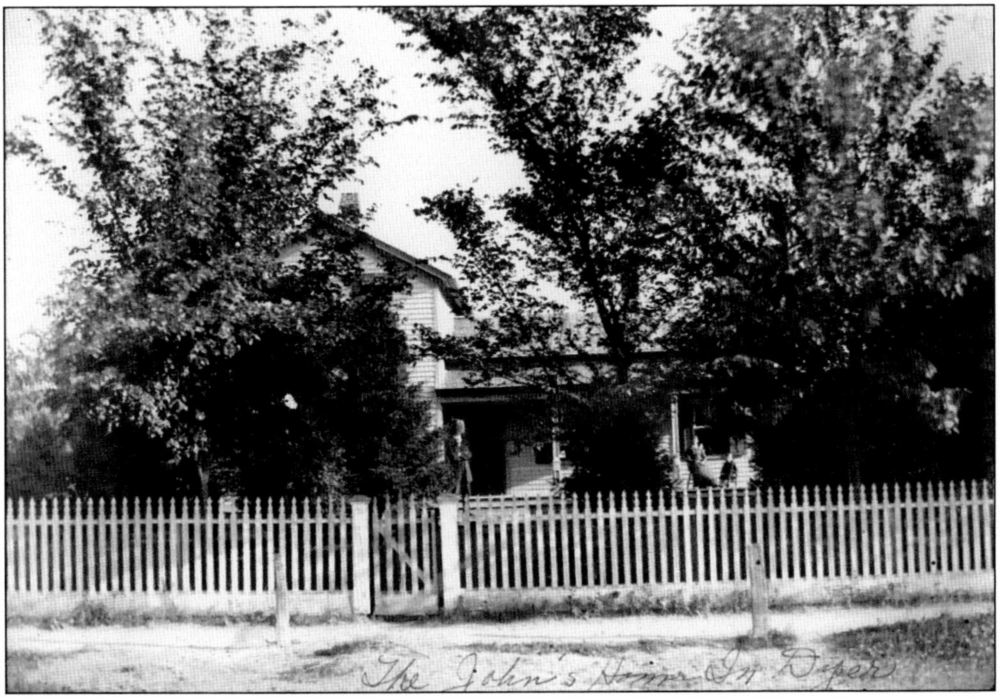

Pictured here is Dyer's second doctor, Dr. John W. Johns, and family. Dr. Johns was born in Lake County in 1845, and earned his diploma from Chicago Medical College in March 1868. He married Carrie Jung and together they had a daughter, Katie, all of whom are seen in this photograph.

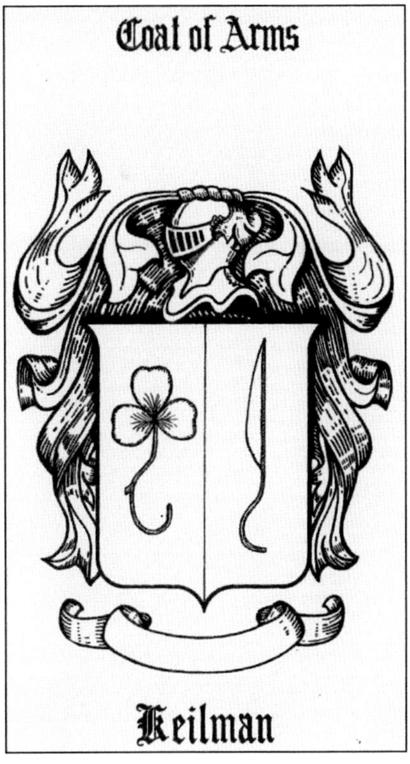

Pictured here is the Keilman coat of arms. Leonard Keilman is considered to be the patriarch of the Keilman clan, one of the largest families in Dyer. Leonard was born in Hesse-Darmstradt, Germany, on May 4, 1833, came to the states, and resided in Ohio with his family. Leonard came to the Dyer area in 1845.

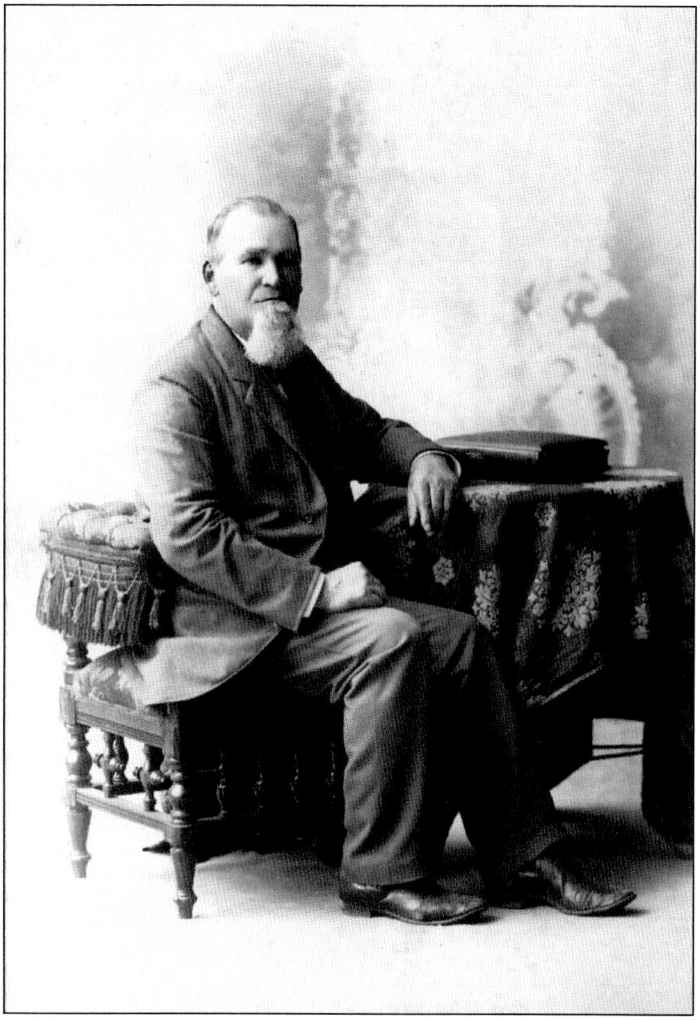

The Henry Keilman family came to Lake County Indiana about 1845. In 1858, Leonard and D. Lowenberg founded the L. Keilman Company that operated the grain elevator. It was a dominant business in Dyer.

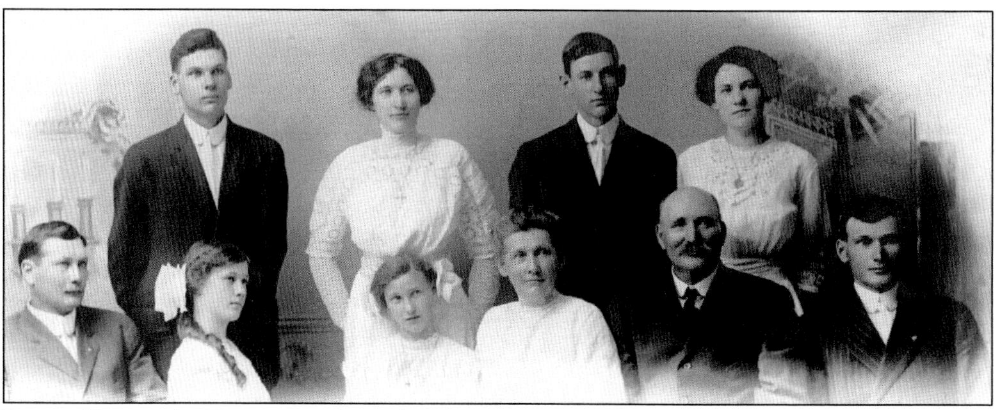

Pictured here is the Henry L. Keilman family. From left to right are (first row) William, Veronica, Helen (Mulhollan), mother Margaret (Schafer), father Henry L., and Frank; (second row) Raymond, Emma, Leonard, and Frances (Kahler). Henry L. Keilman helped organize the First National Bank, served as its president, and was the first chairman of the board of trustees.

Raymond Keilman was one of eight children of Henry L. and Margaret (Schaefer) Keilman, grandson to Leonard Keilman. He is pictured here in his World War I military uniform. Many members of the Keilman family served their country during World War I and World War II.

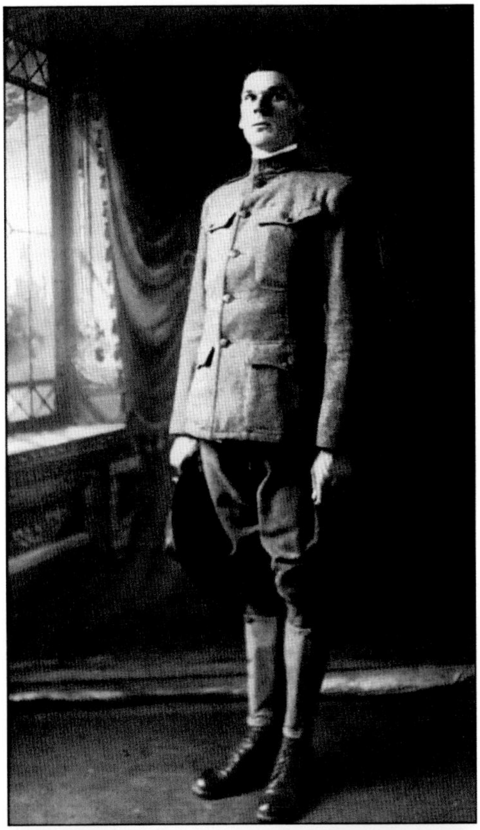

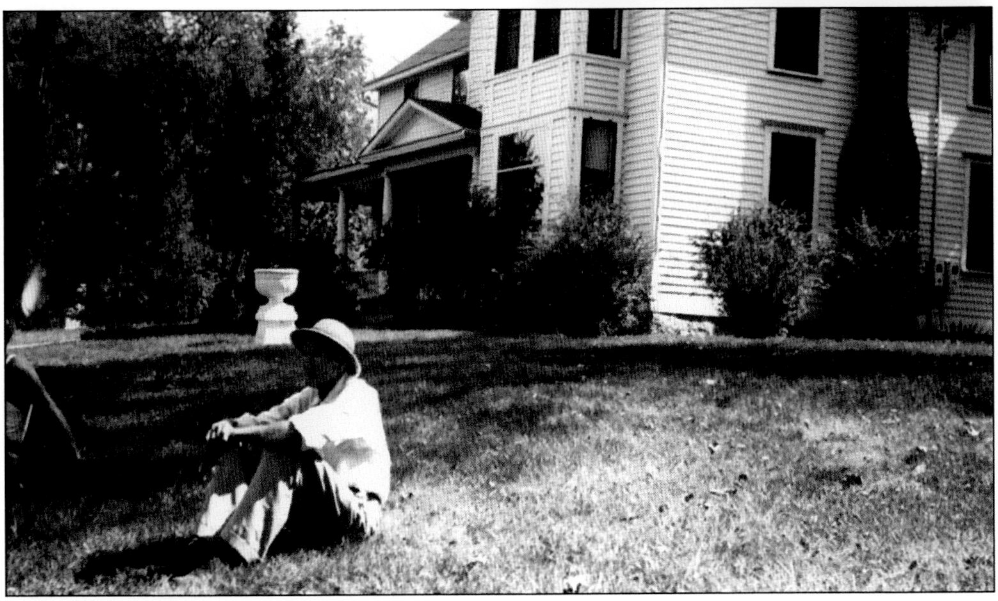

This picture, taken in September 1955, features Frank L. Keilman sitting in front of his brother Henry L. Keilman's house. Both were sons of Leonard Keilman. His farm was located on Hart Street. Although not in its original location, the house still stands today near the corner of Hart and Seventy-seventh Streets.

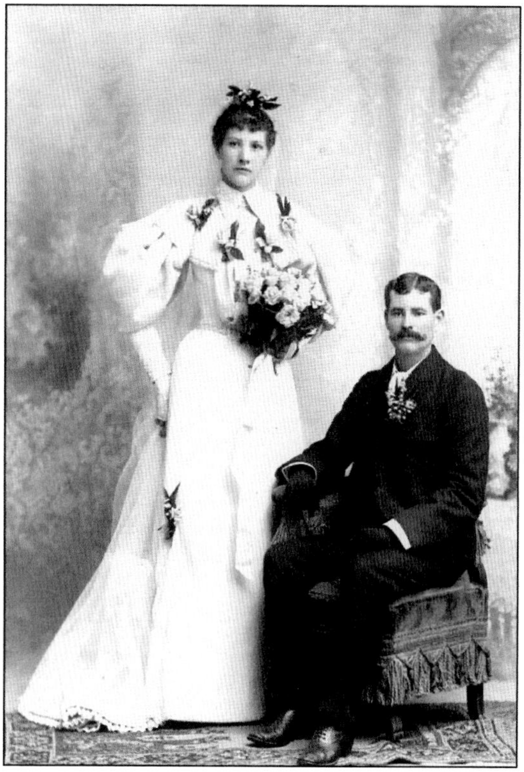

This 1895 photograph features, from left to right, Emma (Schafer) and John Keilman. John, son of Leonard Keilman, owned and operated the John L. Keilman building and dry goods store. The building stood until the early 1990s, when it was torn down to widen Route 30, the old Lincoln Highway.

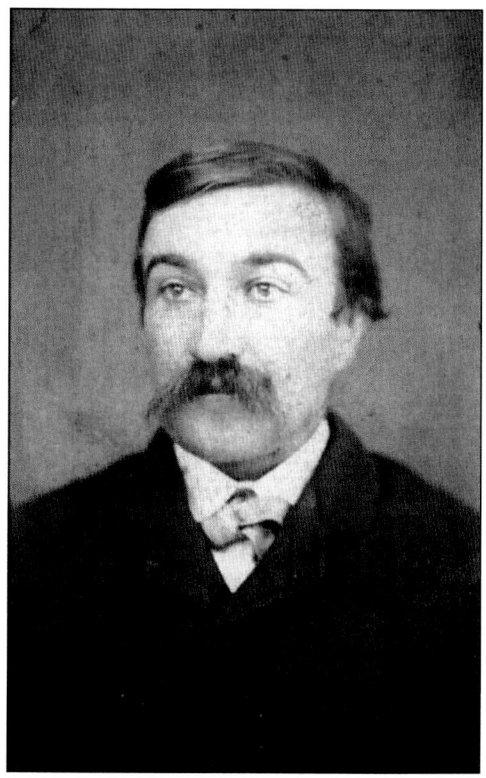

John L. Keilman, son of Leonard, was a founder of the First National Bank in Dyer. He married Emma Schaefer. John owned a dry goods store that stood on the northeast corner of Hart Street and the Lincoln Highway. In 1925, he retired and sold his business to Andrew Peschel and Helmuth Schwab.

Featured here is Catherine Keilman, known as Aunt Katie, at a young age. She grew up in the Leonard Keilman home, once located on the Sauk Trail turned Lincoln Highway. She witnessed Native Americans using the Sauk Trail and its conversion into the Ideal Section of the Lincoln Highway.

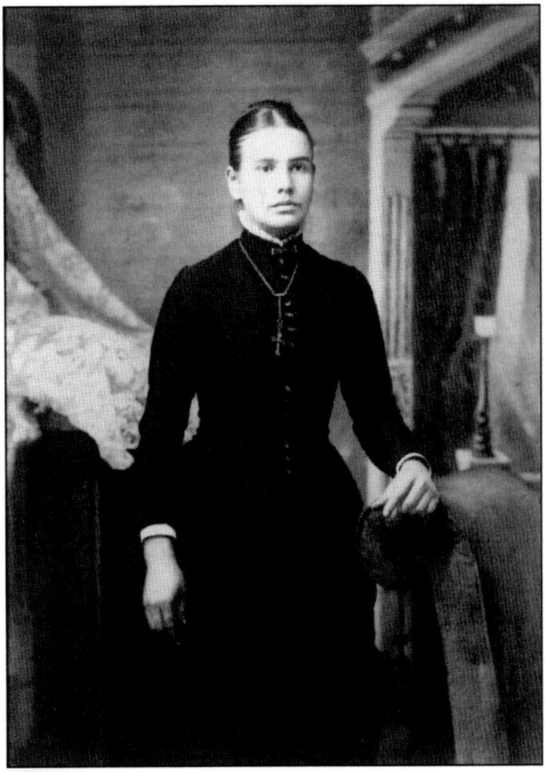

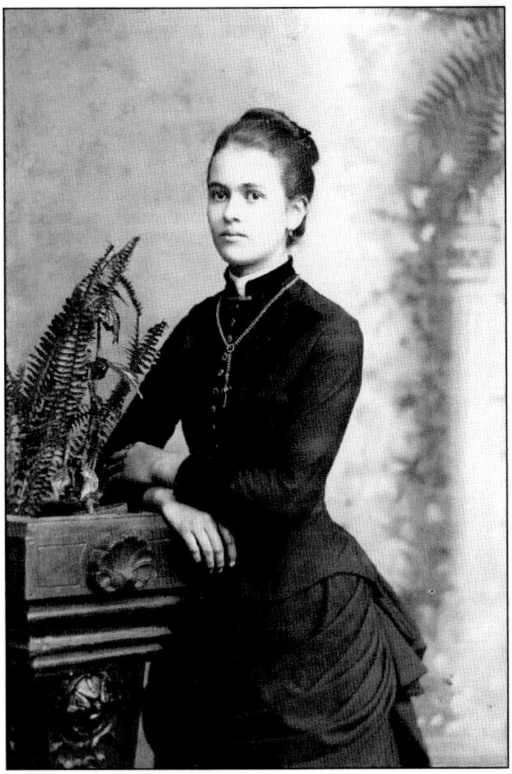

Aunt Katie was a daughter of Leonard Keilman. She was born on November 1, 1859, and lived a full 100 years. She lived to see Dyer incorporated into a town and the Sauk Trail turn into the Ideal Section of the Lincoln Highway.

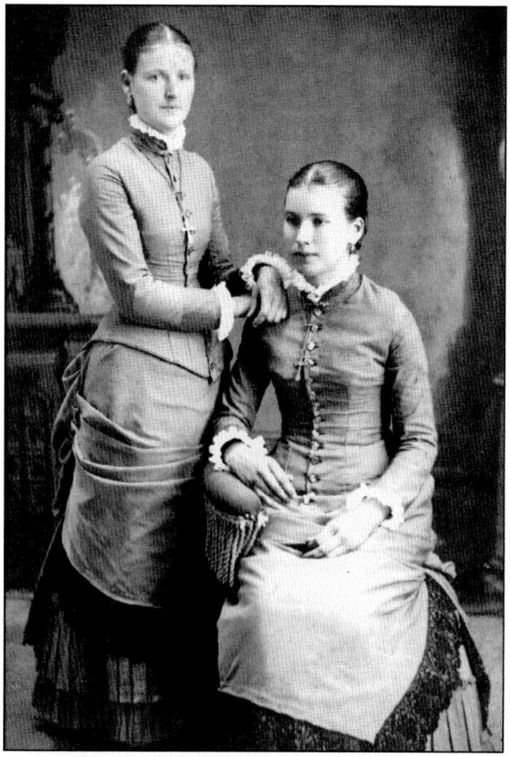

Pictured are Leonard Keilman's daughters Mary (left) and Elizabeth, also known as Lizzie. They were sisters to Catherine, or Aunt Katie Keilman. All three sisters grew up in Dyer, their house being located on the old Sauk Trail. They were known for making quilts to be auctioned off for church fundraisers.

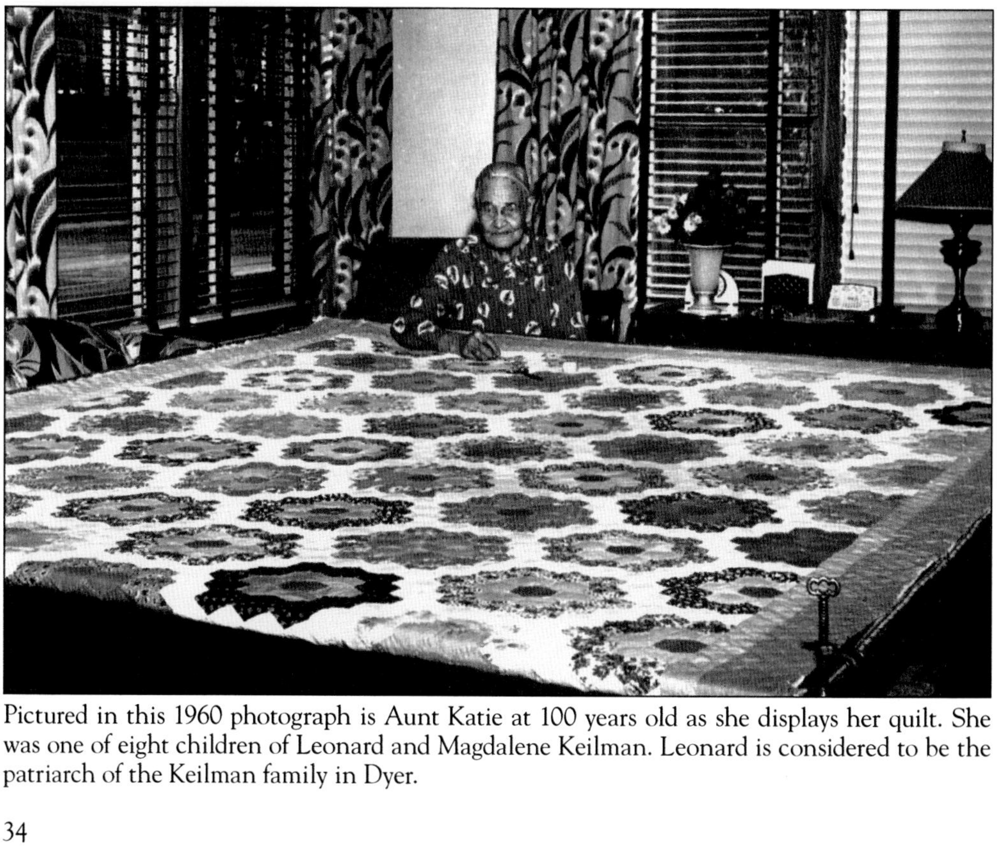

Pictured in this 1960 photograph is Aunt Katie at 100 years old as she displays her quilt. She was one of eight children of Leonard and Magdalene Keilman. Leonard is considered to be the patriarch of the Keilman family in Dyer.

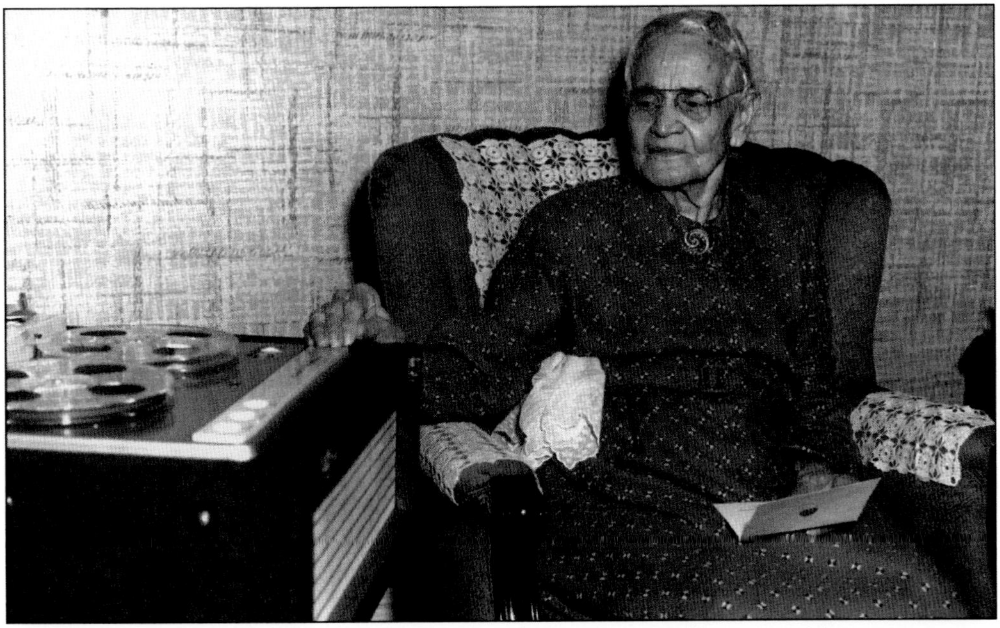

Aunt Katie, shown here in her later years, shared her stories of what it was like growing up in Dyer with her fellow residents. Most fascinating were her recollections of watching the Native Americans walking the Old Sauk Trail and witnessing the Union soldiers march through the area during the Civil War.

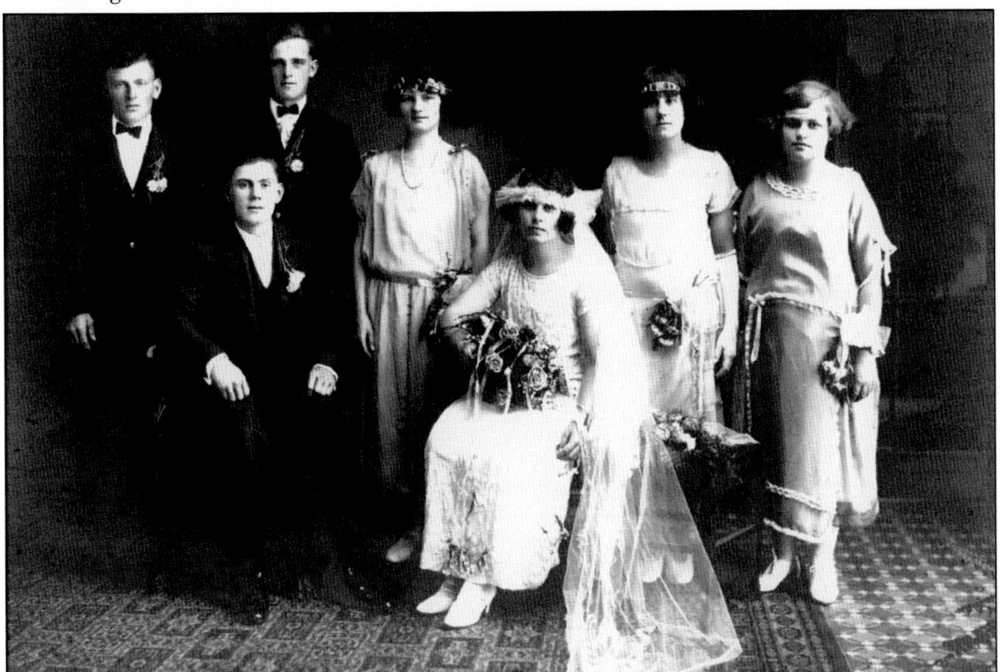

This is a photograph of the Clarence J. and Gertrude B. (Jung) Keilman wedding party, taken on August 26, 1924. From left to right are (first row) Clarence Jacob Keilman and Gertrude (Jung) Keilman; (second row) Ed Austgen, Michael Jung, Frances (Jung) Austgen, Margaret (Keilman) Jacobs, and May (Jung) Willy.

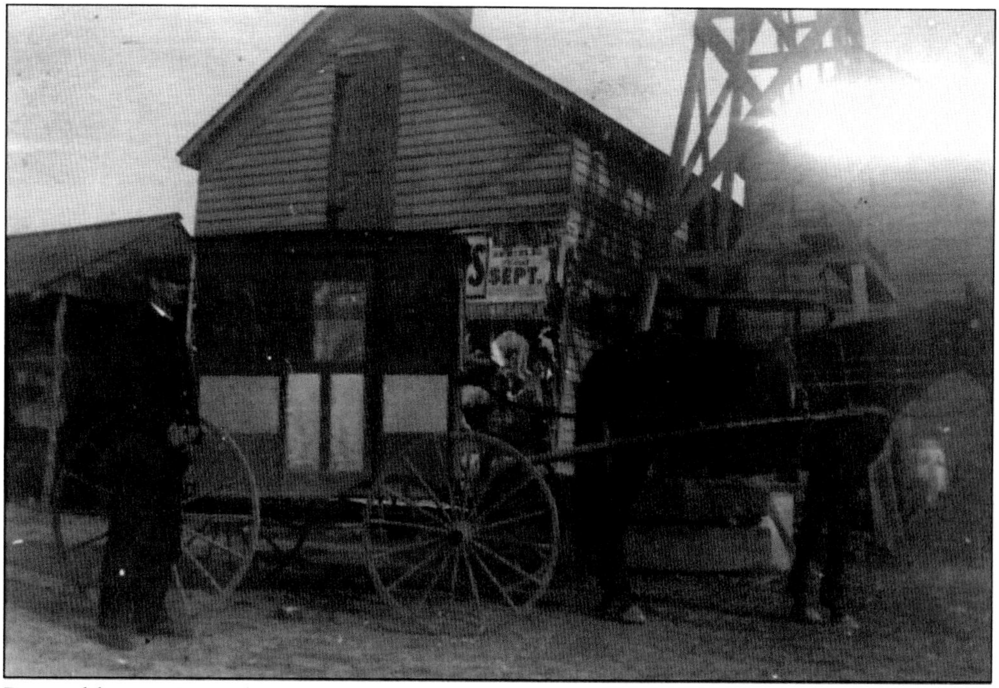

Pictured here is Pete Klein, postmaster during the early 1900s. His predecessors were Charles Sauter who served for two years, Francis Densburger for three to four years, Julius Neising for two years, Claudius Austgen in 1876, and following him, Nick Scherer. Mail service was slow until the railroads made transportation quicker.

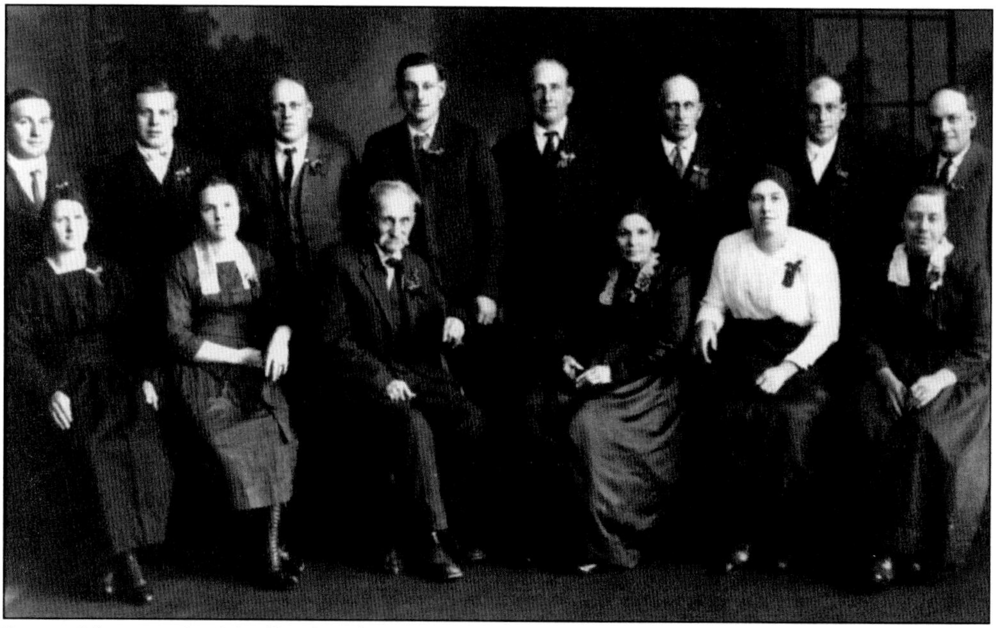

Pictured here is the Moeller family. From left to right are (first row) Katherine, Mary, father Henry Sr., mother Katherine (Govert), Mathilda, and Elizabeth; (second row) John, Joseph, Jacob, Aloyius, William, Henry Jr., Peter, and Theodore. Their homestead was located where Meyer's castle stands today. John Moeller was a Dyer town marshal.

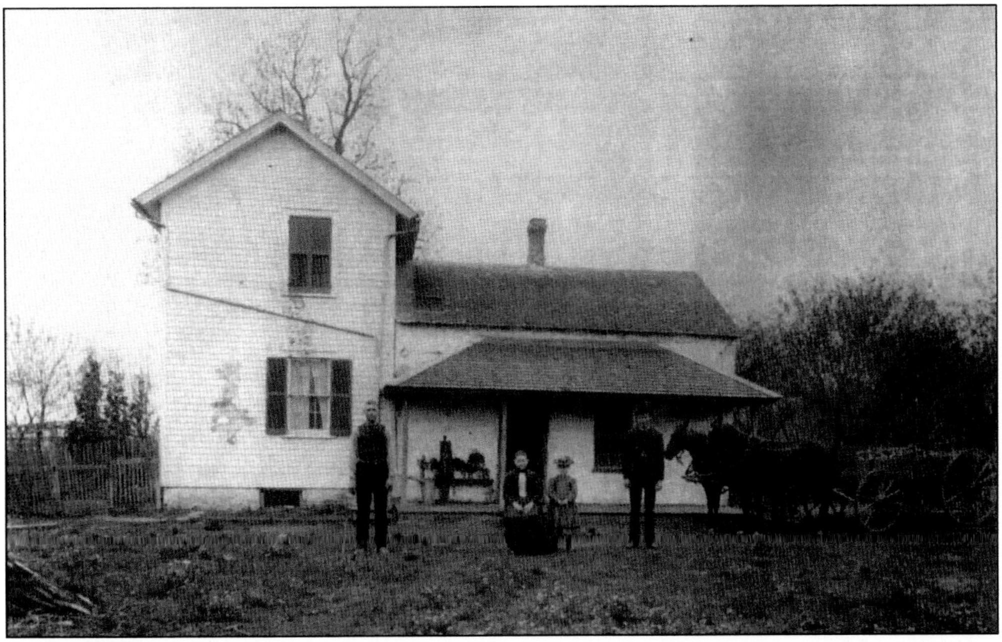

This photograph features the Mangold family: Michael, mother Barbara, Katie, and father Joseph. Their home was built around the original log cabin and was located on the south end of town. Their land was left to the church when Katie passed away. Bibich Elementary school now stands on part of that land.

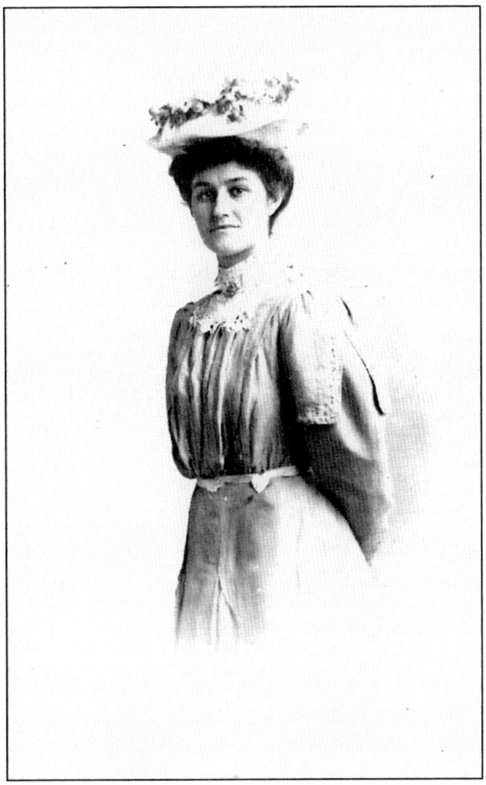

Pictured here is Catherine (Katie) Mangold, who was born in 1887 and lived until February 1965. She lived her whole life in a renovated 125-year-old cabin. Upon her passing, her farmland was donated to St. Joseph Church. The land was then sold off for developing.

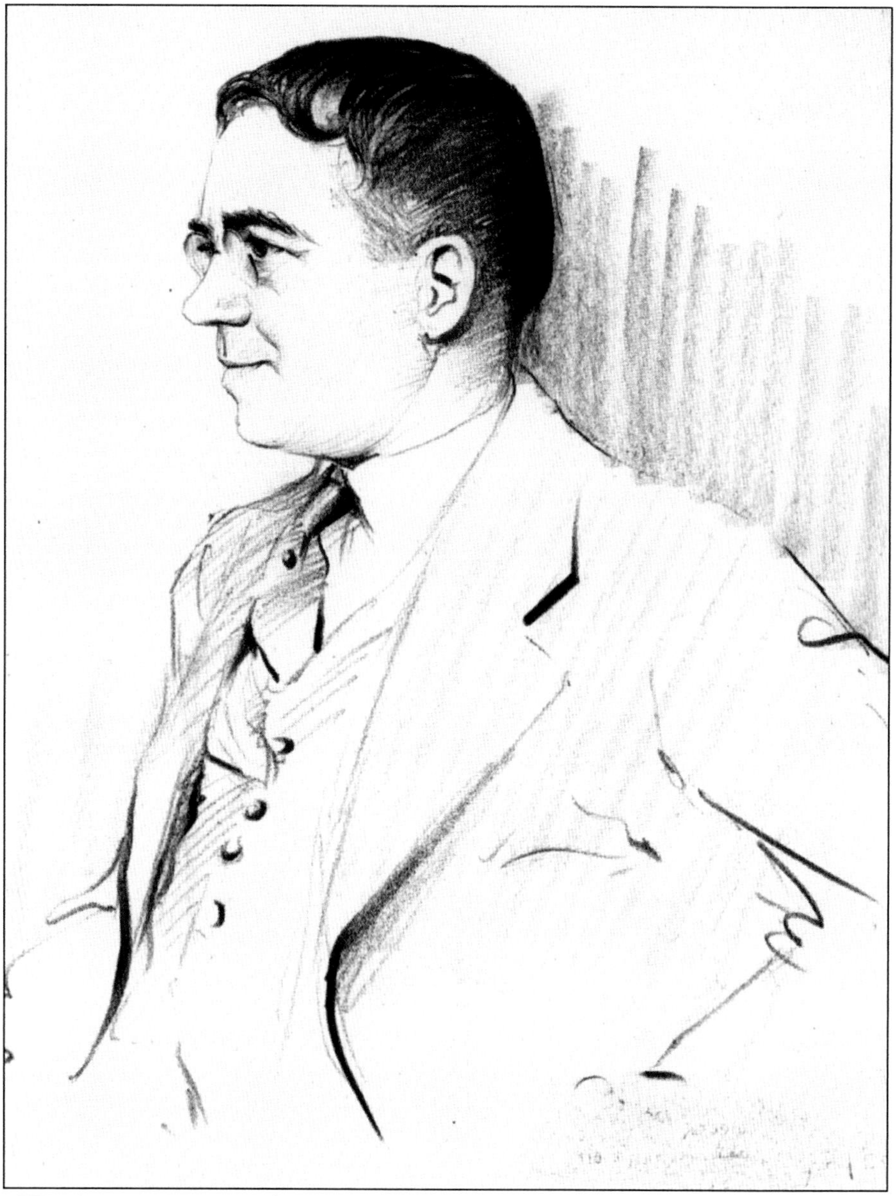

One of Dyer's most prominent homes is Meyer's mansion. The story starts with Joseph Earnest Meyer, pictured here, who was born in Kenosha, Wisconsin, on September 5, 1878. He was orphaned after his father died and sent to live in an orphanage where he learned printing and botany. He purchased land in Hammond where he grew medicinal herbs, which he sold door-to-door. The land became the Indiana Herb Gardens, later renamed the Indiana Botanical Gardens. Eventually Meyer would move himself, his wife Cecilia, and his eight children to Dyer. He selected some land on the Lincoln Highway to build a home and gardens. He hired himself an architect, Cosbey Bemard Sr., whom he instructed to design a mansion based on an old Scottish castle. Construction started in 1929 and finished in 1931. The three-story mansion was a Jacobethan Revival structure. Joseph passed away in 1950. The large tracts of land surrounding the mansion eventually became the Castlewood subdivision and the castle itself is now Rodizio's, an Argentine-style restaurant.

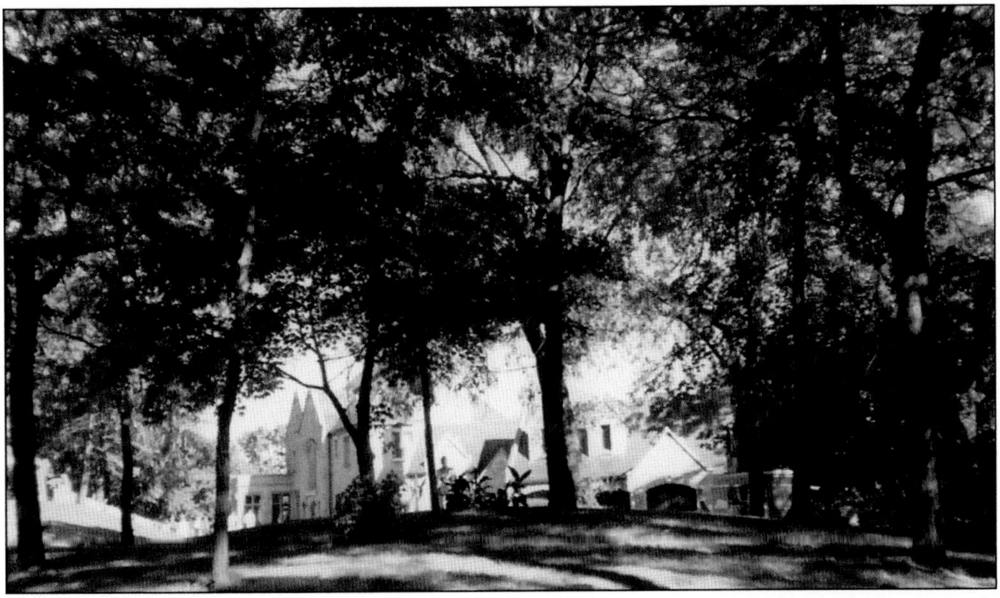

Pictured here is Meyer's castle; built in the Jacobethan Revival style based on a Scottish castle Joseph Meyer had once seen. Meyer, after earning his fortune growing and selling medicinal herbs, built this home in 1929. He lived in the mansion until his passing in 1950.

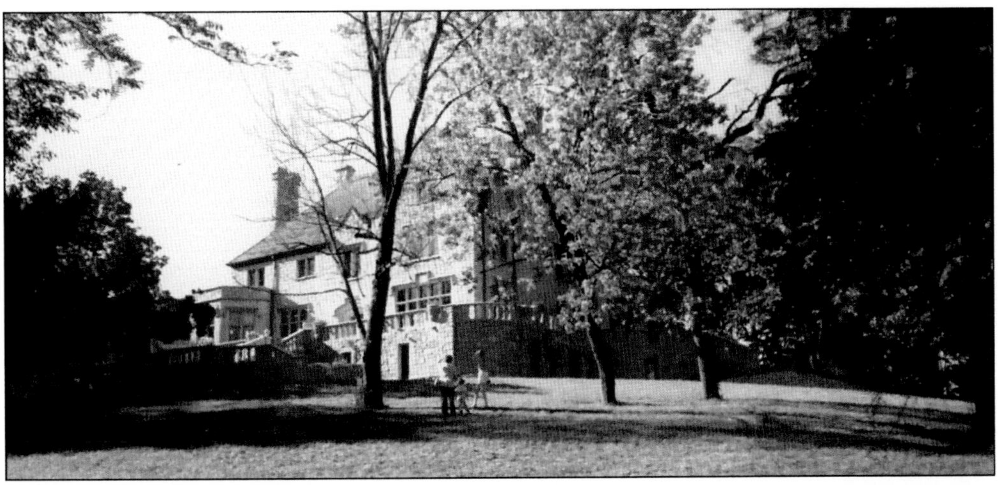

Meyer's castle, also called Meyer's mansion, was built on what is now the last remaining sand dune in Dyer. The sand dune, once called Indian Hill, and the castle, are located on the Lincoln Highway. Today, the mansion houses Rodizio's Argentinean restaurant.

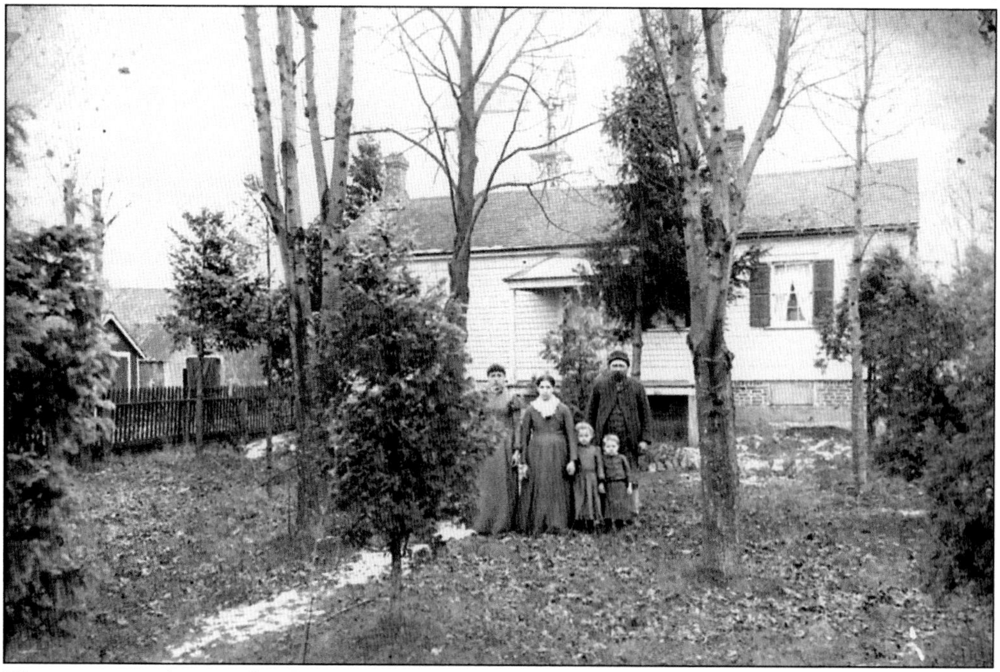

This picture, taken at the dawn of the 20th century, is of the Nondorf family on their farm. Henry and Margaret Nondorf owned much farmland in Dyer. Their son George married Louis Leinen, had 10 children, and operated his own farm that produced milk, eggs, and poultry.

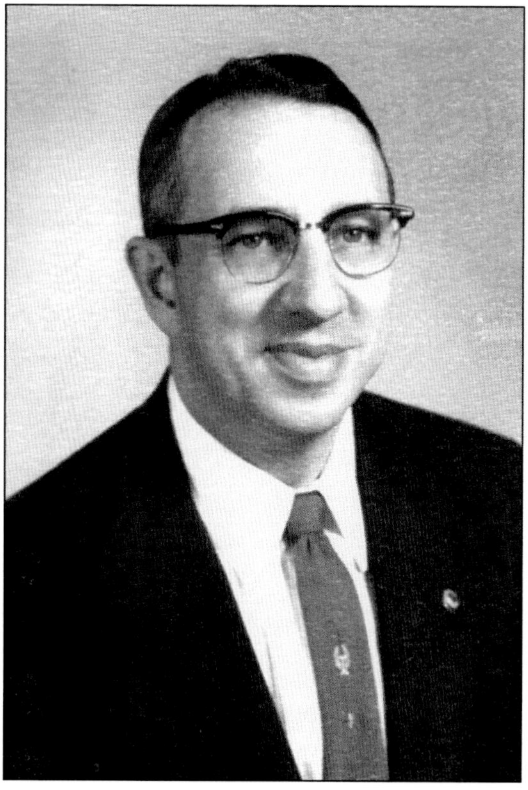

Featured here is A. Erwin Peshel, also known as Mister Dyer. He served as a volunteer fireman for 39 years, was the treasurer of the Lion's Club, was active in the Boy Scouts, coached Dyer Little League, was a member of the chamber of commerce in Dyer and Schererville, and volunteered for the Salvation Army.

This early 1920s photograph features Julius, son of Andrew and Helen Peschel. They were the owners of the Peschel grocery store. Julius died at a young age after a tonsillectomy. He had two brothers, Frank and Erwin. Julius is shown here warming up for baseball in the field behind the Mount Mercy Sanitarium.

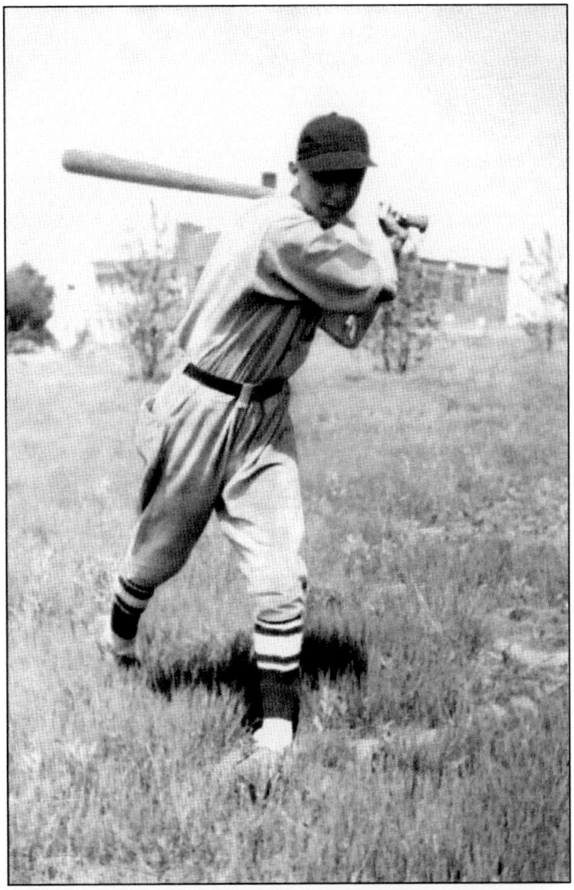

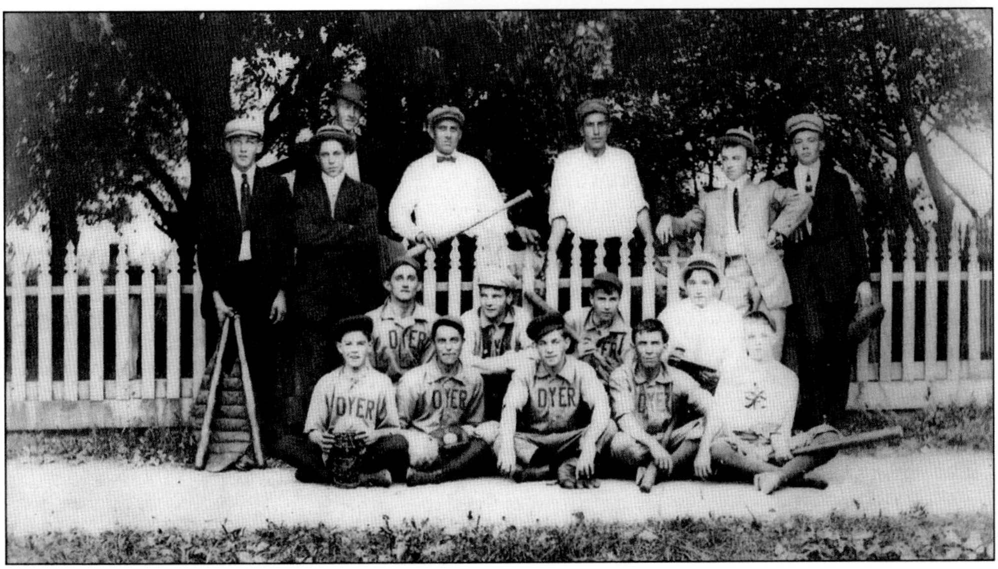

Pictured in this photograph is an early 1900s Dyer baseball team. They used to play in a cow pasture behind the hospital located on the Lincoln Highway. The team members maintained the playing field themselves, taking great care to remove the cow patties.

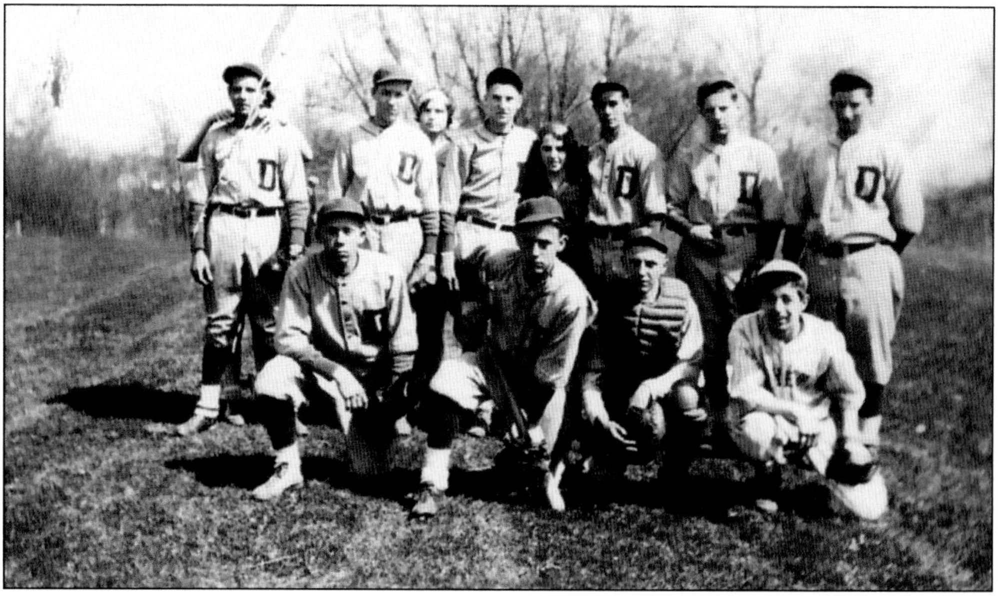

Pictured here is the 1929 Dyer championship baseball team. Sports played a big part in the lives of the townspeople. Dyer had a sports club named the Owls. Baseball was played in an open field behind the Mount Mercy Sanitarium. Care was taken not to step where the cows had been.

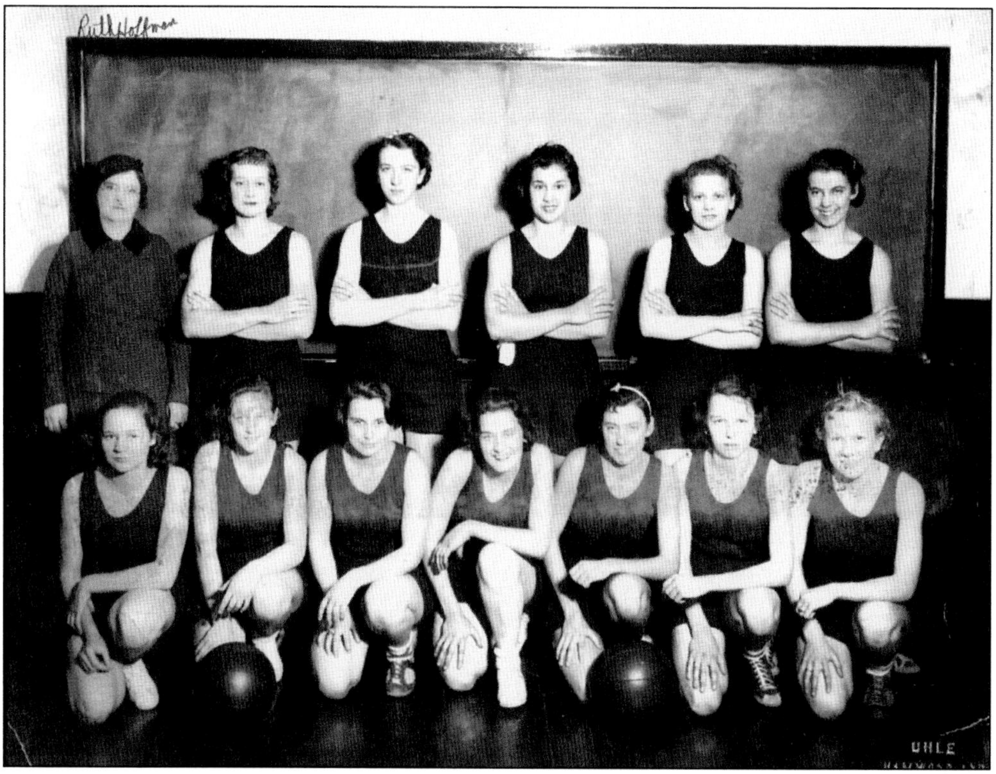

Featured in this photograph is an early women's basketball team. Sports in Dyer were open to boys, men, and later on, women and girls. It was entertainment made available to participants and players alike. Today, baseball, softball, and soccer are common sports played in the town parks.

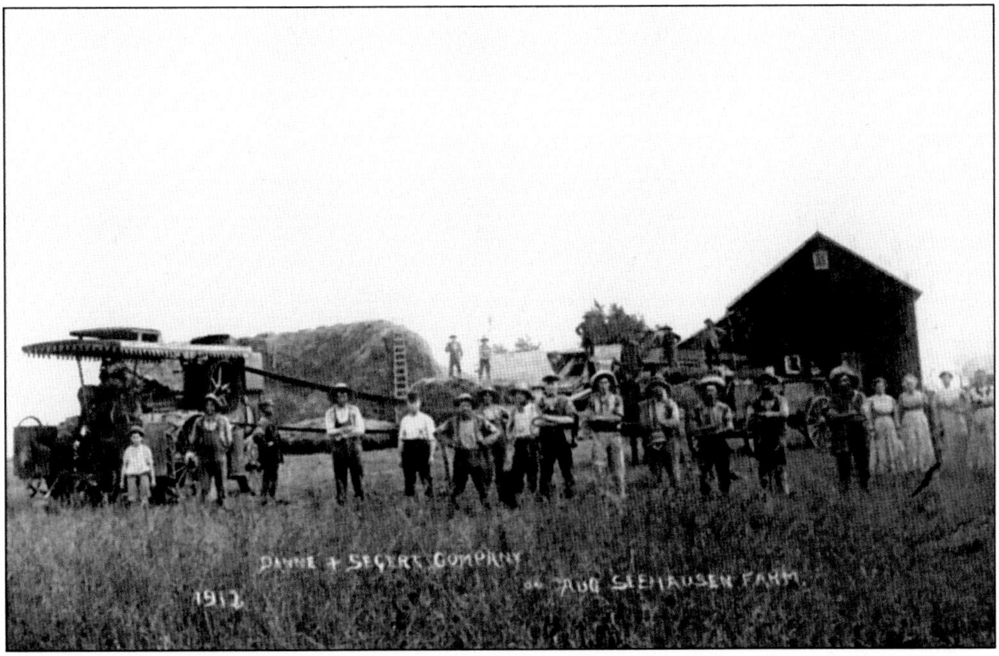

This 1912 photograph features the Danne and Segert Company on the August Seehausen farm. The Seehausen farm was located south of the Dyer downtown business district. Most of the area residents were farmers and the businesses in town catered to their needs, from blacksmithing to sales of seed and grain.

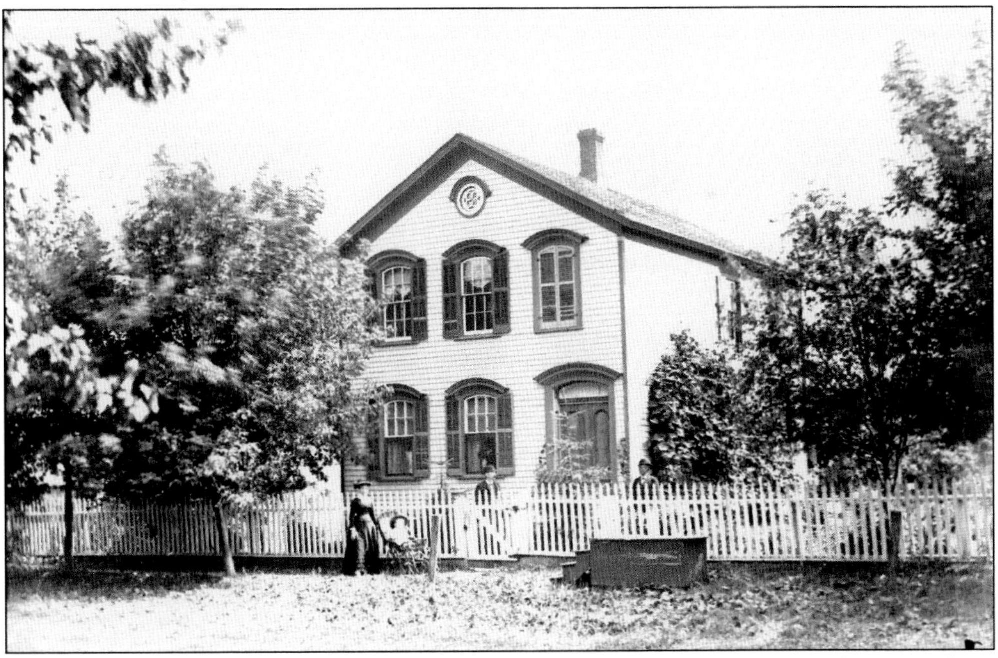

This 1883 photograph shows the William Severin family in front of the Severin home. William Severin and his family lived on a farmstead south of town before moving onto Hart Street near the business district of Dyer. They had nine children, one of whom assisted in starting the Dyer Union Sunday School.

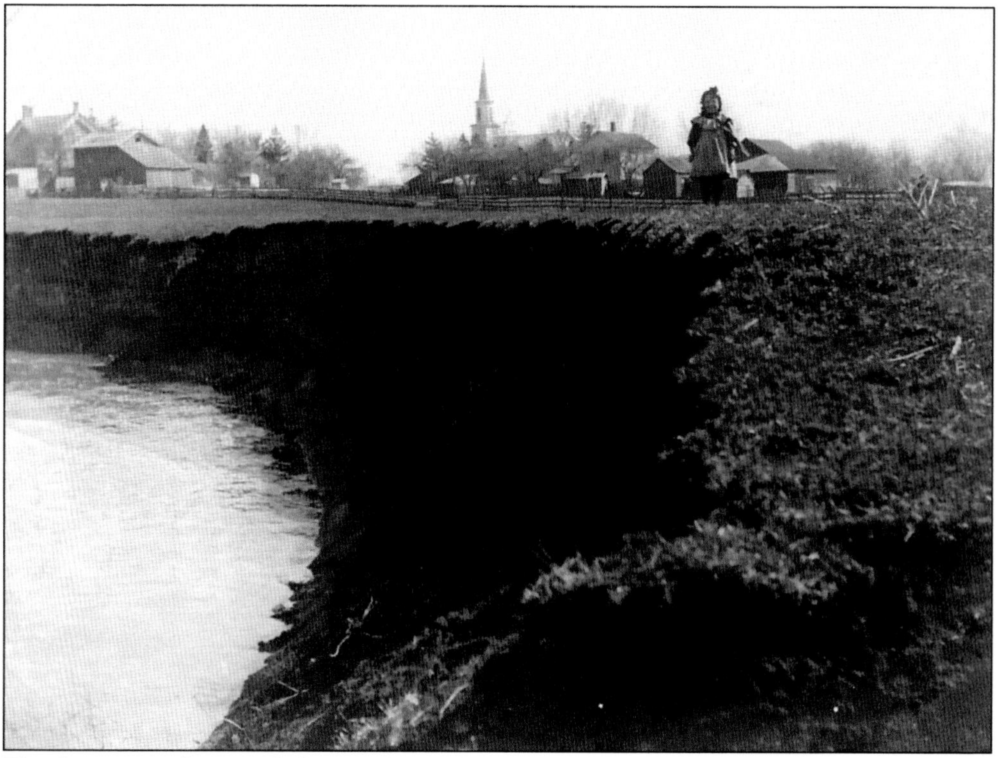

This late 1800s photograph features little Elnora Scheidt standing along Plum Creek with the original St. Joseph Church in the background. Though deepened and widened to drain the land, today the creek has a tendency to overflow its banks due to overdevelopment in the area.

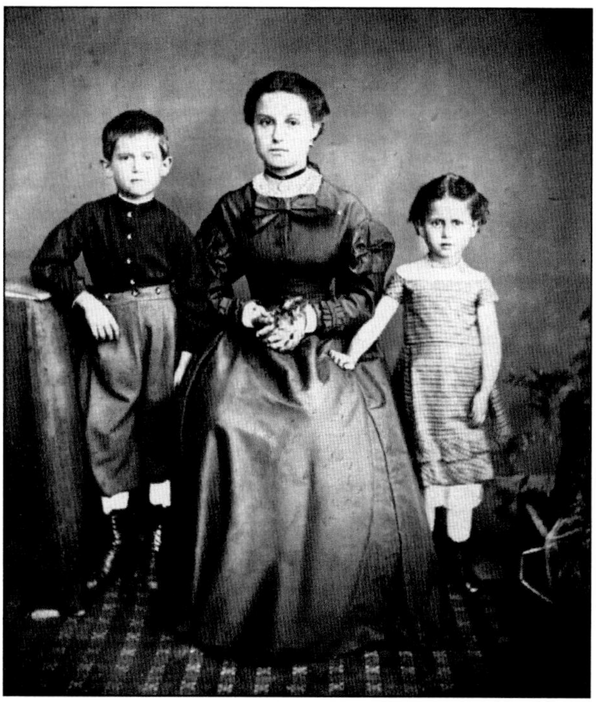

Pictured here are the descendents of Frank Scheidt: Edward, Mary Scheidt (married to Phil Keilman), and Barbara Jean. Frank Scheidt was from Strassberg, Illinois. He came to Dyer in 1893, where he opened a barber shop on the Lincoln Highway. At one time, Frank served as president of the First National Bank.

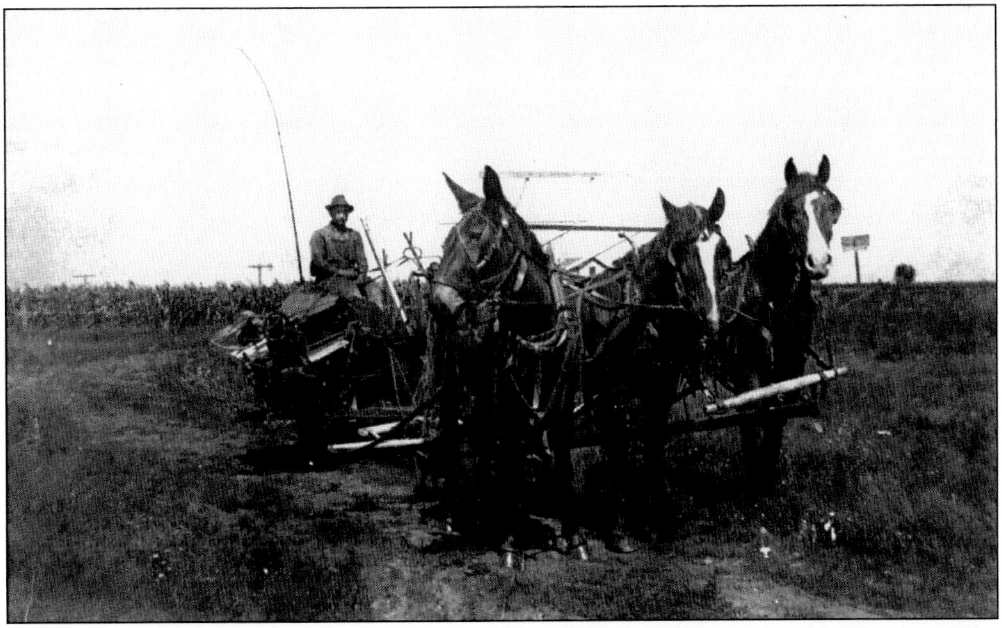

This photograph, taken around 1918, features John Schmitt on a thresher at the Hart farm. The farm was owned by Aaron Hart but was operated by a Mr. Maniniger. The Hart property called Hartsdale was located northeast of the downtown. Aaron Hart made an arrangement with the railroads, allowing them to run on his property in exchange for free passage.

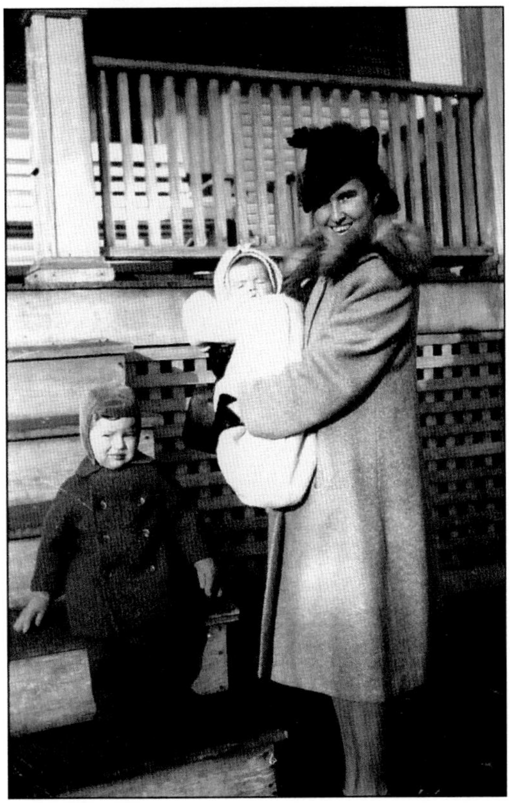

Pictured here is young Bill with his mother Henrietta Schulte, who is holding her newborn daughter Emily. Henrietta's father-in-law Henry Schulte purchased a blacksmith shop from Jacob Schaeffer and ran it until 1914. Henry served on the first town board, representing the third ward, from 1910 to 1915.

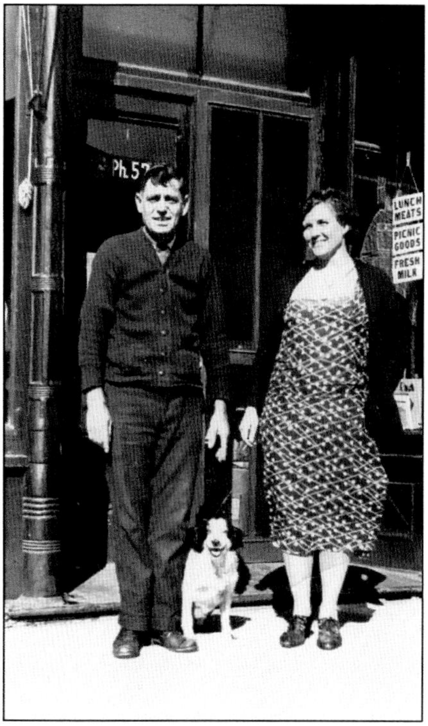

Pictured here are Helmuth and Ella (Seehausen) Schwab in front of their general store, co-owned by Andrew Peschel. Their store was in the John L. Keilman building, which stood on the corner of Hart Street and the Lincoln Highway. Helmuth Schwab was raised by August and Catherine Stommel.

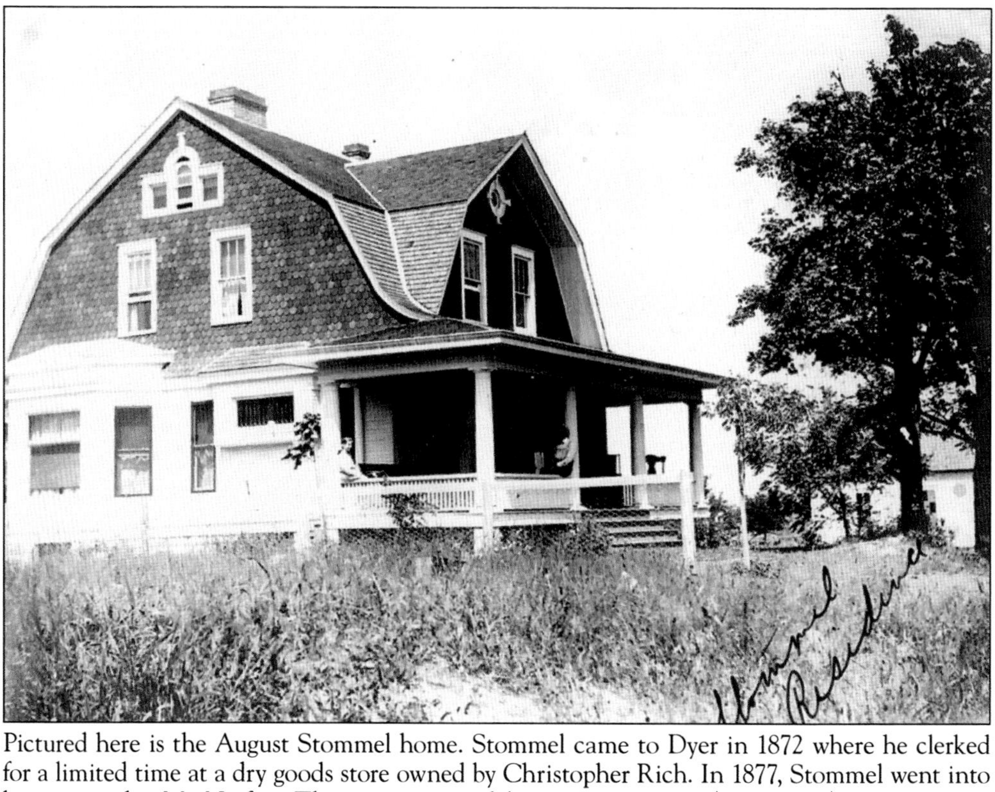

Pictured here is the August Stommel home. Stommel came to Dyer in 1872 where he clerked for a limited time at a dry goods store owned by Christopher Rich. In 1877, Stommel went into business with a Mr. Neifing. This was a successful venture reporting $18,000 to $20,000 a year.

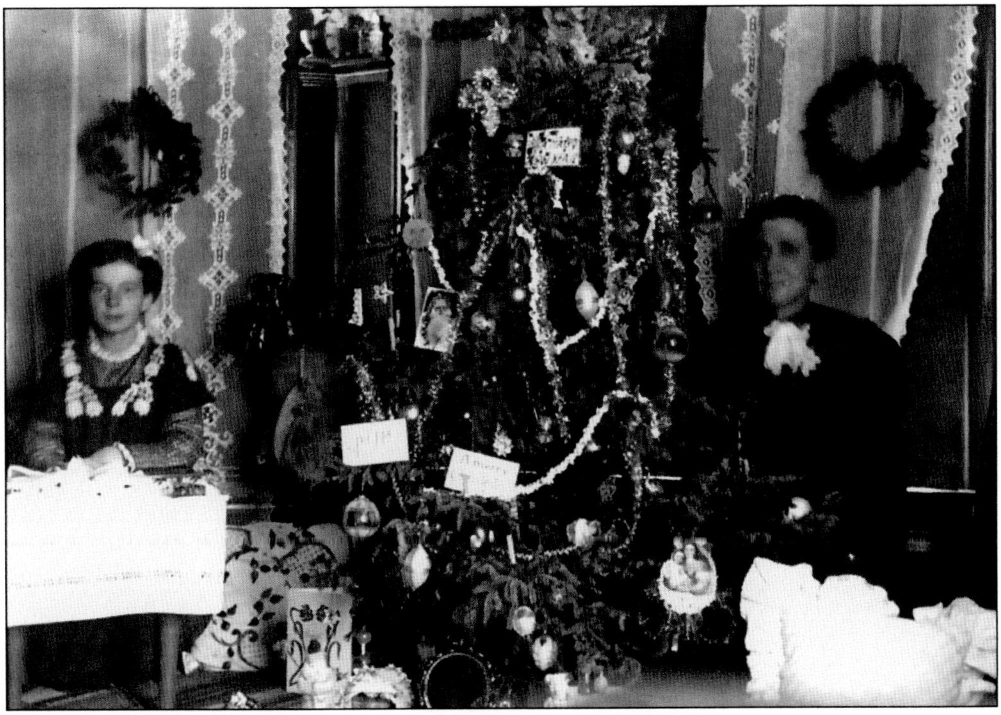

This photograph depicts Christmas at the August W. Stommel home in 1910. Pictured here is August's daughter Ruth with his wife Catherine. August and Ruth had three sons, all of whom died in their infancy. The Stommel family also raised Helmuth Schwab, who became a prominent business owner in Dyer.

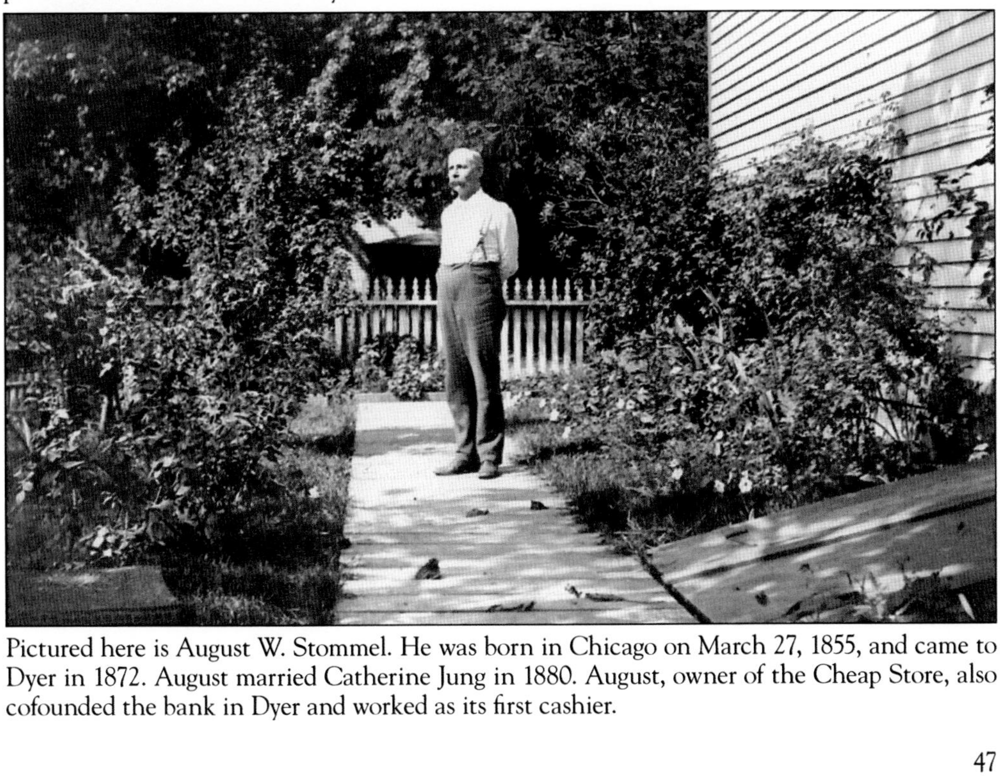

Pictured here is August W. Stommel. He was born in Chicago on March 27, 1855, and came to Dyer in 1872. August married Catherine Jung in 1880. August, owner of the Cheap Store, also cofounded the bank in Dyer and worked as its first cashier.

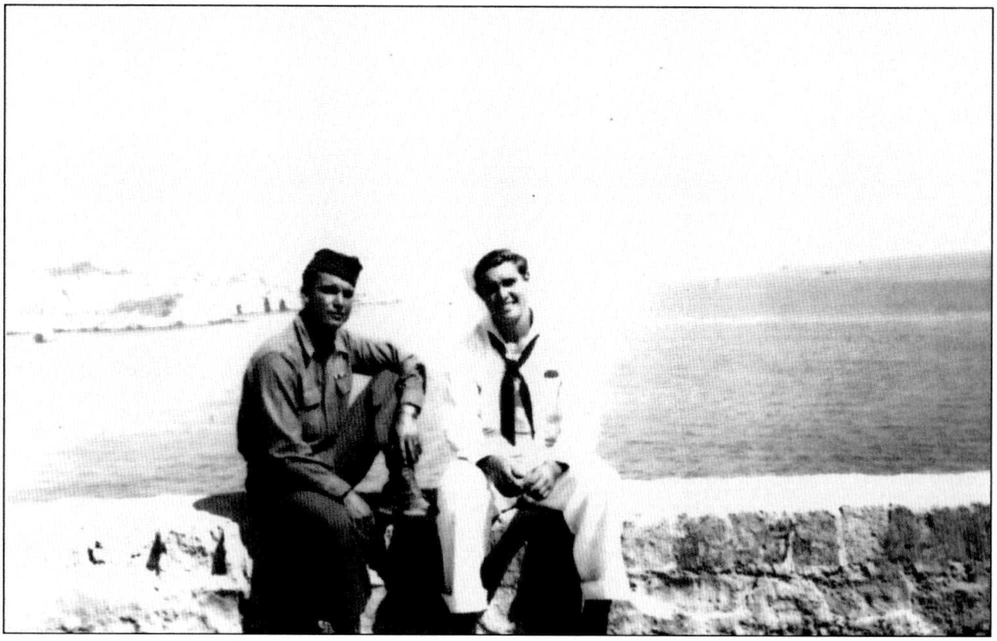

Cyril (left) and Gerald Teutemacher met in Italy during their service in World War II in 1944. Cyril was assigned to anti-aircraft units in Italy during World War II. Many Dyer residents have answered the call of duty during wartime, if not actually serving in the armed forces, then performing public duty at home.

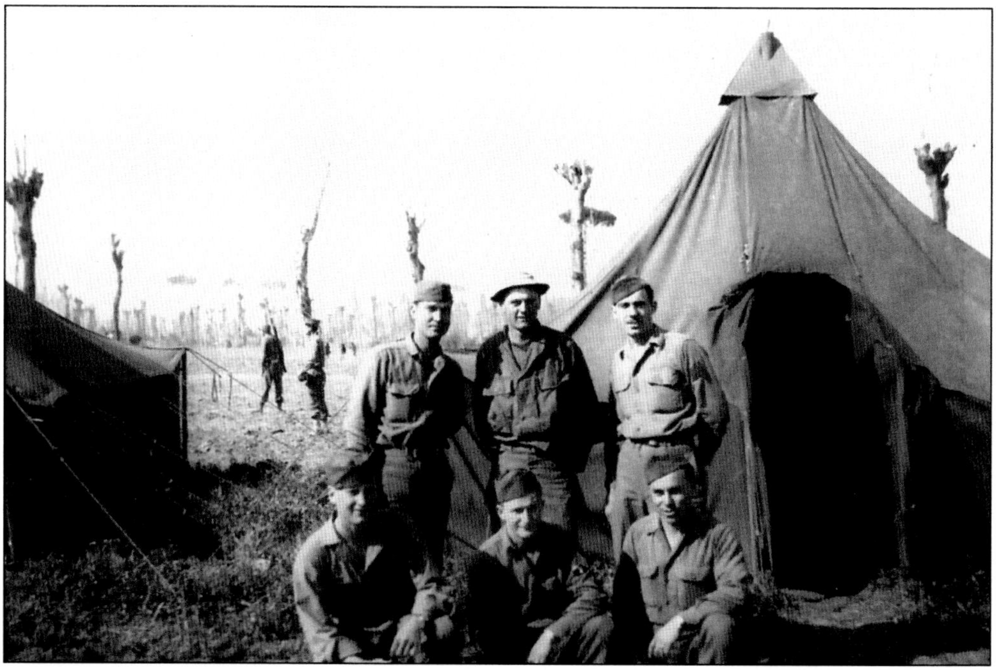

Featured in this photograph are men from the Calumet region who met in Italy in 1944 while serving in World War II. From left to right are (first row) Bob Mattix of Griffith, Clayton Jones of Crown Point, and ? Franz of Merrillville; (second row) Cyril Teutemacher of Dyer, Ambrose Rietman of Dyer, and Frank Brodner of Merrillville.

Two

BUSINESSES

Dyer saw its first business in 1856. It was a store, owned by John Streets. Two years later he converted it into a saloon. A distilling plant opened in 1863 that lasted only a couple of years. In 1870, a door and blind factory had been established, but succumbed to fire in 1872. The year 1870 was also the year Joseph Peschel opened a hardware store. Jacob Schaeffer ran a blacksmith shop but sold it to Henry Schulte, who owned it until 1914. Joseph and Kate (Beiriger) Schaller owned and operated the Dyer Hotel.

The Dyer Creamery had its start in 1893 on Fagen Street, close to Plum Creek. The creamery was a co-op where local farmers could process and ship their goods. The creamery moved behind the old inn on the corner of Route 30 and Hart Street. Here the creamery expanded and became one of the first businesses ever to produce powdered milk. Towards the end of the Dyer Creamery's existence, its biggest clients were Nestle, Heath, Brach, Cook, World's Finest, Ambrosia, Cadbury, and other confectioneries. At the closing of the Dyer Creamery in the early 1990s, it was owned and operated by Wayne's son Mark Wallar.

In the early 1900s, Dyer had a cigar factory. There was a tin shop on Hart Street, just south of the Lincoln Highway, that was owned by a member of the Peschel family. The shop was sold to Nick Austgen, who made it into a harness shop in 1902. This business eventually became Austgen Hardware Store.

Hartman, Kallenberger and Gettler was a name-brand sauerkraut once produced here in Dyer. The pickle and sauerkraut factory opened in 1917. It was owned by Louis Hartman, Matt Gettler, Joe Gettler, John Burge, and a Mr. Kallenberger.

Another notable business was the Fitch Brother's Garage. Before Ford developed the assembly line, small businesses like the Fitch Brother's Garage did the assembly work. Ford and Case car parts were shipped via railway to the garage, where the brothers would assemble them and ship them back.

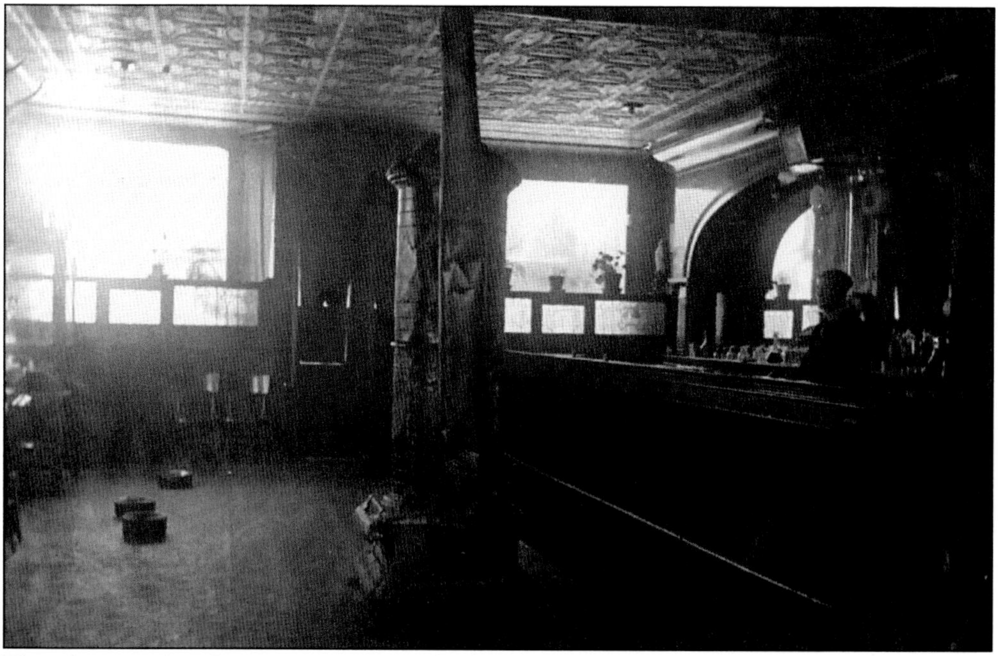

This photograph, taken in 1900, gives a look into the inside of State Line Hotel and saloon. It served food and drink and offered lodging to many weary travelers, traveling salesmen, and farmers, some hailing from 30 miles away to do business with the grain elevator in town.

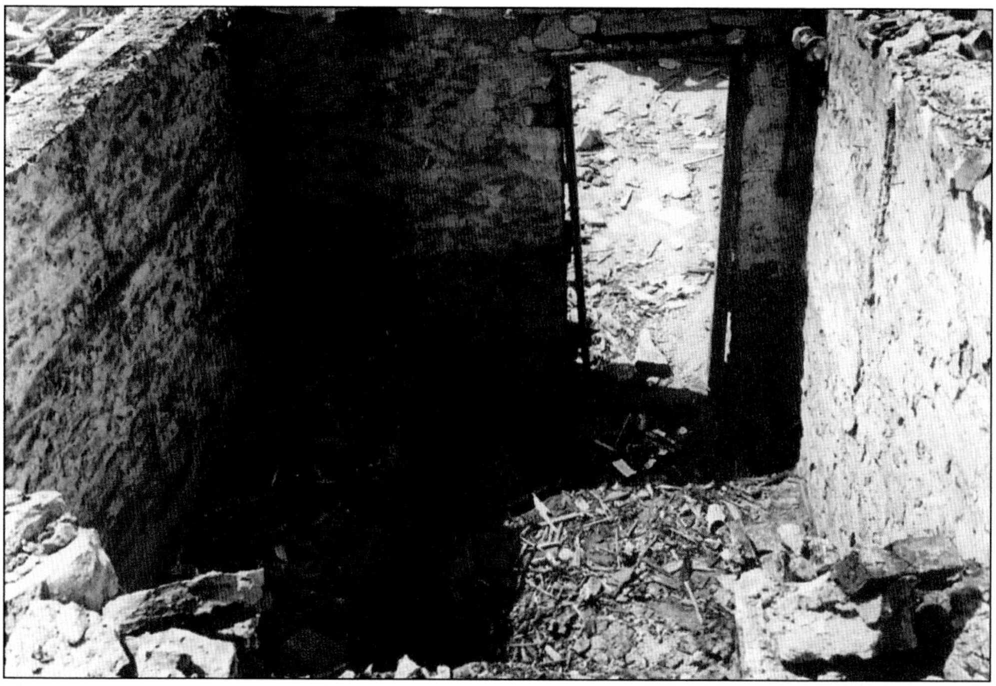

This 1994 photograph shows a hidden room located in the basement of the old State Line Hotel. It was rumored to be a part of the Underground Railroad. There is no evidence supporting this rumor, however. The Underground Railroad has been documented to come through the area along the Sauk Trail.

Pictured is the Cheap Store, opened in 1877 by August Stommel and a Mr. Neifing, which sold new merchandise. The store was taken over by August's brother Charles Stommel. The property changed hands a few times, becoming the Hoffman General Merchandise store, a grocery store, and a five-and-ten owned by Kenny and Louise Coomes.

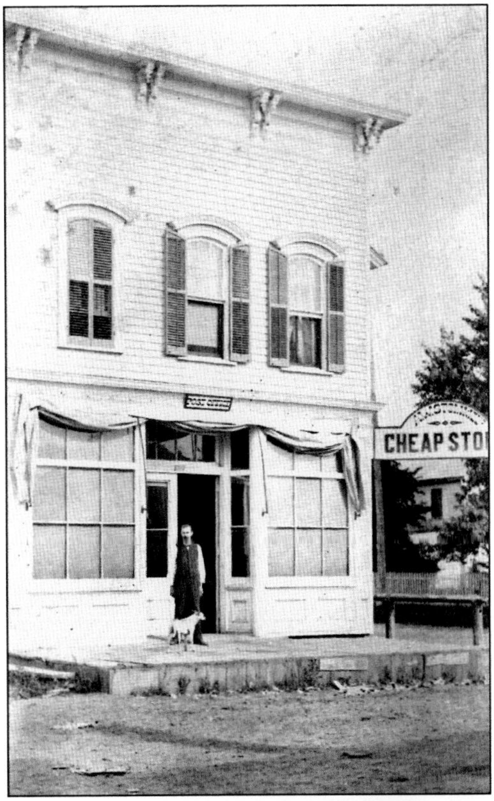

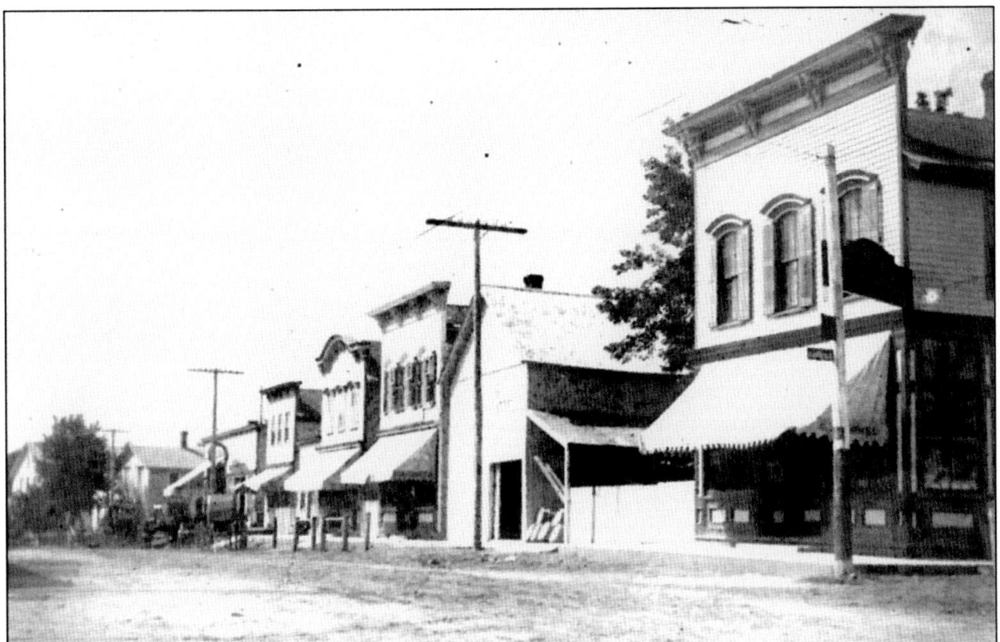

This picture features the Cheap Store, far right, in the late 1800s. Henry C. Batterman was a blacksmith and wagon merchant who owned the harness and hardware shop, pictured just to the left of the Cheap Store.

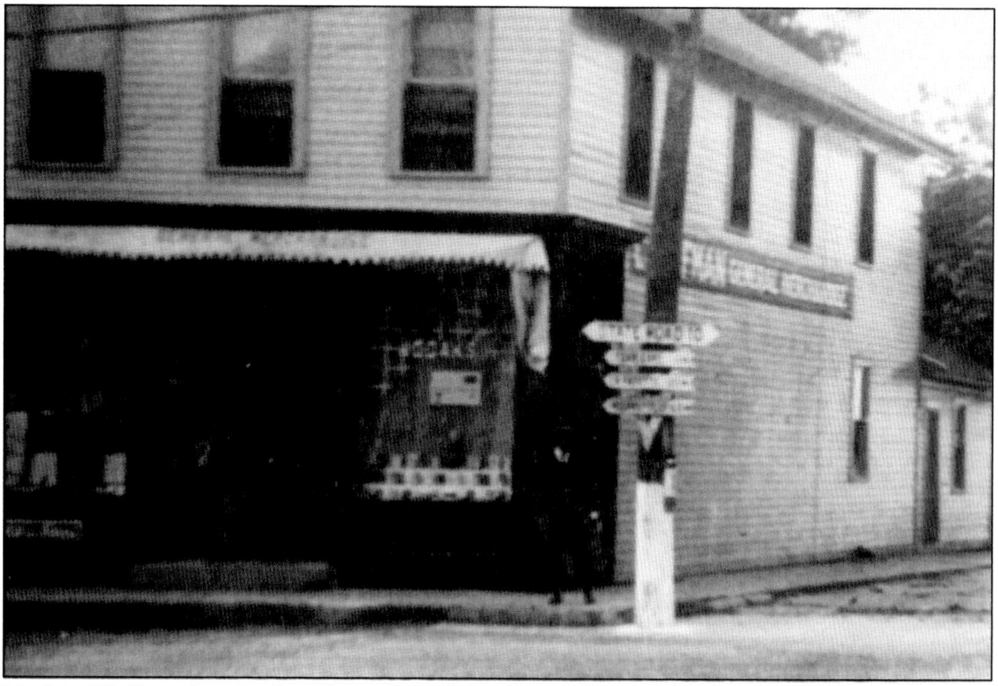

Mathias Hoffman bought the Cheap Store from August Stommel and made it into the Hoffman General Merchandise store. Mathias's son Leo took over the store. Eventually Kenneth and Gilbert, sons of Leo, operated it after Leo's retirement. They moved the store to Joliet Street where it became an IGA Supermarket.

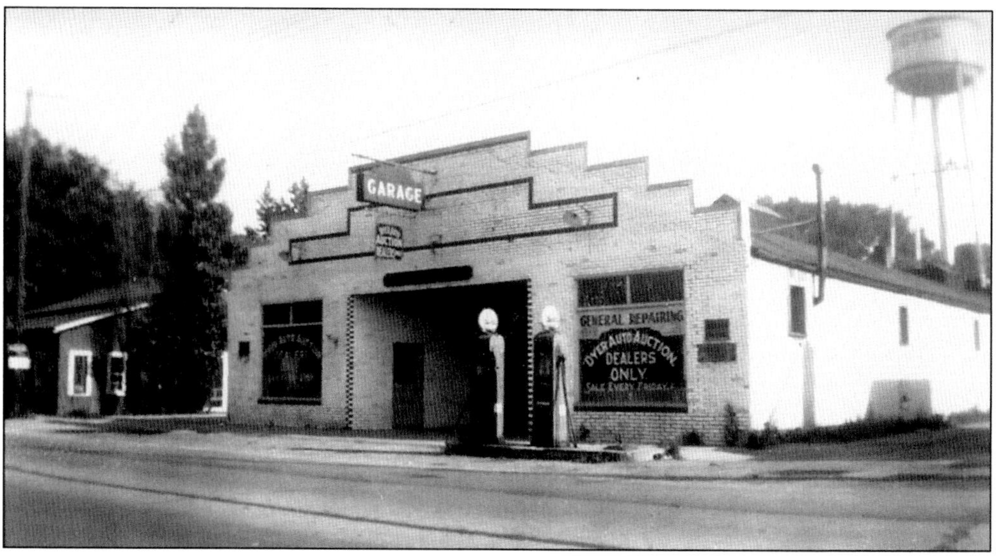

Featured here is the Dyer Auto Auction. In its early history, this was the site of the Hoffman Grocery Store and IGA. Original owner Mathias Hoffman passed the business to his son Leo. Leo passed it on to his two sons Kenneth and Gilbert. They ran the store as an IGA Supermarket before it became the Dyer Auto Auction.

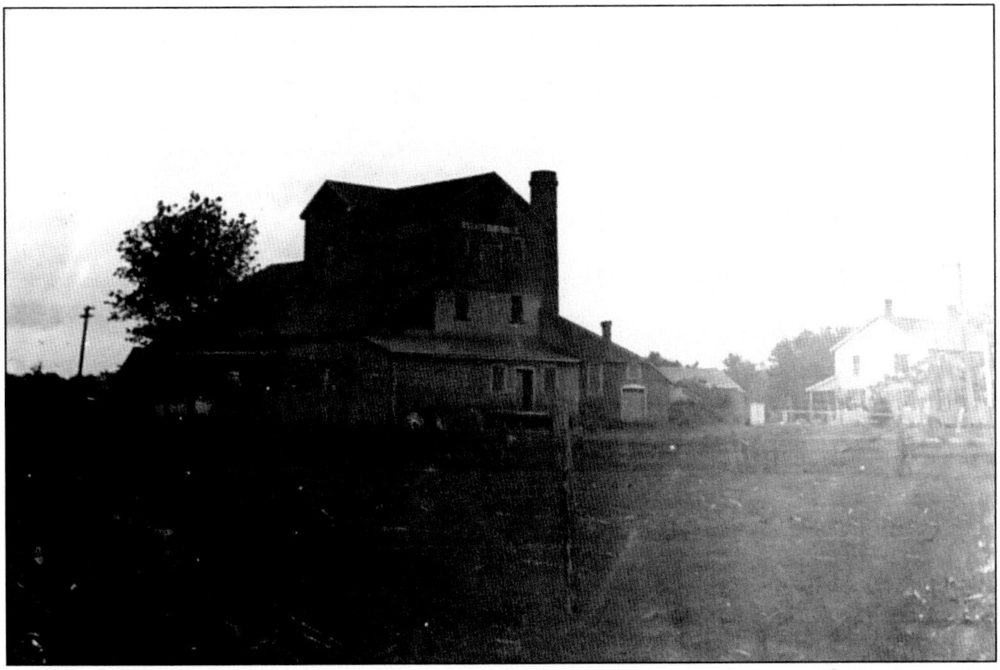

The Dyer Flour Mill, located on Matteson Street near the grain elevator, was built in 1856 and operated by two French brothers, August and John DeBrueil. Eventually they decided to go into the grain business and sold the mill to Scheidt and Davis, who then later sold it to Charles W. Friedrich.

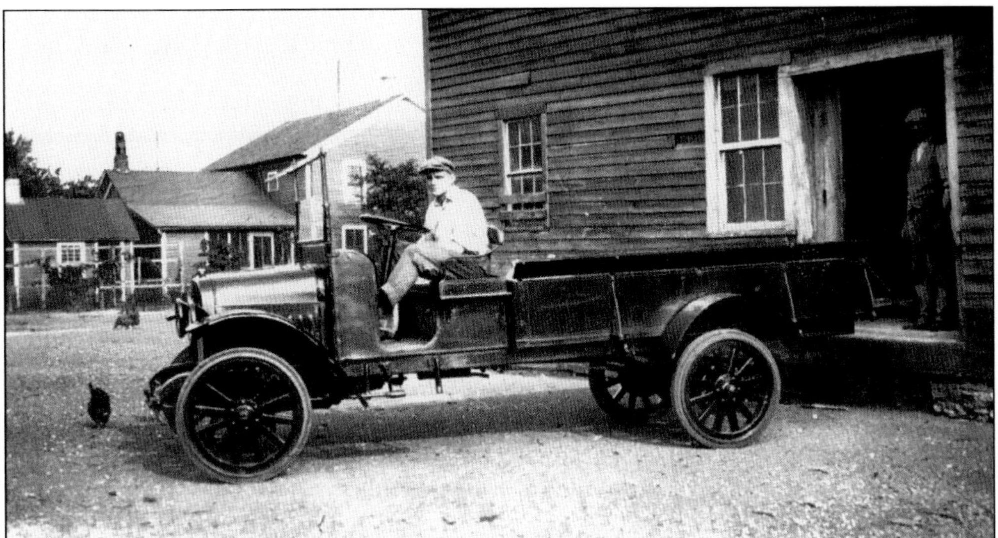

Featured here is Carl Friedrich, son of flour mill owner Charles W. Friedrich, in a Maxwell truck at the old flour mill. He worked with his father at the flour mill, helping his brother William when he took over after their father's retirement. This picture was taken in August 1916.

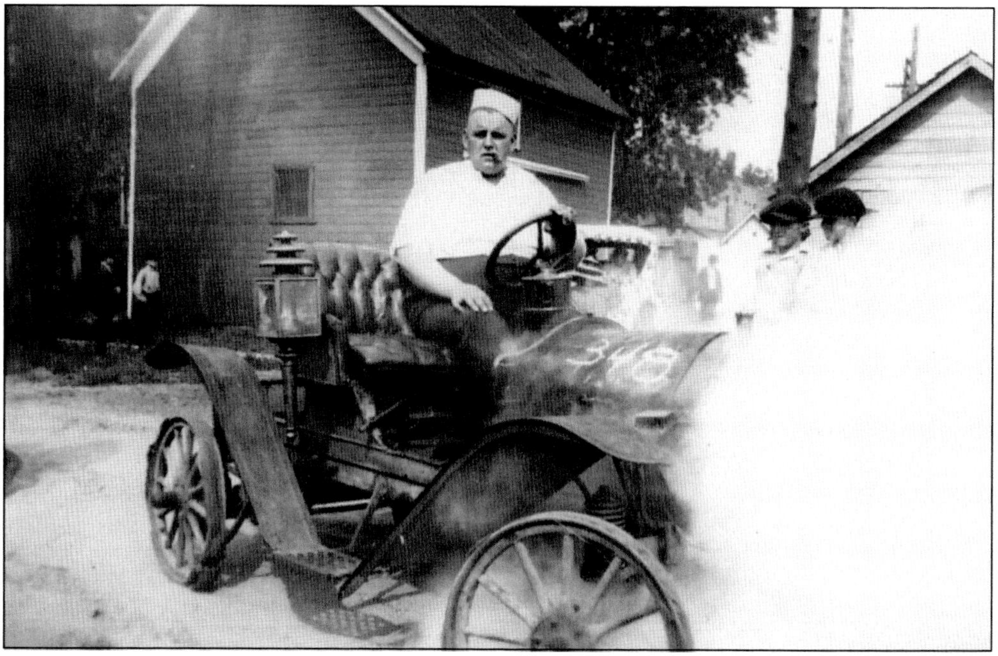

Pictured here is William H. Friedrich, son of flour mill owner Charles W. Friedrich, in a Brush Runabout. He married Ida Ross of North Judson. William took over his father's flour mill when Charles retired. Eventually William and Ida left Dyer to live in Chicago.

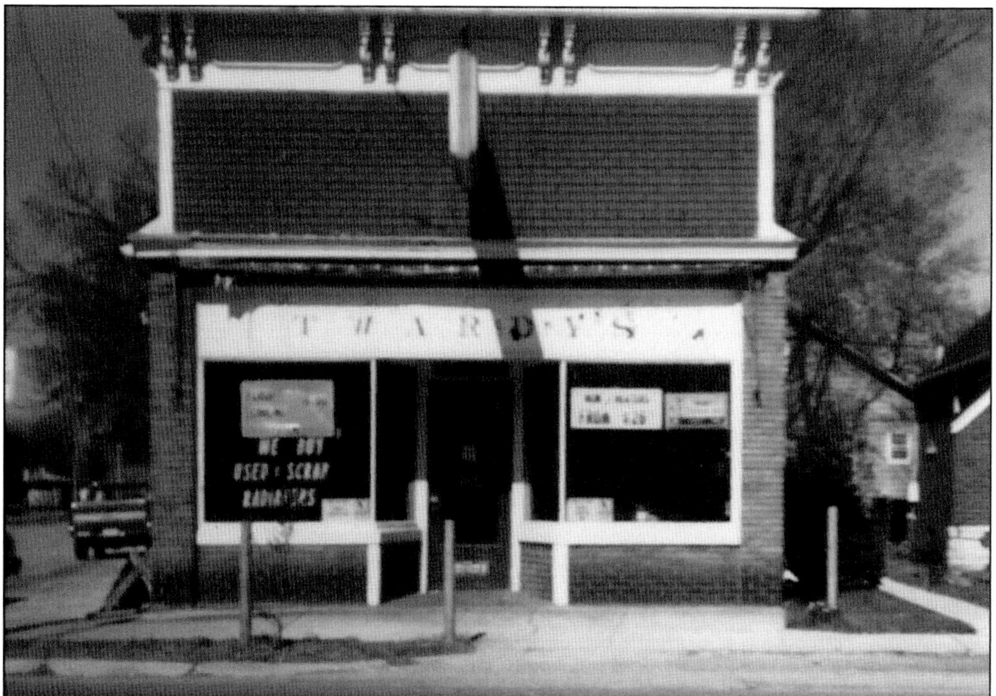

Pictured here is the Twardy's Radiator Shop, which is no longer in business. This building is the original Dyer Meat Market built and operated by Michael Fagen in 1895. People came from as far as Chicago to purchase the fine goods from this store. This photograph was taken in May 1988.

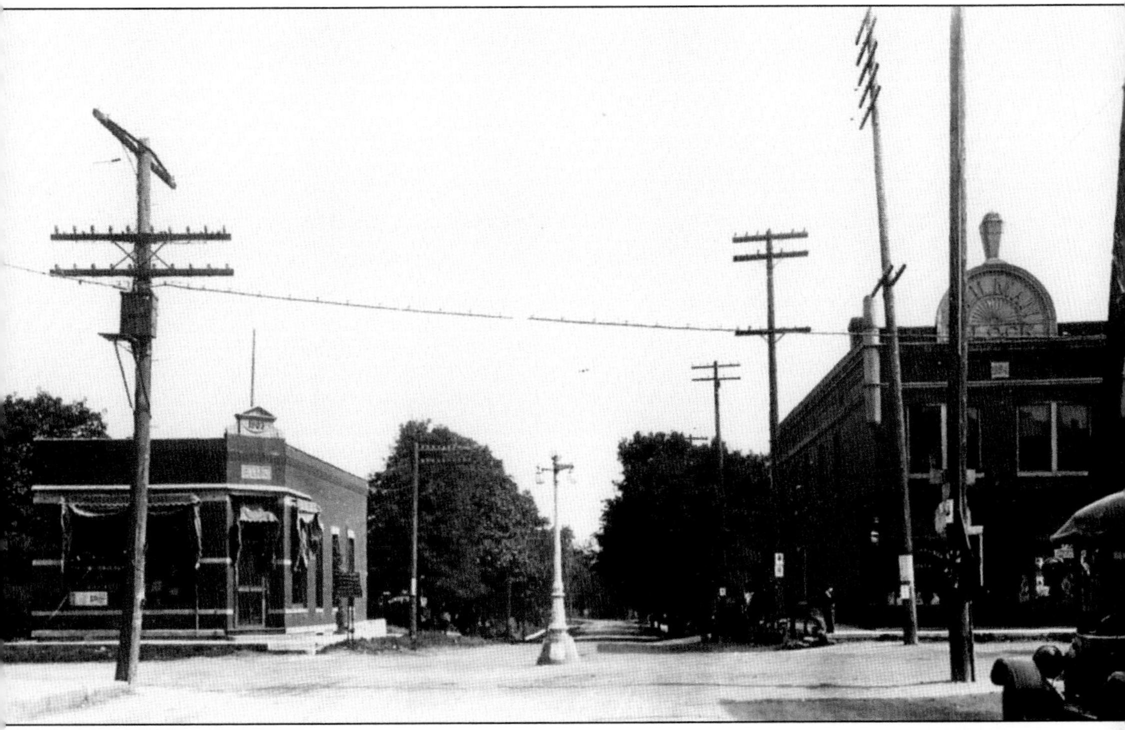

This is a photograph of Hart Street, once called Adeway, facing north away from the business district of Dyer. The Sauk Trail is in the foreground, running east and west. This picture was taken around 1900. Hart Street and the Sauk Trail, later the Lincoln Highway, were the main crossroads in Dyer. At the crossing was the business district. The bank, general stores, pharmacies, the creamery, blacksmiths, restaurants, the State Line Hotel and Saloon, the Dyer Hotel, and many taverns could be found in this area. Further north were the railroads, grain elevator, flour mill, Hartman's Hotel and saloon, Fagen Funeral Parlor, and sauerkraut factory. Some residents lived in this immediate area but most lived on farms in the outer regions of Dyer's borders. Some of the business owners were farmers themselves. While the businesses basically served the farmers' needs, they also benefitted by having the Lincoln Highway built. This increased traffic running through the town. Many travelers would stop for overnight lodging, food and drink, or any other supplies they found a need for.

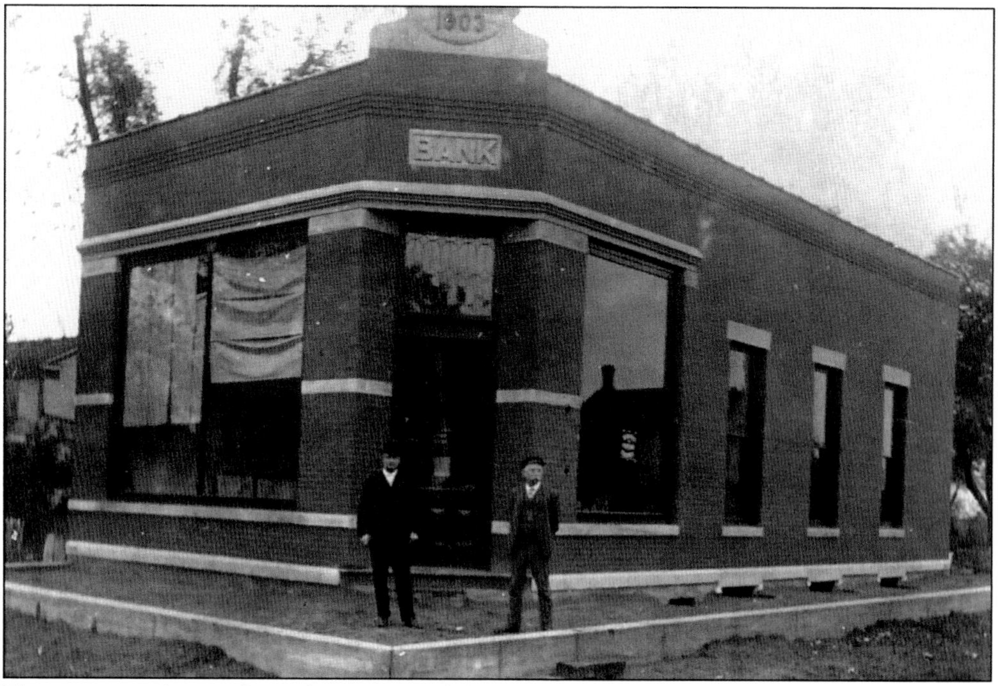

This picture, taken in the early 1900s, is of the First National Bank of Dyer. Posing in front are two of its five cofounders, William N. Gettler (left) and August W. Stommel. Cofounders John L. Keilman, John L. Kimmett, and Henry L. Keilman are not pictured. The bank was established in 1903.

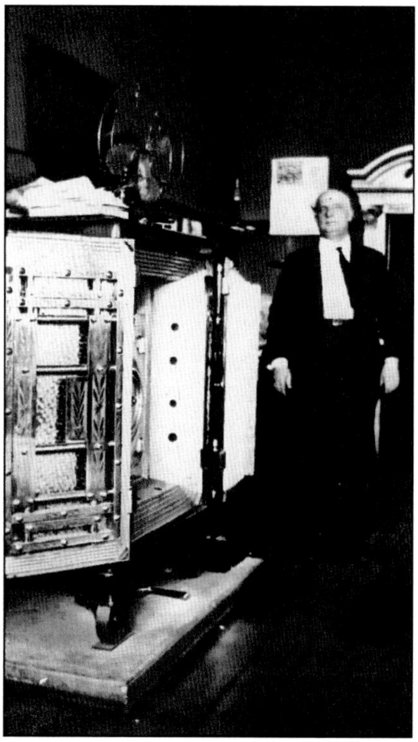

William N. Gettler poses with the safe inside the First National Bank of Dyer. He was one of the founders of the First National Bank of Dyer, worked as a cashier from 1903 to 1939, and became the president of the bank. William also served as Dyer's clerk-treasurer for 29 years.

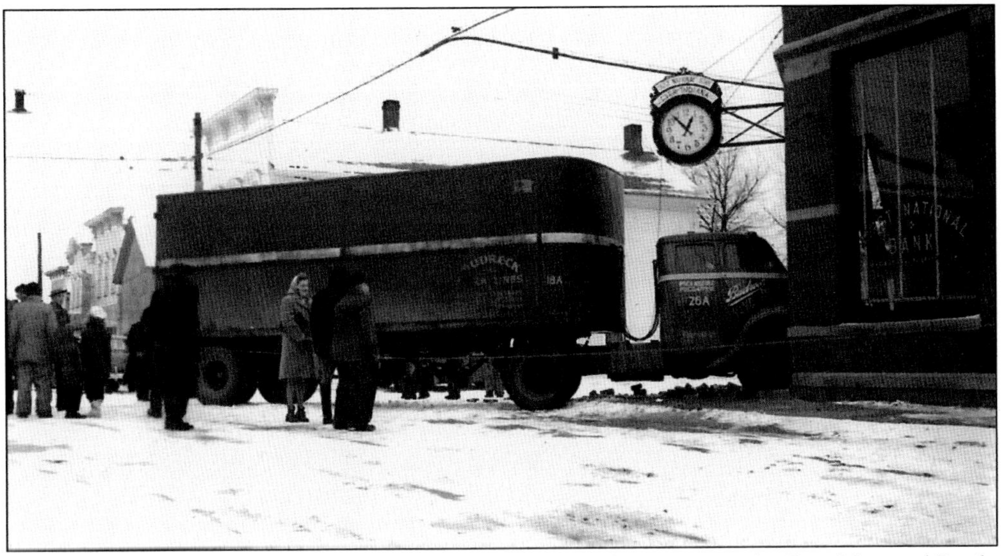

This 1940s photograph features a Budreck whiskey truck that ran into the First National Bank. In 1947, the bank changed to Gary National Bank. In 1982, it became Gainer Bank. In 1994, it relocated to the northwest corner of Route 30 and Calumet Avenue and became NBD, Bank One, and in 2005, it switched to Chase Bank.

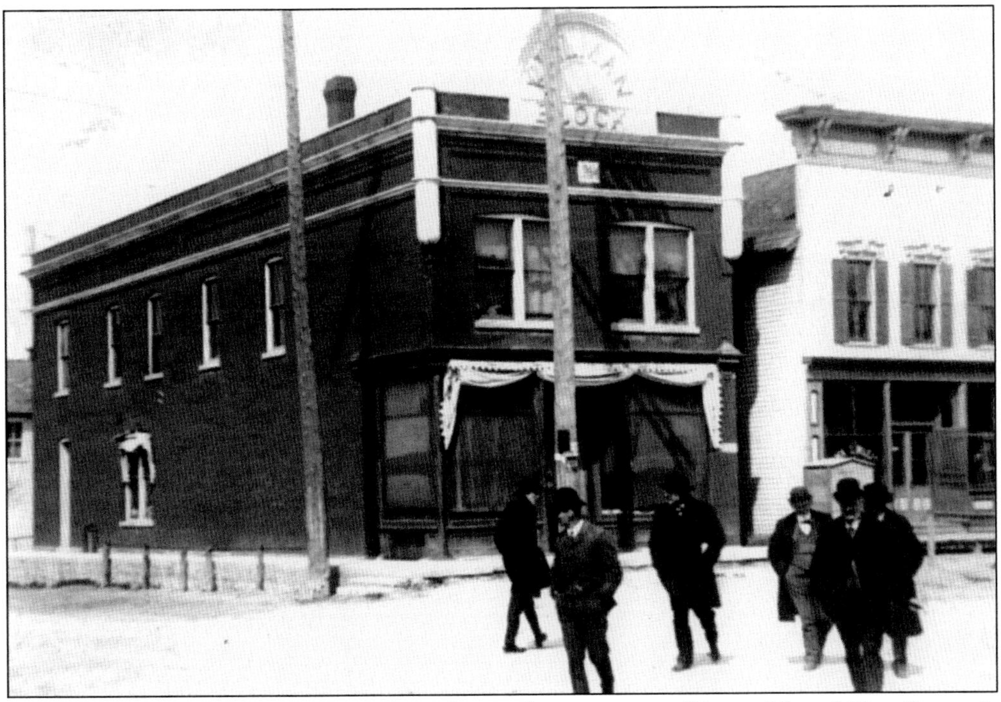

The John L. Keilman building stood on the northeast corner of Route 30 and Hart Street. It housed a dry goods store until 1925, when Peschel and Schwab turned it into a general store. In 1949, Leo Putz turned it into the Royal Blue grocery store. The building became the Lincolnway Building that housed various offices.

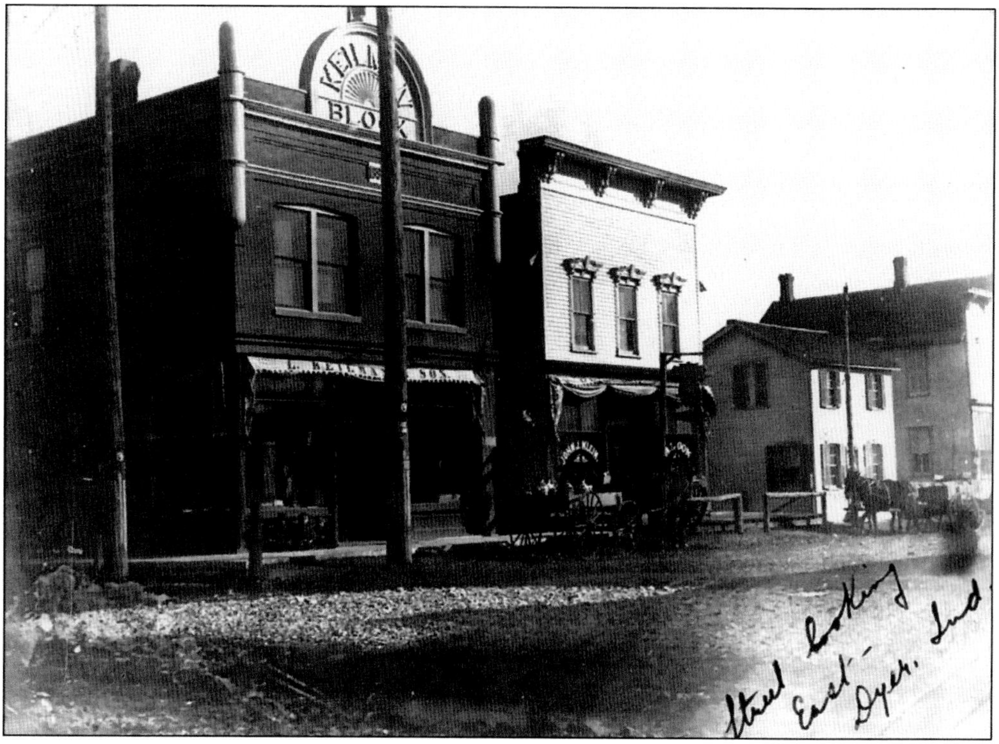

The building on the left is the Keilman building. To the right of that is the John J. Klein Saloon. There were a total of seven saloons in Dyer during the early 1900s. Not only did they serve the townfolk, but the many voyagers traveling by railway and road.

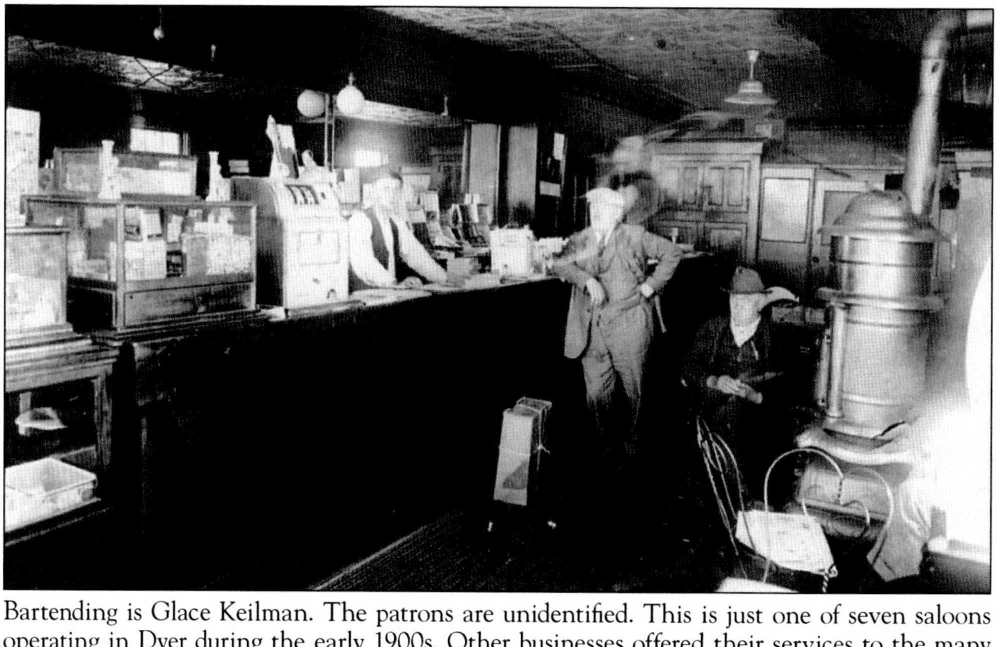

Bartending is Glace Keilman. The patrons are unidentified. This is just one of seven saloons operating in Dyer during the early 1900s. Other businesses offered their services to the many travelers coming through Dyer as well. There were three hotels and a livery stable for travelers to house or rent horse and carriage.

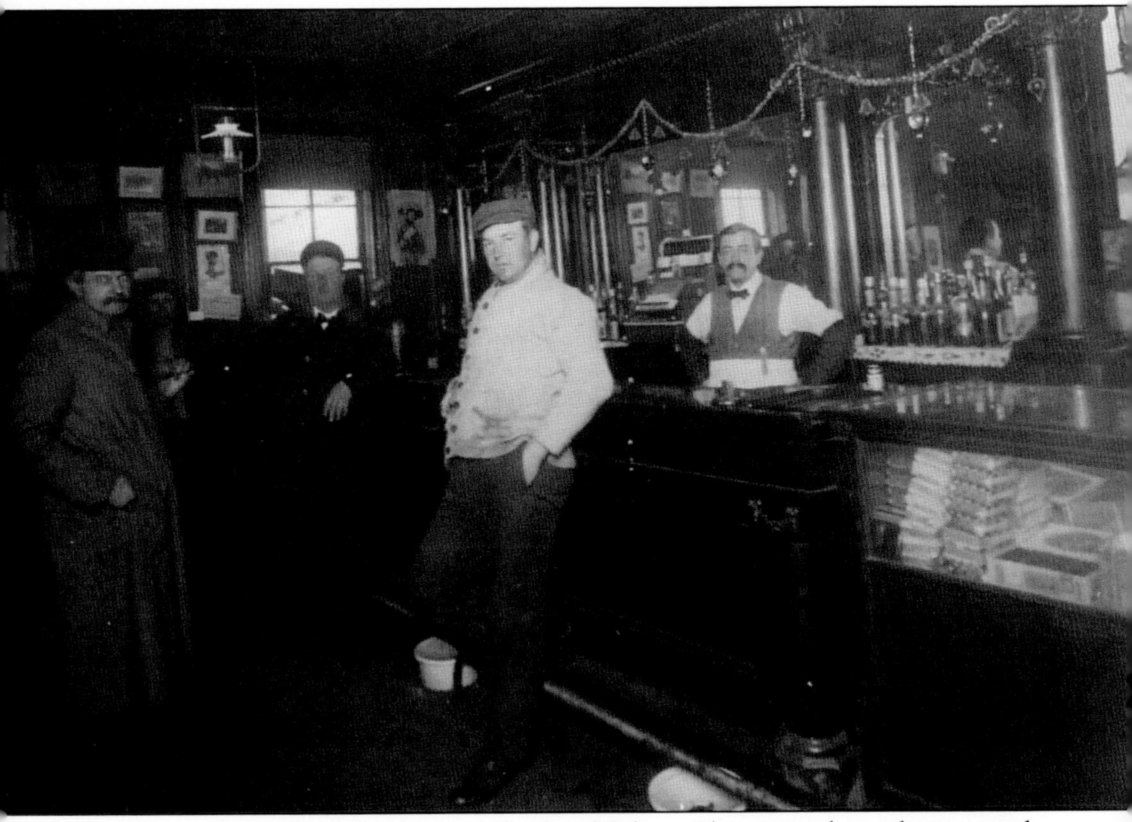

Pictured here is the inside of the Hartman Hotel and Saloon. The seven saloons that operated in Dyer during the early 1900s never seemed wanting of patrons. Locals and out-of-towners paid visits to these taverns. Much was offered to wet the whistles and the appetites of the customers. Many out-of-town farmers coming to Dyer to deliver their crops to the grain elevator would stay the night at one of the hotels and visit the saloon for food and drink. In addition to the hotels and saloons, other services were available to the passing travelers. Many salesmen came to town by horse or by train. Those who came to town to sell their goods and supply the general stores with their wares would visit the livery, which was located behind the State Line Hotel. Here they could lodge their horse overnight or rent a horse to travel to the other local towns to promote their merchandise.

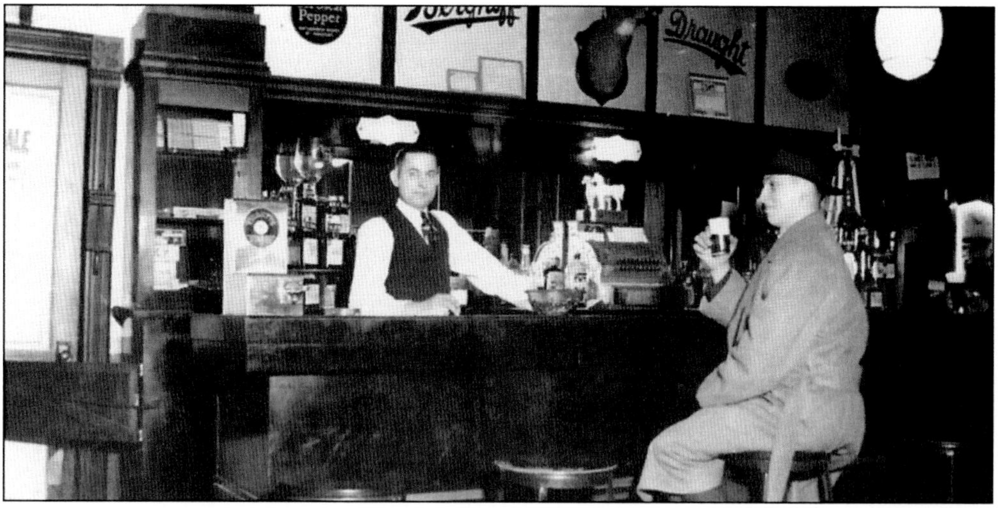

This 1930 photograph features Greiving's Tavern, once located on the Lincoln Highway, also called Joliet Street. Identified are owner Henry Greiving, bartending, and Francis Peschel, who is enjoying his drink at the bar. Greiving Street was named after Henry Greiving. Francis was the son of Andrew Peschel, co-owner of the Peschel and Schwab store.

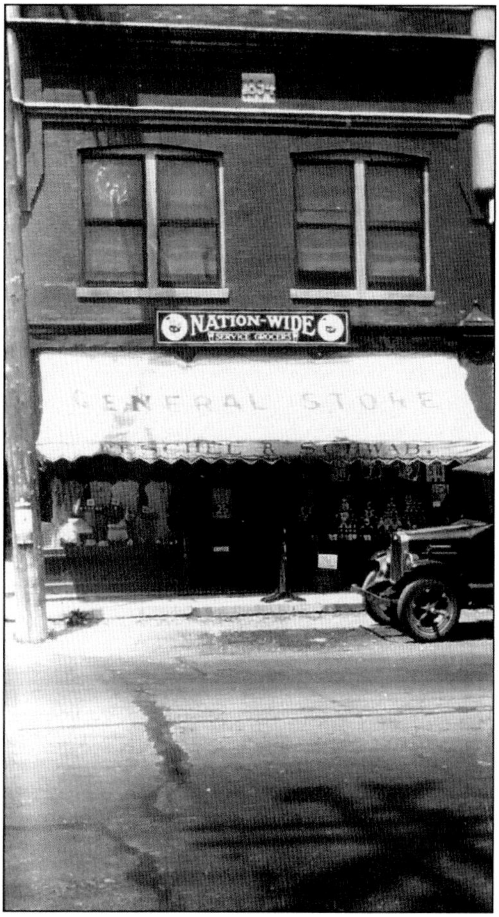

Pictured here is the Peschel and Schwab general store. It started as John L. Keilman's dry goods until purchased by Andrew Peschel and Helmuth Schwab when John Keilman retired in 1925. Schwab later bought out Peschel's share of the business. Schwab then turned it into a grocery and meat market.

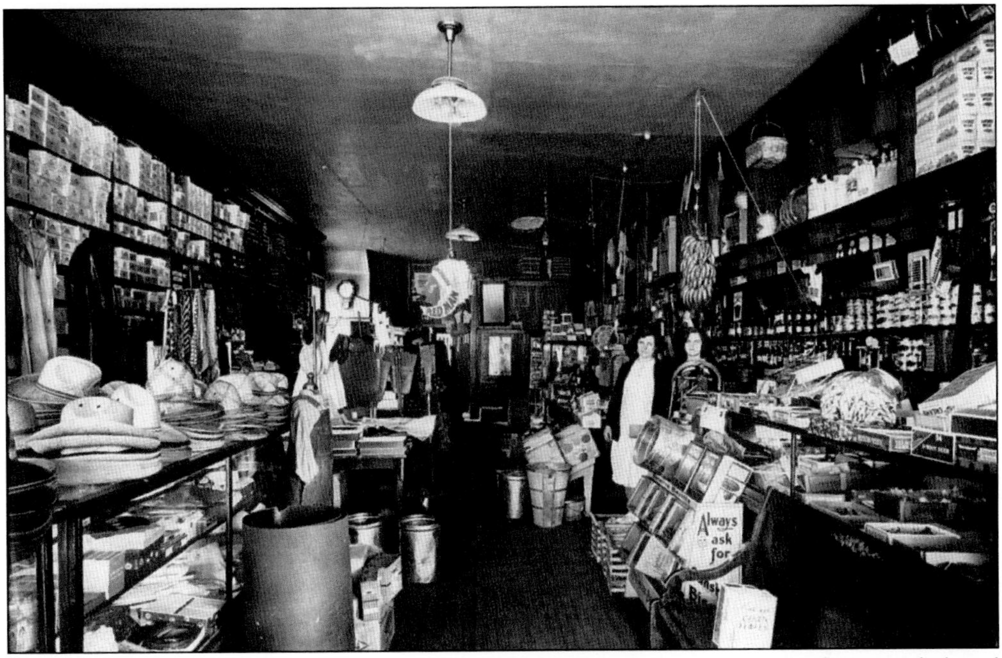

This picture, taken in the 1920s, is of Schwab's General Store, run by Andrew Peschel and Helmuth Schwab. It began as a dry goods store owned by John L. Keilman until he sold it to Peschel and Schwab. It stood in the John L. Keilman building on the northeast corner of Hart Street and U.S. 30.

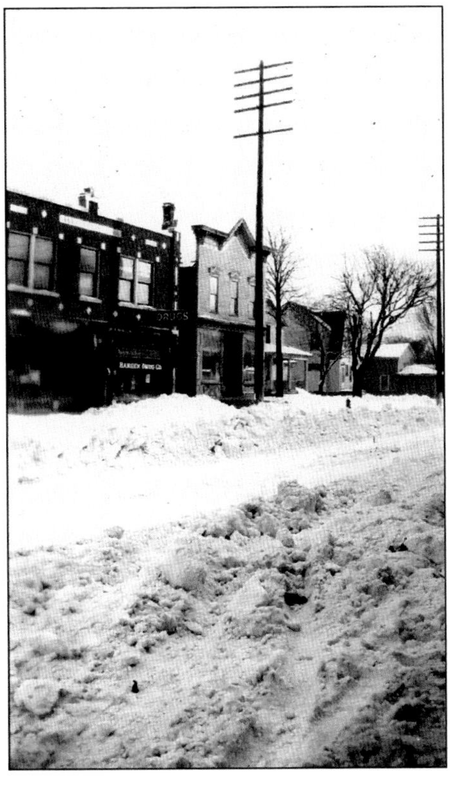

Pictured on the left is the Schilling building, housing Hansen's Drug Store, in 1923. The white building to the right is where the town's first meetings took place, then owned by Henry Schulte, trustee of the third ward.

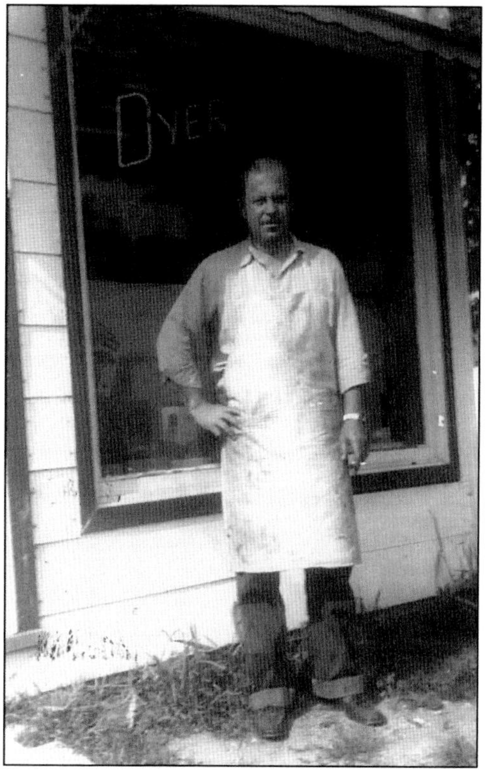

Marvin McBee poses in front of his shoe repair shop, once located on Schulte Street just south of the Lincoln Highway near where the town hall stands today. He and his wife used to drive the buses in the 1960s for the school system. This photograph was taken in 1955.

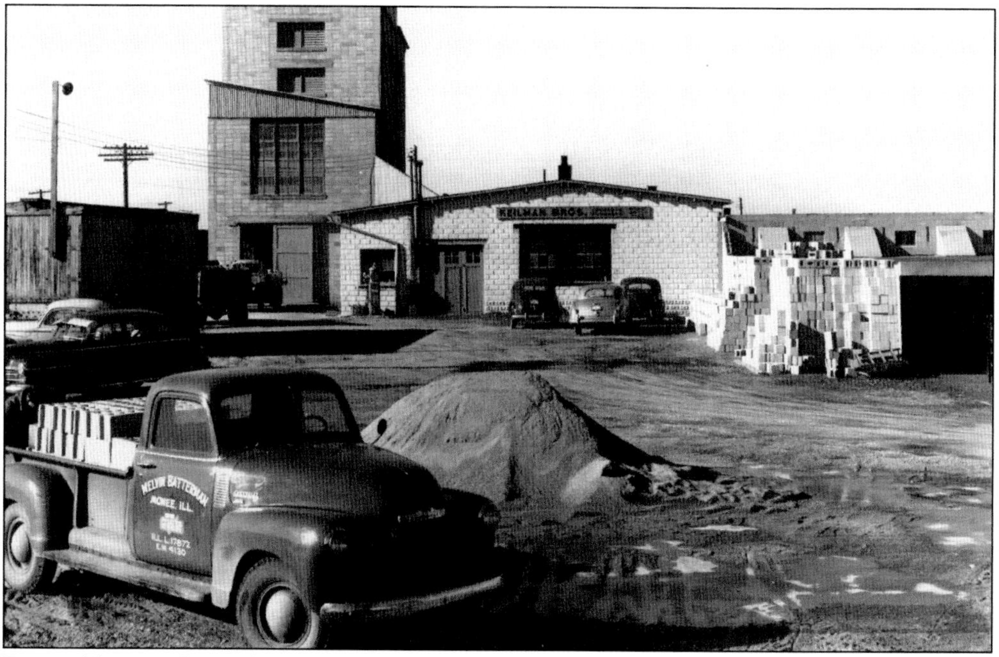

Pictured here is the Keilman Brothers Concrete Products plant, located just outside of Dyer in Illinois. This business was started by brothers Frank and Leonard Keilman, sons of Henry L. Keilman. Many members of the Keilman clan were very industrious. They were farmers, business entrepreneurs, and sometimes both.

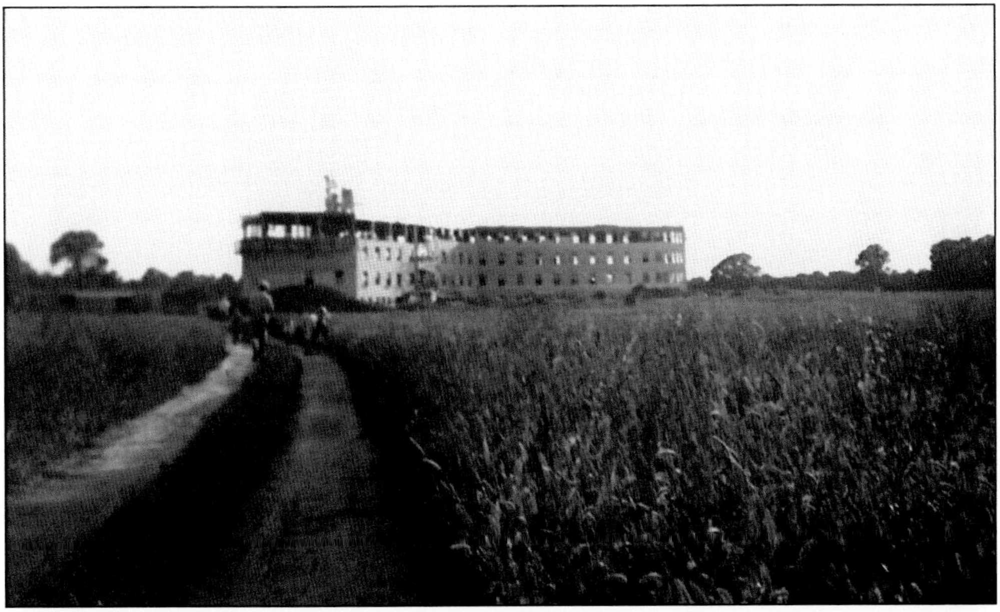

Pictured here is the Mount Mercy Sanitarium while under construction. John Lawler sold land to the Sisters of Mercy, who in 1942 constructed Mount Mercy Sanitarium on the 87 acres of land. At the time it was capable of housing 75 patients.

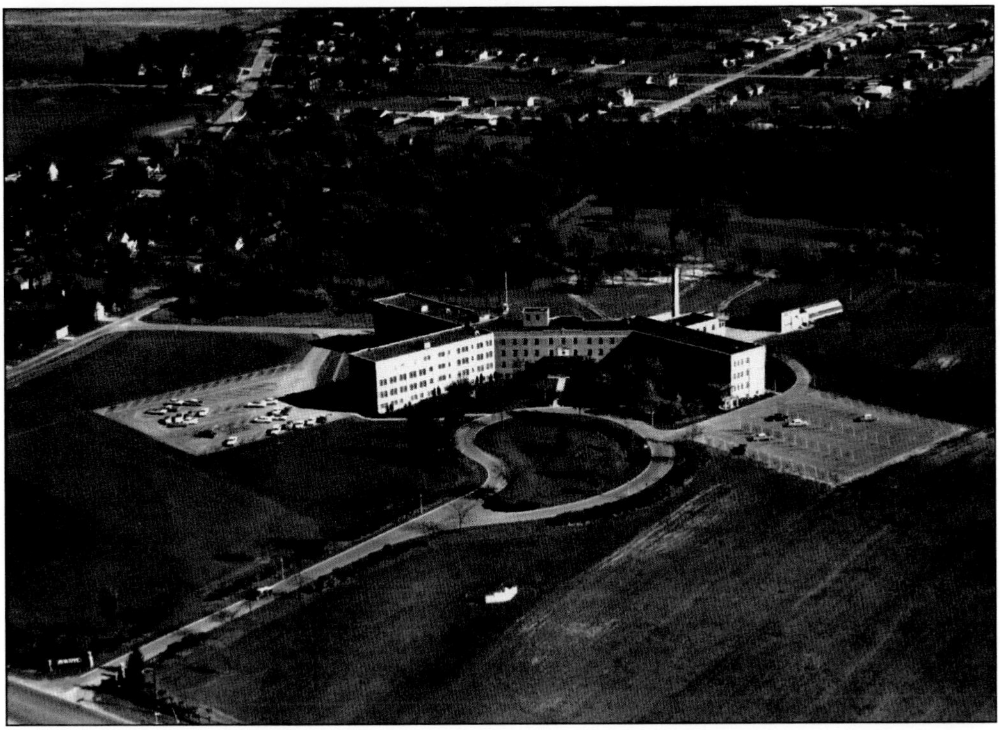

In 1952, the sanitarium was converted into a general hospital and renamed Our Lady of Mercy, pictured here in 1960. In 1972, the hospital expanded to 258 beds, 95 of which were for psychiatric care. The hospital converged with St. Margaret hospital in Hammond and is now called St. Margaret Mercy, south campus.

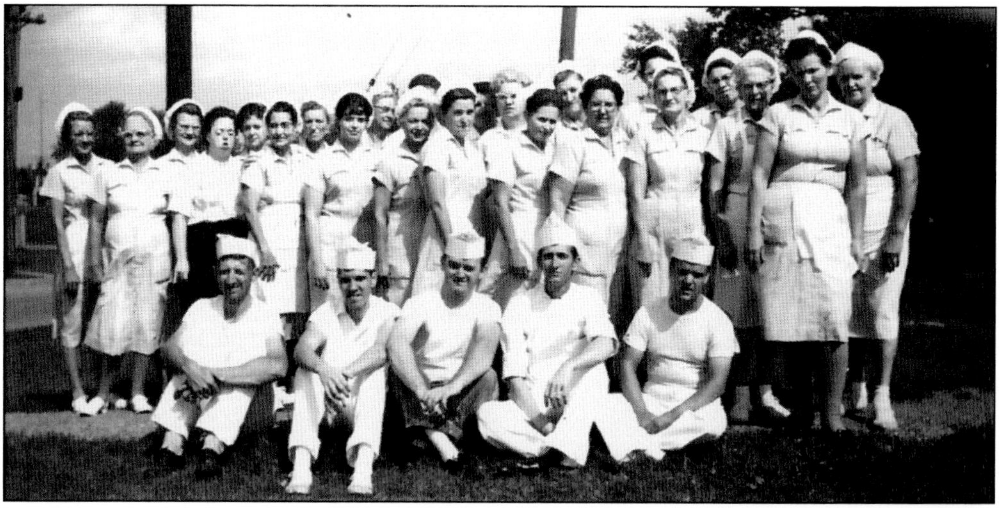

In addition to bringing medical care to the residents of Dyer, the hospital also brought job opportunities. This can be seen in this photograph of Our Lady of Mercy hospital staff of 1963. Today, a walking trail through the woods on the hospital property is open to the public.

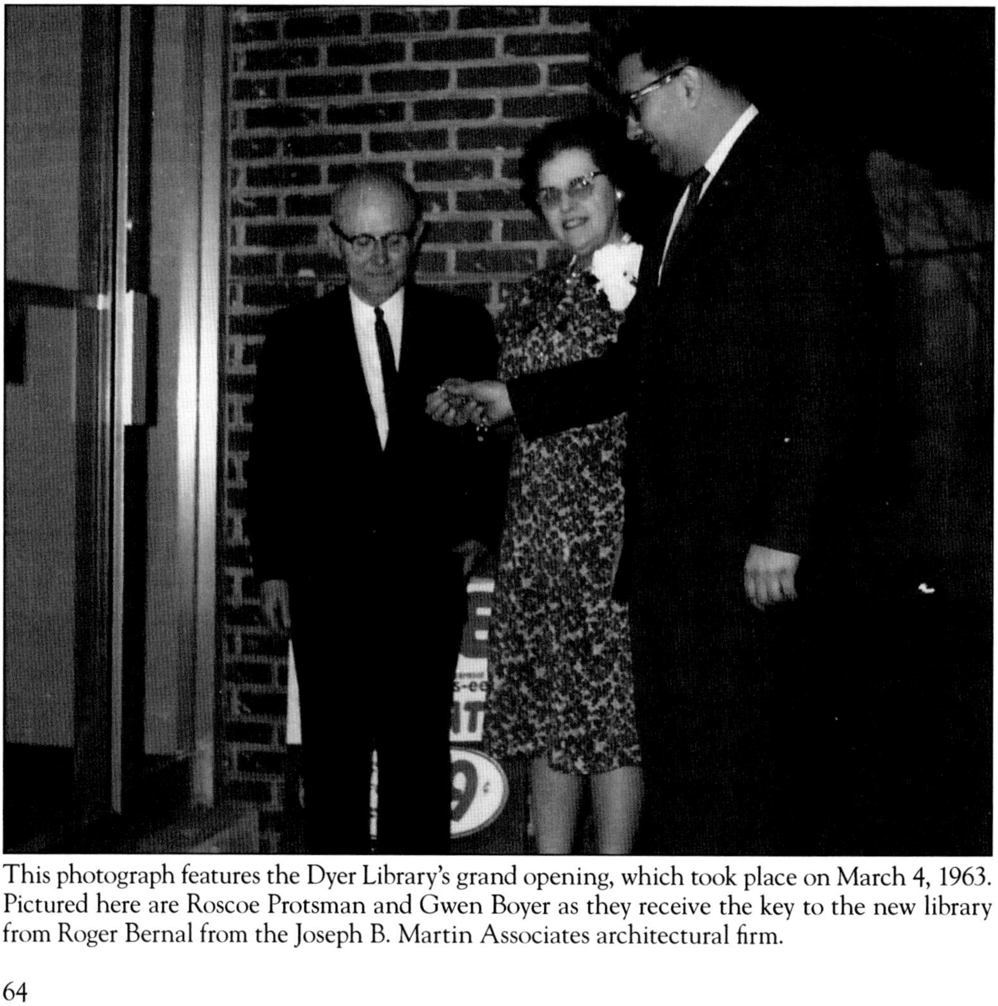

This photograph features the Dyer Library's grand opening, which took place on March 4, 1963. Pictured here are Roscoe Protsman and Gwen Boyer as they receive the key to the new library from Roger Bernal from the Joseph B. Martin Associates architectural firm.

Three

Churches

In 1867, Rev. Jacob Schmitz built the people of Dyer their first Catholic church, St. Joseph's. It was a small, whitewashed construction costing between $4,000 and $5,000. A rectory was built in 1869, but replaced in 1950 by Father Edmund A. Ley. In 1878, the parish became one of the first missions for the Franciscan Sisters, whose convent was built in 1901 along with the St. Joseph Catholic School. Unfortunately, the original church succumbed to fire in 1902. The church that stands today was built in 1903, dedicated by Father Joseph Flach on November 26 the same year, costing $18,000. Eventually a newer convent was built in 1924 by Father George Lauer and was later attached to the church itself.

In 1901, St. Joseph Church started a parishioner school. The schoolhouse was a wooden structure located north of the church, south of the cemetery. In 1938, a two-story brick structure with four rooms was built to house the pupils. An addition of four more classrooms was made again in 1956.

The church's Baldwin pipe organ has some history as well. It was featured in Chicago's 1933 Century of Progress International Exhibition before being purchased and finding a home at St. Joseph's. The Baldwin pipe organ's asking price was between $3,000 and $4,000. When the organ was finally purchased, local farmers removed part of the church's roof and lowered the instrument by block and tackle, since access to the choir loft was too narrow to carry it up.

In 1880, the Union Sunday School of Dyer was founded by Mrs. F. N. Biggs and George Davis. The Dyer Union Congregation was established September 30, 1981. North of Sauk Trail on the west side of Hart Street, the Dyer Union Protestant Church was erected for less than $1,000 under Rev. E. A. Palmquist, and was dedicated on October 11, 1891. It was the first Protestant church in Lake County. In March 1962, the congregation voted to join the United Presbyterian Denomination to which the First United Presbyterian Church was erected on Hart Street, south of the old Sauk Trail.

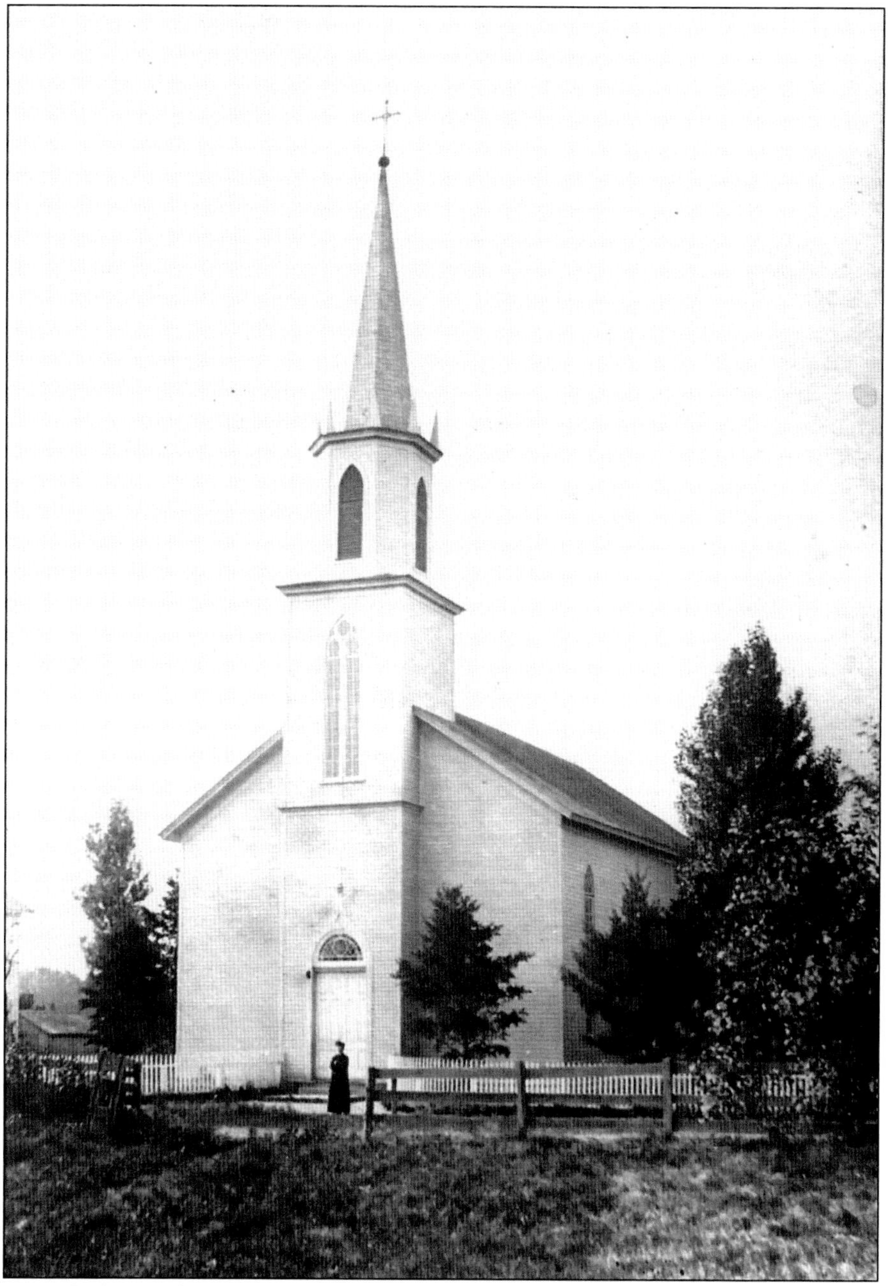

Before a Catholic parish came to Dyer, residents of that denomination would attend masses in St. John at the St. John Church. Reverend Werhrle, residing in Turkey Creek, would come to make visits with the town's parishioners. In 1867, Rev. Jacob Schmitz built the people of Dyer their first church, St. Joseph Church. It was a small, wood-frame whitewashed construction (pictured here) costing between $4,000 and $5,000, and sat on four acres of land along the Sauk Trail. A rectory was built in 1869, but replaced in 1950 by Father Edmund A. Ley. In 1878, the parish became one of the first missions for the Franciscan Sisters, whose convent was built in 1901 along with the St. Joseph Catholic School. Unfortunately the original church succumbed to fire in 1902. In 1903, a new redbrick church was built to replace the old white, wooden structure.

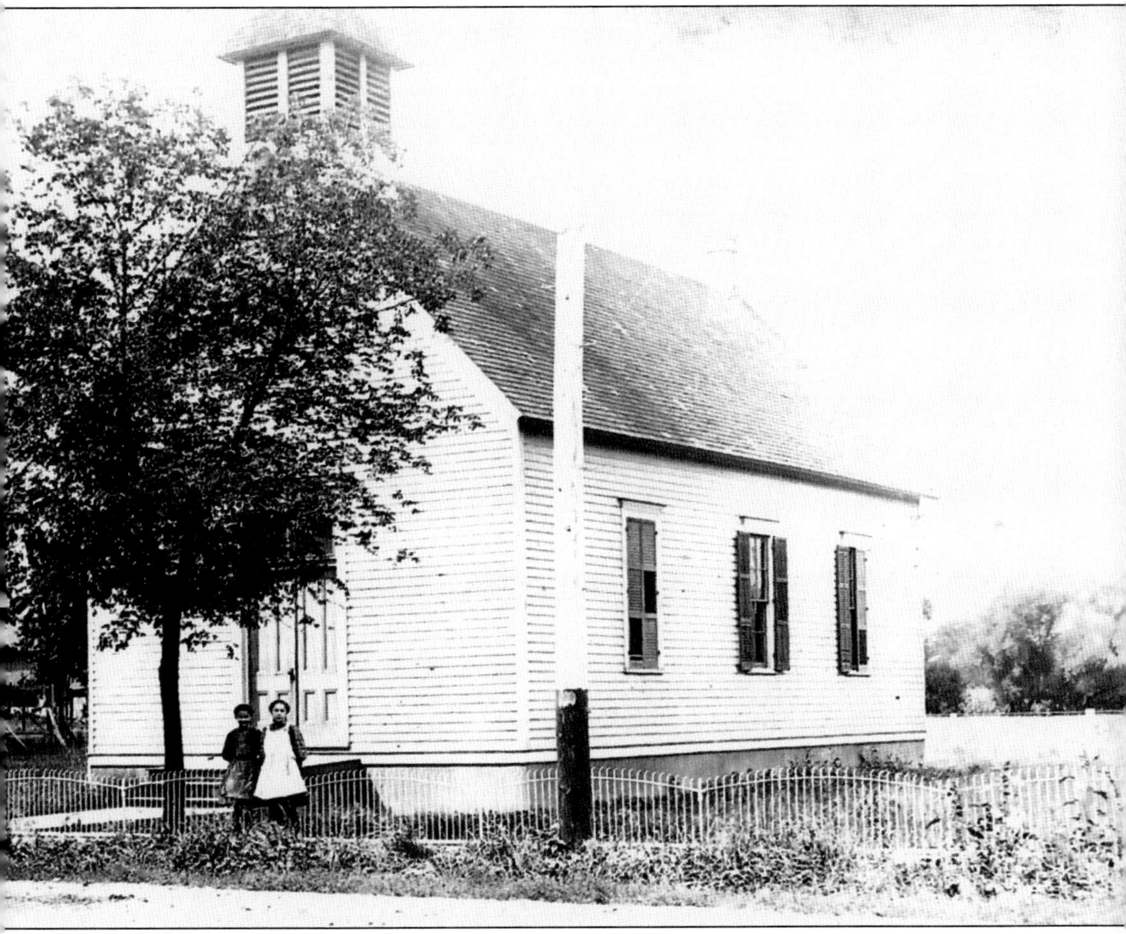

Pictured here is the Dyer Union Church. In 1880, the Union Sunday School of Dyer was founded by Mrs. F. N. Biggs and George Davis. The Dyer Union Congregation was established September 30, 1981. North of the Sauk Trail on the west side of Hart Street, the Dyer Union Protestant Church had been erected for less than $1,000 under Rev. E. A. Palmquist and was dedicated on October 11, 1891. It was the first Protestant church in Lake County. In March 1962, the congregation voted to join the United Presbyterian denomination to which the First United Presbyterian Church was erected on Hart Street, south of the old Sauk Trail. The new church kept the original stained glass windows from the Dyer Union Church. The old Dyer Union Church became home to the Dyer Lions Club for some time. It still stands today and houses Antonio Michael's Salon and Day Spa.

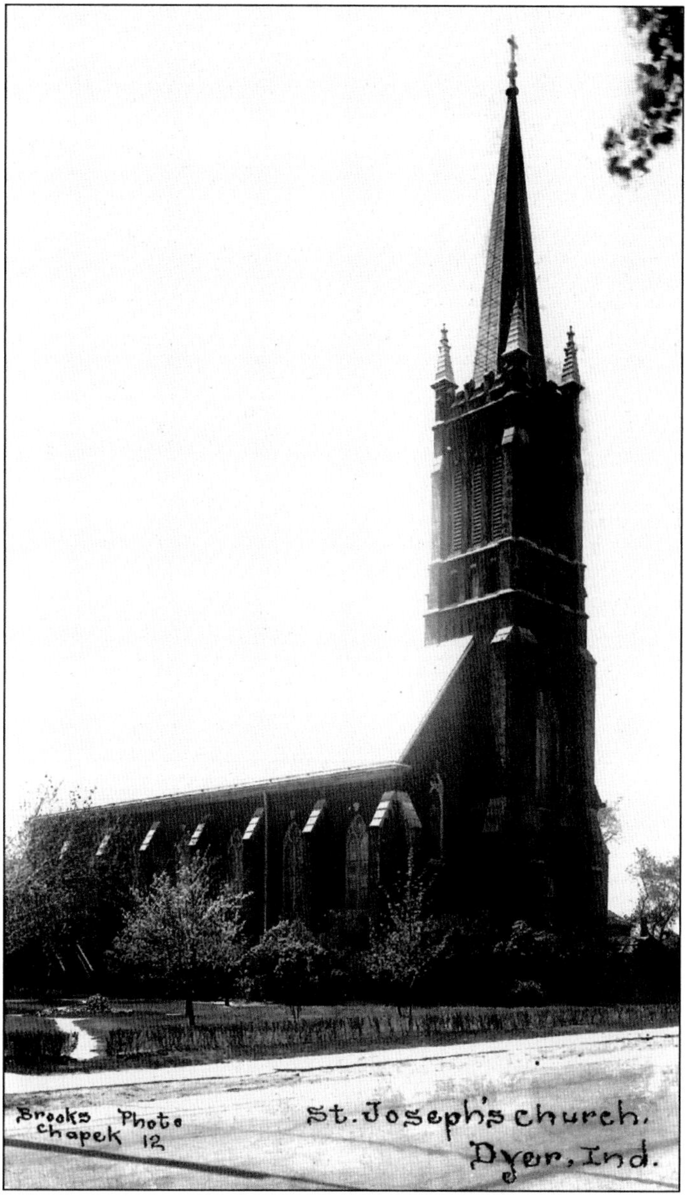

The church that stands today was built in 1903, dedicated by Father Joseph Flach on November 26 the same year, costing $18,000. Eventually a newer convent was built in 1924 by Father George Lauer and was later attached to the church itself. The church's Baldwin pipe organ has some history as well. It was featured in Chicago's 1933 Century of Progress International Exhibition before being purchased and finding a home at St. Joseph's. After the fair, it was being stored in a warehouse at which some of the church's parishioners—Ray Gettler, Alois (Glace) Keilman, Eddie Hartman, Bill Reed, Carl Greiving, Elmer P. Miller, John Theil, and others—examined it for purchase. The Baldwin pipe organ's asking price was between $3,000 and $4,000. Donations were raised through several means. Choir members donated $100 to $150 each, and the Rosary Club donated as well. When the organ was finally purchased, local farmers removed part of the church's roof and lowered the instrument by block and tackle since access to the choir loft was too narrow to carry it up.

When the original St. Joseph Church, then a wooden structure, succumbed to fire in 1902, a new brick church was built in 1903. It was dedicated by Father Joseph Flach, pictured here, on November 26, 1903. The new brick church, which still stands today, cost a total of $18,000.

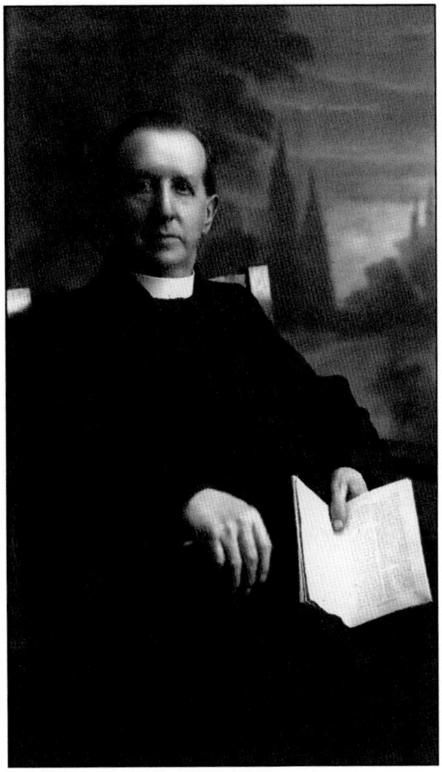

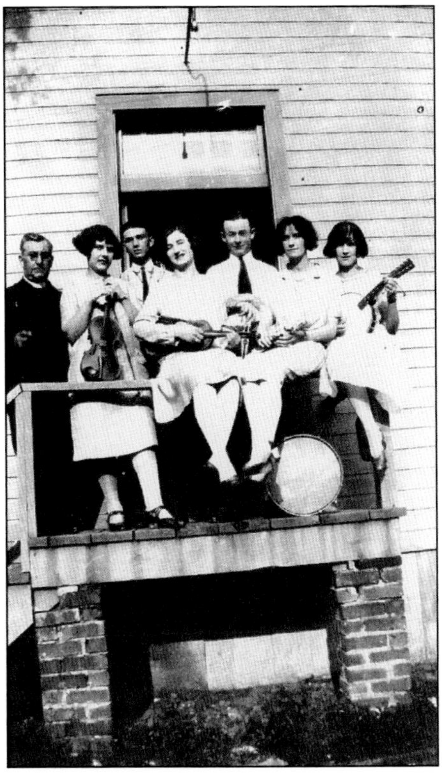

Pictured here is Father George Lauer with local musicians Marion (Berens) Keilman, Alois (Glace) Keilman, Nina (Schulte) Miller, Arthur Hartman, Othilia (Austgen) Keilman, and Lucille (Schulte) Theil.

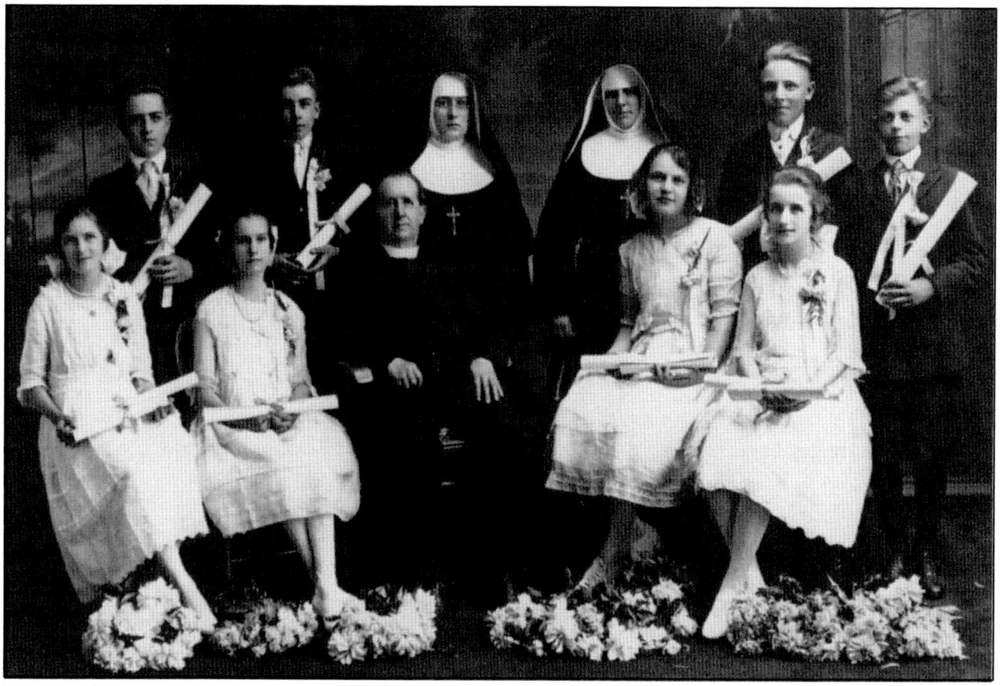

Pictured here are receivers of their diplomas from St. Joseph school. From left to right are (first row) Lucille (Schulte) Theil, Othelia (Keilman) Austgen, Father Flatch, Marion (Berens) Keilman, and Nina (Schulte) Miller; (second row) Ralph Austgen, ? Keilman, unidentified, unidentified, Edmund Gettler, and ? Dubois. This photograph was taken in the late 1800s.

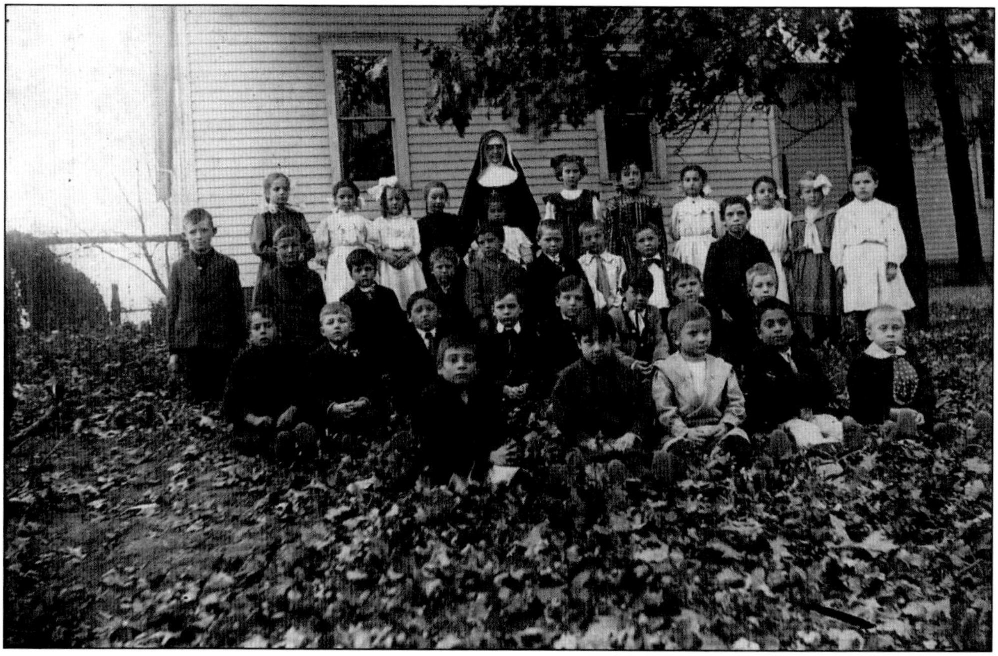

This photograph features St. Joseph's 1912 class in front of the first St. Joseph schoolhouse. The wooden schoolhouse stood until a larger brick school was built in 1938. The original schoolhouse was removed from the property and made into two separate homes.

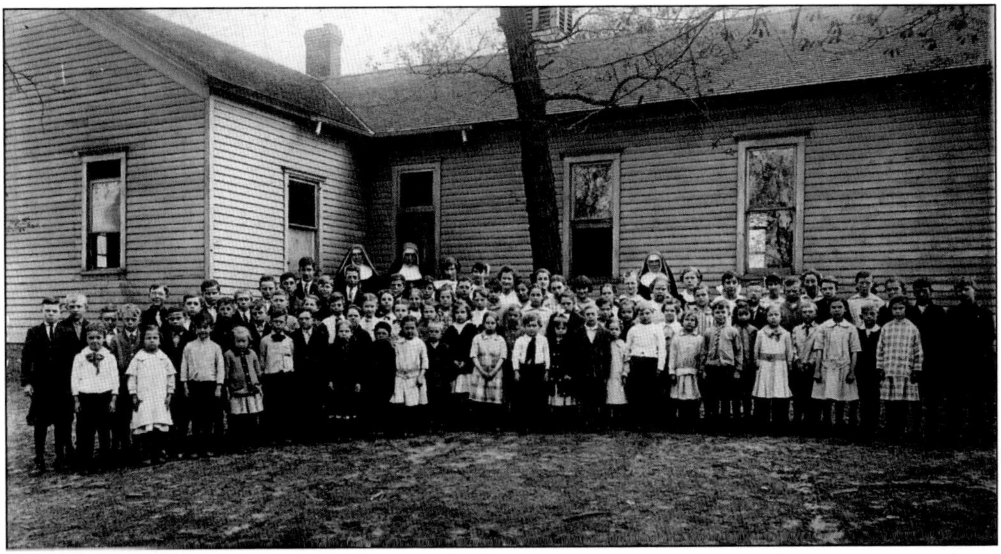

This photograph features students who attended St. Joseph's school around 1914, posing in front of the original St. Joseph schoolhouse. The two separate homes which the schoolhouse was made into still stand today in the town of Dyer.

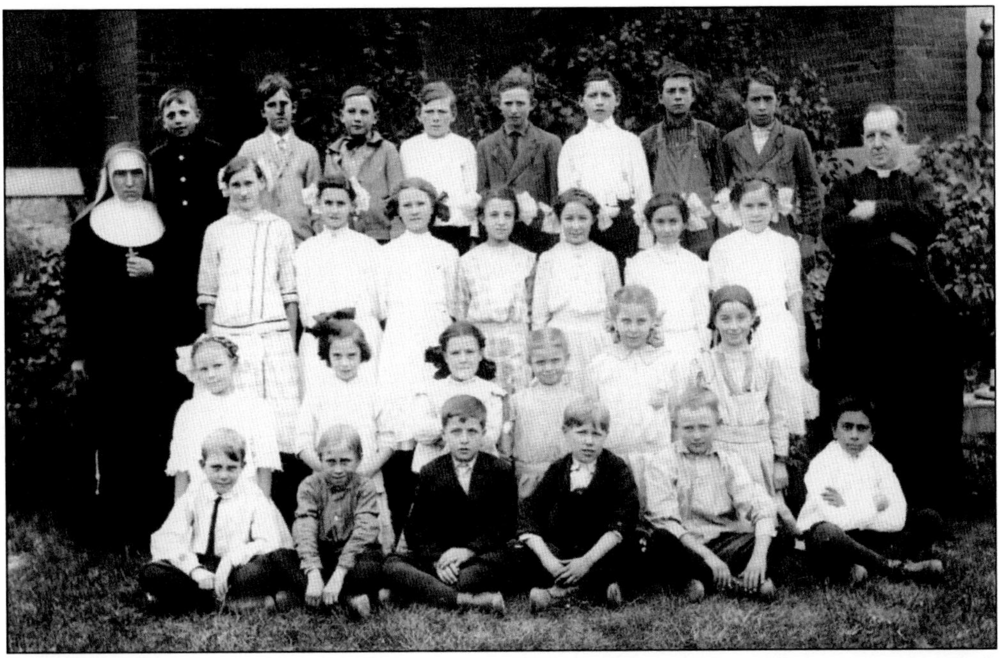

Seen here is St. Joseph's sixth grade class from 1915. From left to right are (first row) unidentified, Mabel Chenard, unidentified, unidentified, Clara Schmitt, Frances Kammer, Carl Miklik, Bill Gettler, Henry Keilman, ? Willy, and Sam Schelfo; (second row) Hellen Keilman, Helen Schaeffer, ? Willy, Matilda Klein, Susan Schmitt, Marie Schaeffer, and Marie Schmidt; (third row) Sister Germaine, Vic Greiving, Andy Keilman, George Chenard, Joe Jung, Leo Willy, Mike Schaller, Joe Shelfo, and Joe Grau.

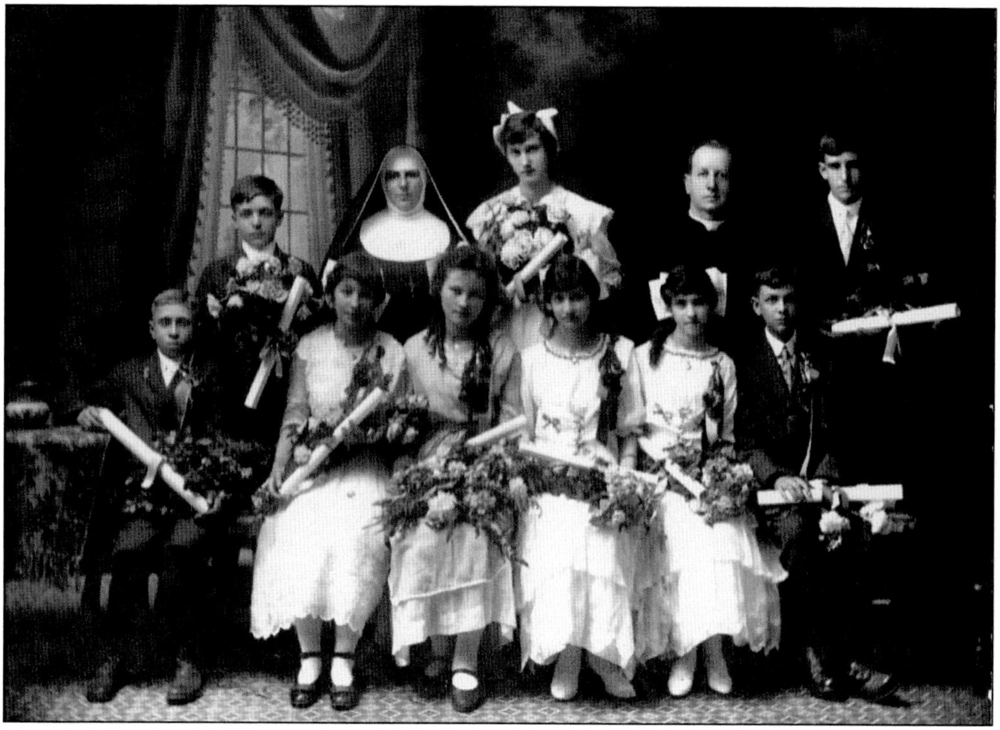

St. Joseph's 1917 graduating class is seen here. Pictured from left to right are (front row) Carl Miklik, Susan Schmidt, Caroline Willy, Helen Schaefer, Marie Schafer, and Alois (Glace) Keilman; (back row) William Gettler, Sister Damaniana, Helen Keilman, Rev. Joseph Flach, and Andrew Keilman.

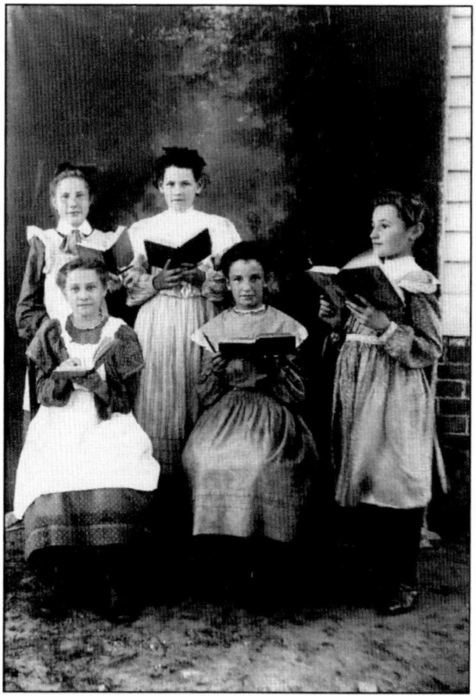

Pictured here are some of the students who attended St. Joseph School. The original schoolhouse was built in 1901. This school stood east of the present day church and west of the cemetery. This photograph was taken around 1920.

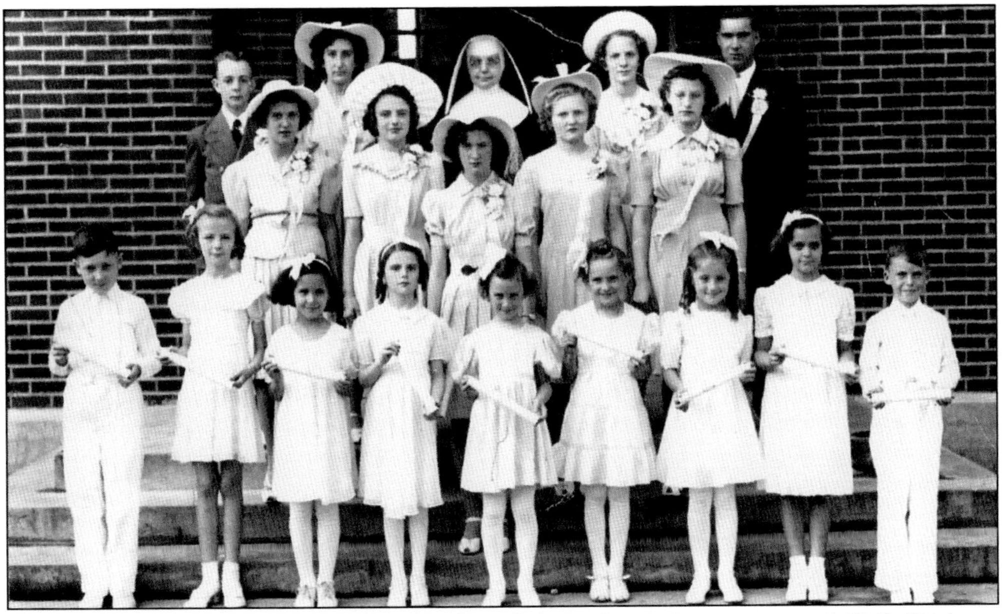

This photograph shows St. Joseph School's eighth grade graduation, around 1942. Diploma carriers, from left to right, are (first row) unidentified, Mary Jane Drangmeister, unidentified, Mary Lou Dumbsky, Margaret Mulhollan, unidentified, Mary Ann Schell, Rosemary Bohney, and unidentified; (second row) Doris Fagen, Margaret Dumbsky, Schirley Dumbsky, Marian Schweitzer, and Lois Keilman; (third row) Paul Keilman, Norma Keilman, Sister Alma, Betty Schweitzer, and Melvin Nondorf.

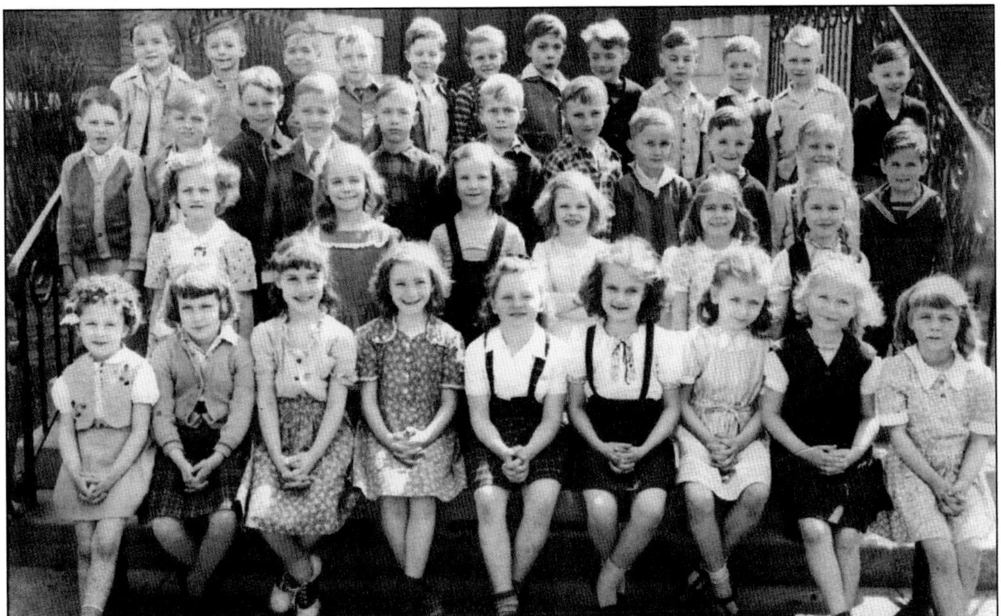

This photograph, taken April 1947, is of the St. Joseph School students, grades one and two. They are seated on the front steps of the church. In the early 1990s, the front of St. Joseph church was modified when the Lincoln Highway was widened. The steps leading to the front entrance are no longer there.

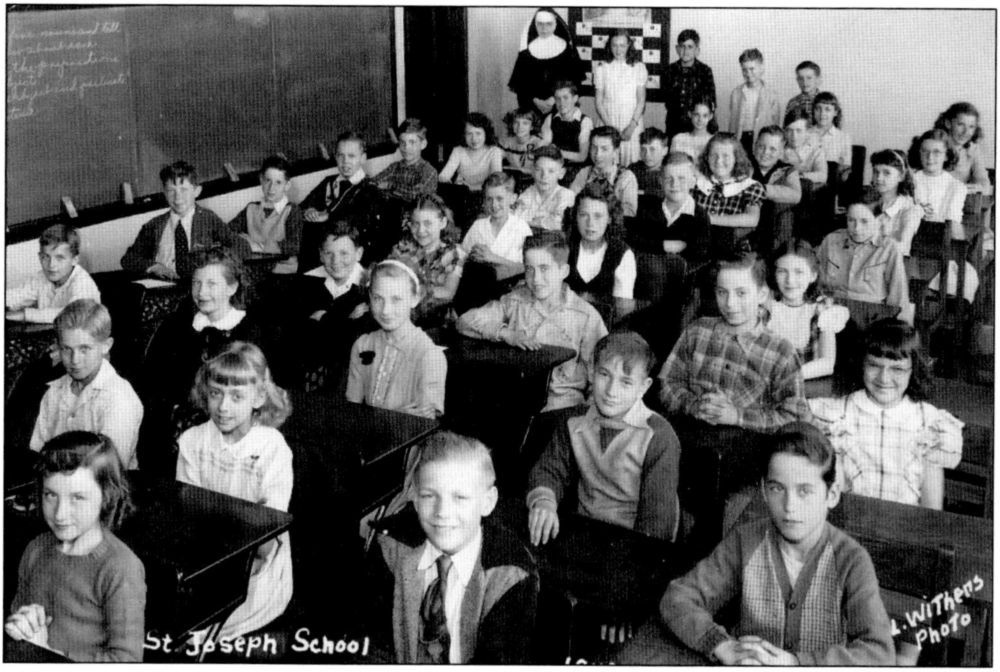

This 1948 picture features Sr. Mary Patrick and grades four, five, and six of St. Joseph School, where she taught. St. Joseph parish was one of the first missions, beginning in 1878, that the Franciscan Sisters assisted upon coming here. Their convent stands between where the church and school are today.

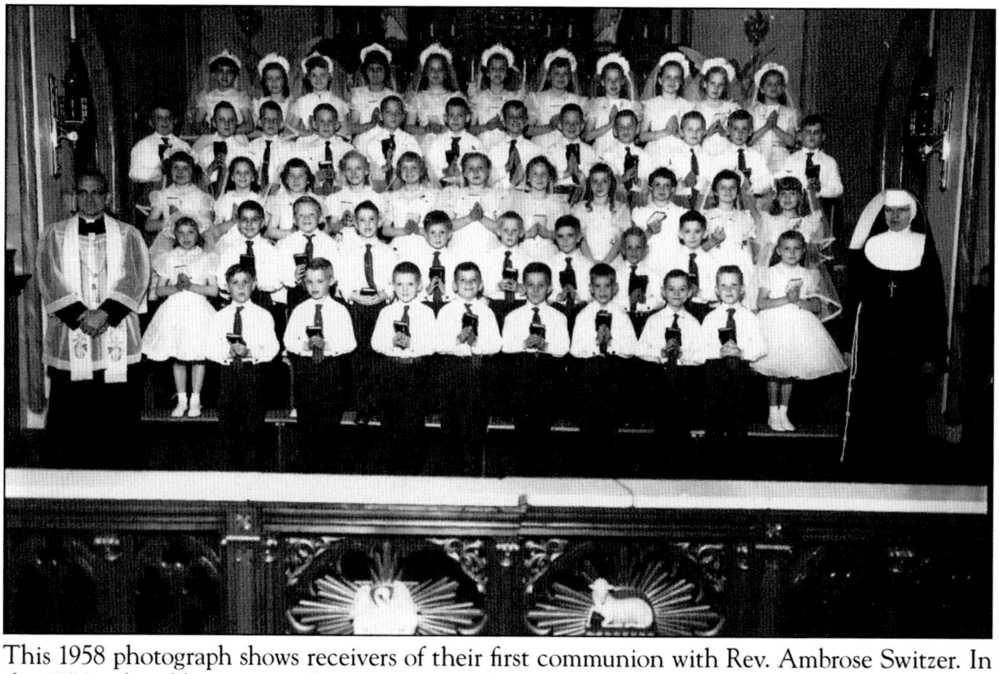

This 1958 photograph shows receivers of their first communion with Rev. Ambrose Switzer. In the 1970s, the old sacristy and communion rail were removed for remodeling. The church also houses an old Baldwin pipe organ that was featured in the Century of Progress International Exhibition in Chicago.

Four

Schools

The St. John Township school system was established in 1853. The children in the northwest part of the township, the Dyer area, attended the district No. 2 schoolhouse. This was a small, one-room school located on the corner of what is today known as Seventy-seventh Street and Patterson Avenue. In 1866, enrollment at this particular schoolhouse reached 77. As parochial schools opened within the township enrollment declined, leading to the district No. 2 schoolhouse closure in 1907.

The population in the area that was to become Dyer was increasing, however, and a second school was built. This was a log cabin–type structure. In 1875, yet another school was erected. This time it was a one story, two-room structure. In these schools, both English and German was spoken; however, many of the early grades needed lessons in English.

In 1898, a larger school was required. This time a two-story building with four rooms was constructed of bricks. This school was to become the St. John Township High School in the autumn of 1908. Three more rooms were added in 1916, and in 1928 the school was again enlarged to include a study hall, gymnasium, and an additional three classrooms.

As the area's population increased, so did pupil attendance. In the 1960s, a new high school was constructed and the old St. John Township High School became Kahler School. This would house both grade school and junior high students. The original building was demolished but a new structure replaced it, keeping the name Kahler School. As time went on, two more schools were built in Dyer. First came Protsman grade school in 1962, followed by Bibich elementary.

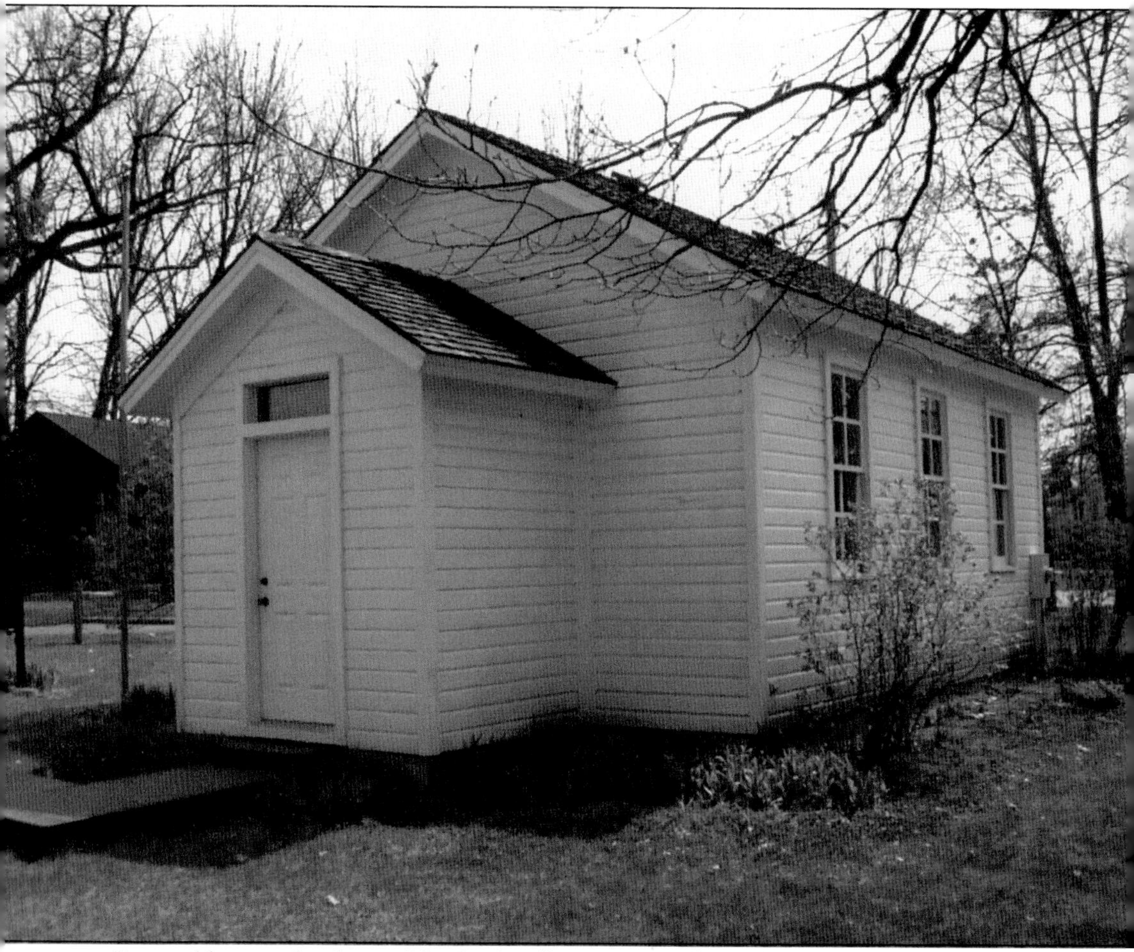

Pictured here is the district No. 2 schoolhouse. It was located on the corner of what is today known as Seventy-seventh Street and Patterson Avenue. It is recorded that a former student boasted that this school owned an enamel drinking cup, which no other school had at that time. In 1866, enrollment at this particular schoolhouse reached 77. As parochial schools opened within the township enrollment declined, leading to the district No. 2 schoolhouse closure in 1907. This did not indicate a lack of need for schools, however. Dyer's population was ever increasing. By 1890 the population was at 250. In 1910, the population increased to 500. In 1950, the number of people residing in Dyer was 1,556. This created a demand for more schools. The district No. 2 schoolhouse is now on display behind the St. John Community Center in Schererville. It is open to the public and is often the focus of field trips for the surrounding schools.

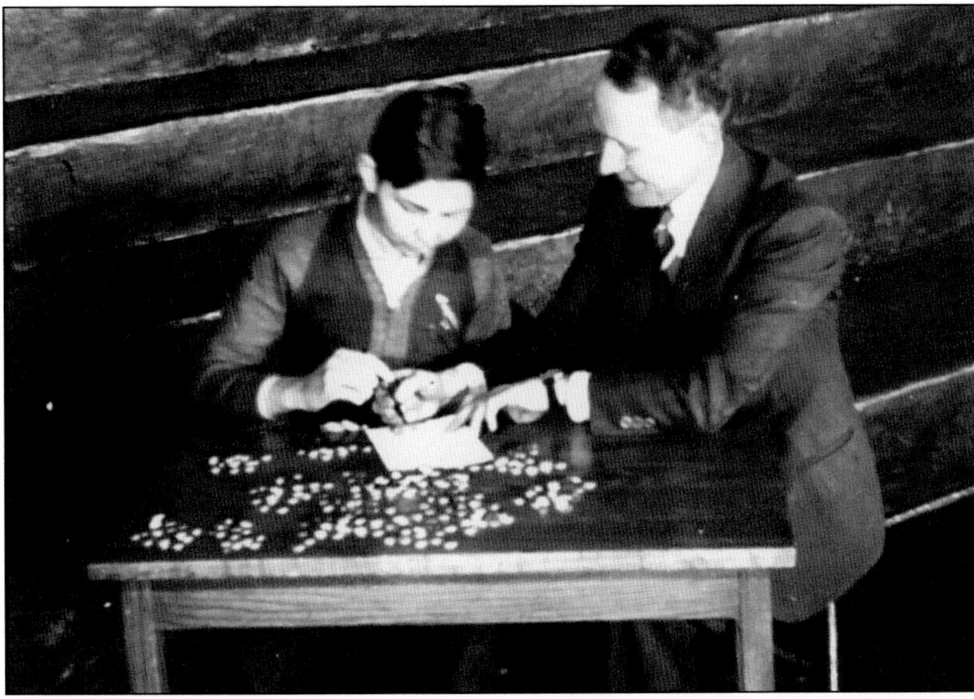

In this photograph, teacher Roscoe Protsman assists Harold Teibel with his studies. Protsman Grade School, named after Protsman for his many years teaching in Dyer, was built on the north side of town in 1962.

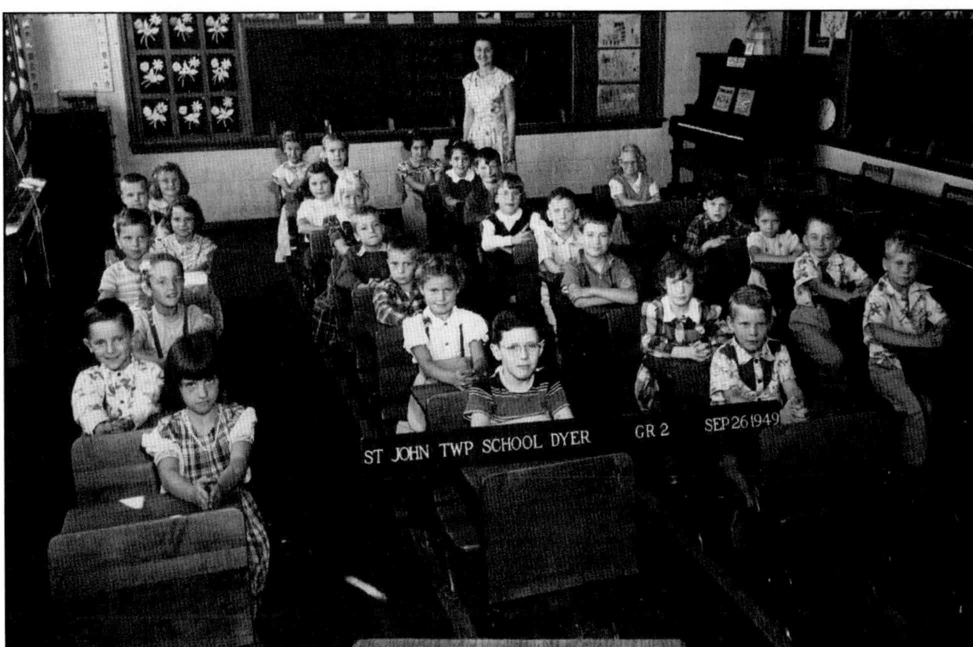

Teacher Miss Schaller poses with her second grade class on September 26, 1949. A student council has been in existence since 1937. Its contribution to the student government has been instructional assembly and homecoming programs, just to name a couple.

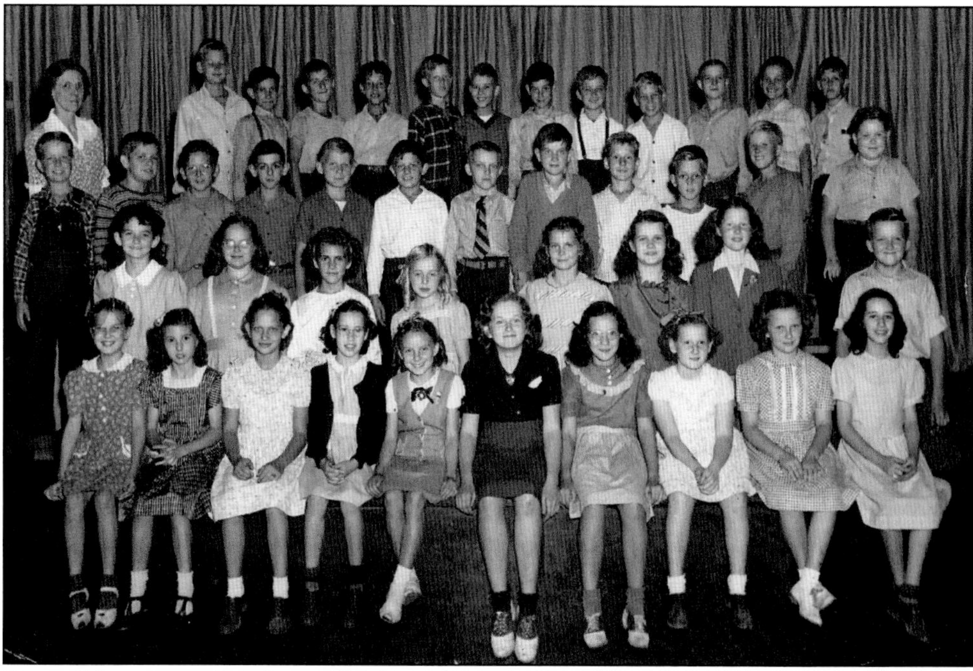

Pictured here is teacher Agnes Kahler and her St. John Township School fifth grade class in 1949. In 1959, the name of the St. John Township Grade School was changed to Kahler School in honor of Kahler. Her teaching career lasted from 1917 to 1961.

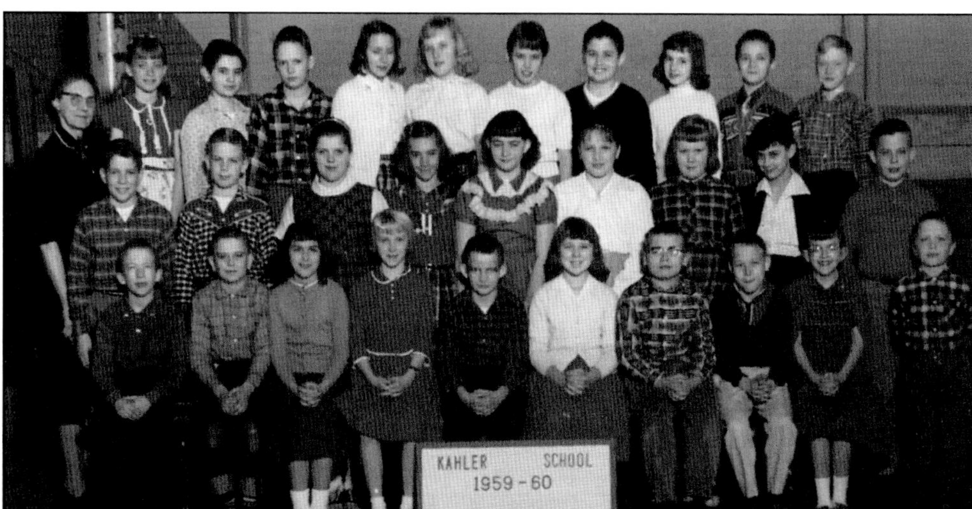

Pictured here is teacher Kahler with her fifth grade class of 1960. Kahler taught in the Dyer school system from 1917 to 1961. When St. John Township High School changed to a junior high school it was named after Kahler.

Roscoe Protsman directed the drama club of St. John Township High School. Protsman also directed an annual variety show called *Plum Creek Review*. In this photograph Don Austgen and Ruby Pheifer perform the *Lambreth Walk* for a talent show.

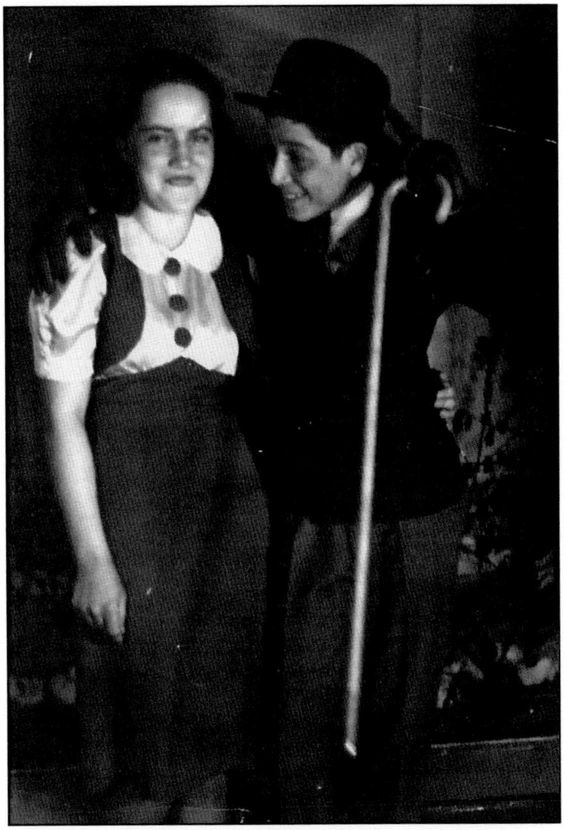

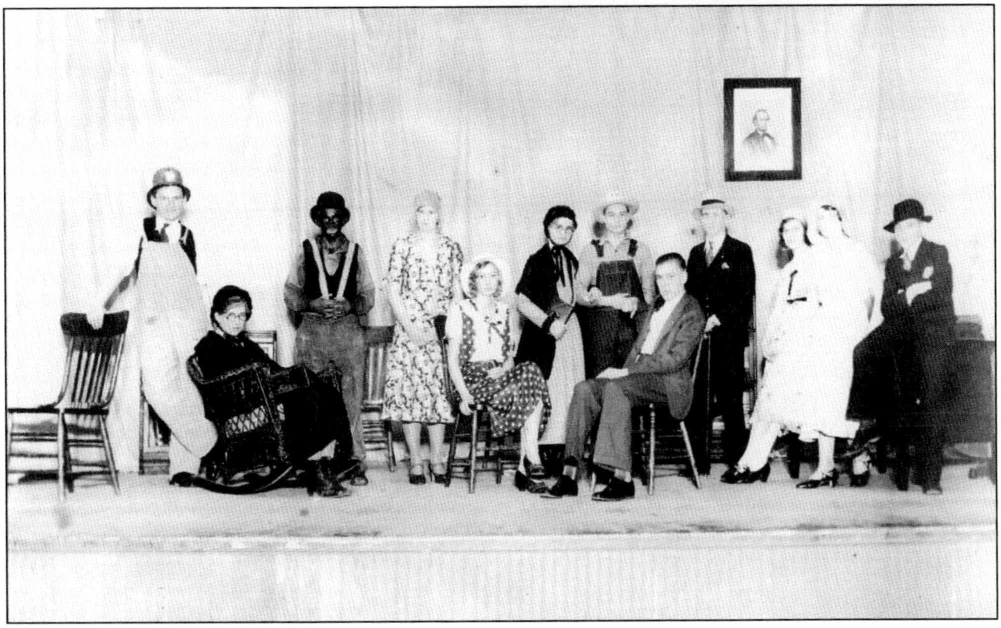

Featured here is the cast of *The Boomer*. This play, performed in 1932, was a St. John Township High School junior class play. In addition to Protsman directing the drama club, he was instrumental in beginning the orchestra with Vada McPherson.

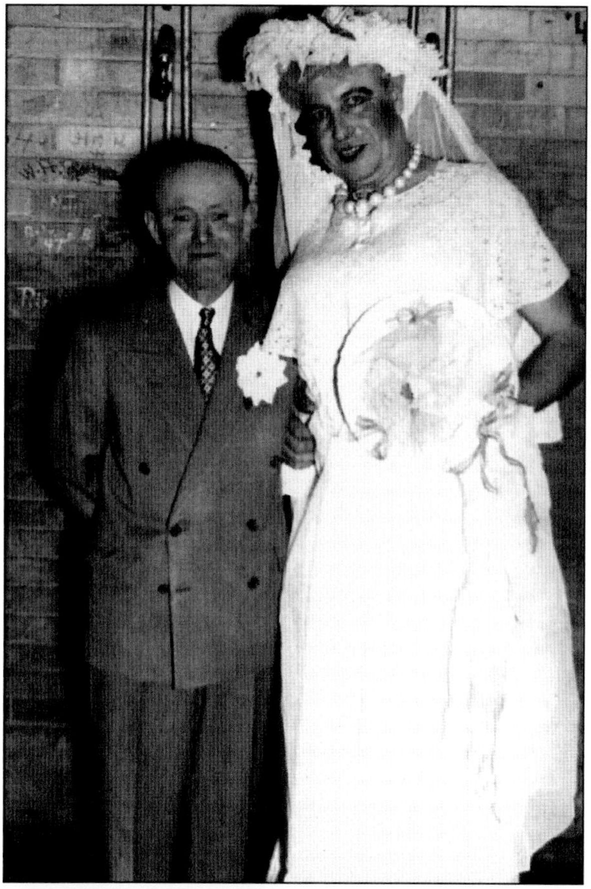

Teacher Roscoe Protsman used to facilitate variety and minstrel shows in addition to his work with the St. John Township High School drama club and orchestra. He is seen here with teacher William Smallwood, who is dressed for a performance. This photograph was taken in 1944.

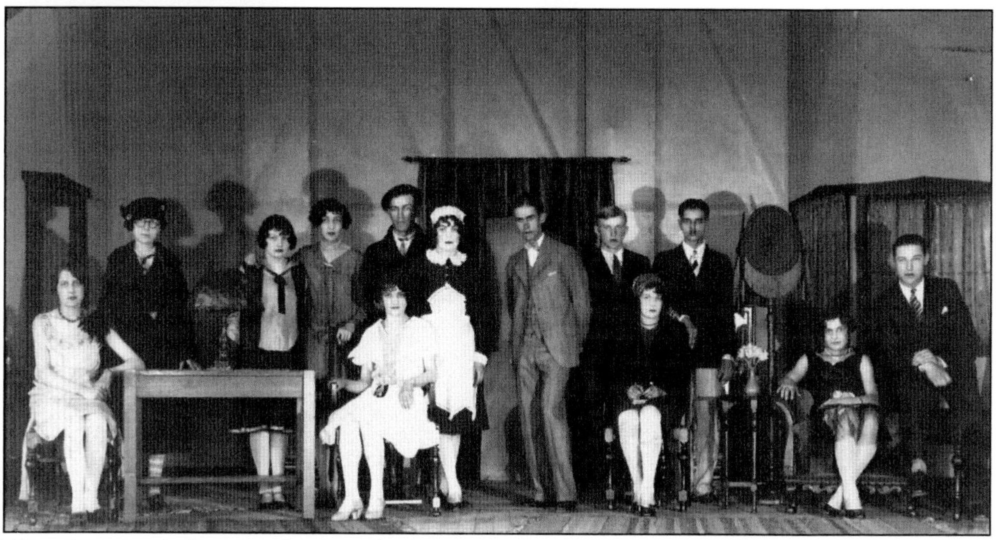

This photograph features the St. John Township High School drama club in 1944. The *Plum Creek Review* variety show that they used to perform was named after the creek running through Dyer. Many of the town residents were entertained by talent shows, plays, and variety shows performed by the drama club.

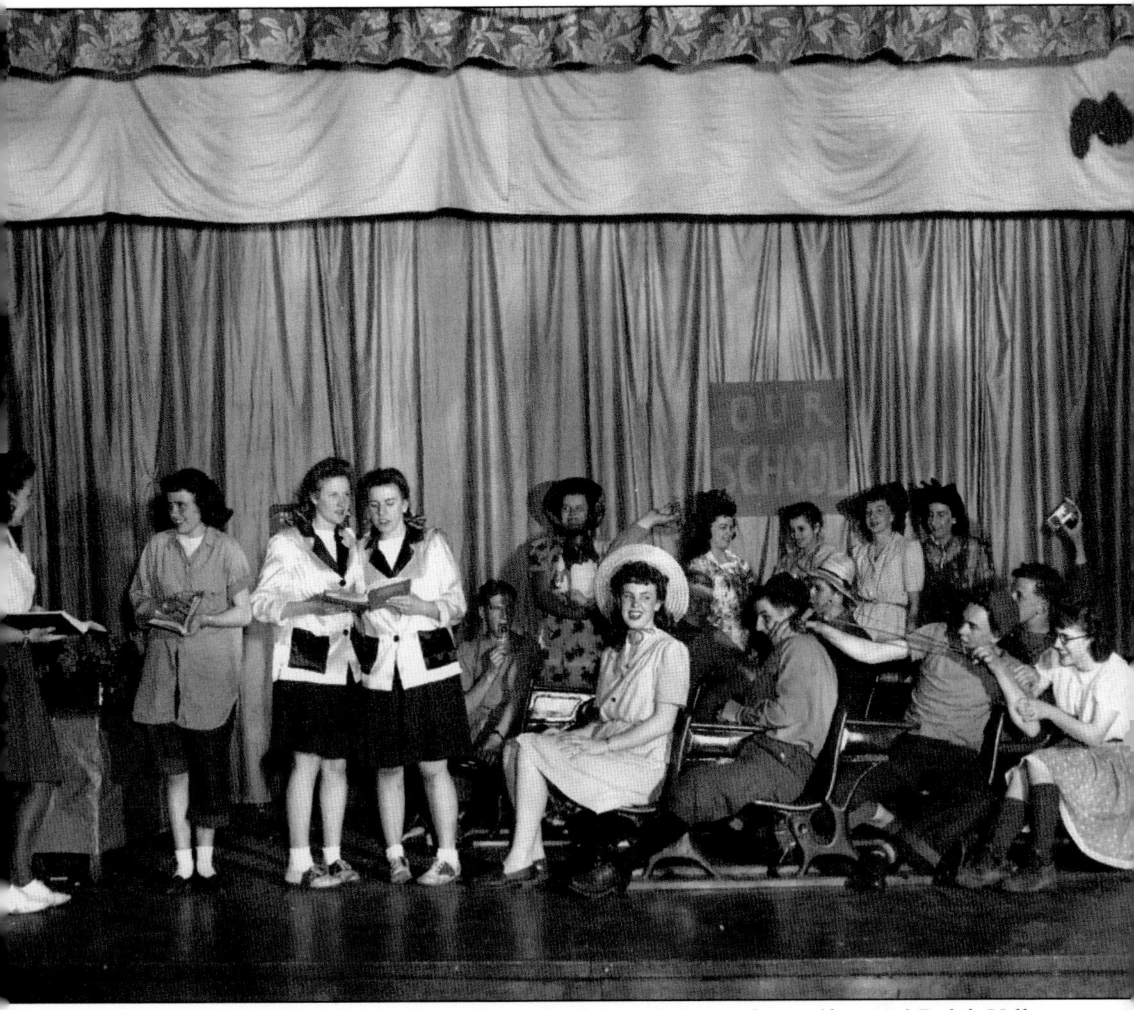

Pictured here is the 1946 cast from *First Day at School.* From left to right are (first row) Ralph Hill, Barbara Phillips, L. Rinkenberger, Vesty Redar, Ray Gallas, Paul Keilman, Wilfred Hoerning, and Ruth Funk; (second row) Betty Teibel, Marge Dumbsky, Betty Hilbrich, Rosella Bohney, Doris Ford, Pat Schnick, Mart Davis, Betty Schweitzer, and Norma Keilman. In addition to theater, other activities were offered to the students. Sewing classes came to the schools in 1920. In 1923, a glee club was formed. The *Dyer Flyer*, a monthly paper, came out in 1927. The local schools offered opportunities for students to play sports as well. In 1925, the first baseball and track teams were introduced and basketball was made available in 1928. These sports were open to both boys and girls. Football came to the schools in 1941. It was discontinued but later returned in 1948.

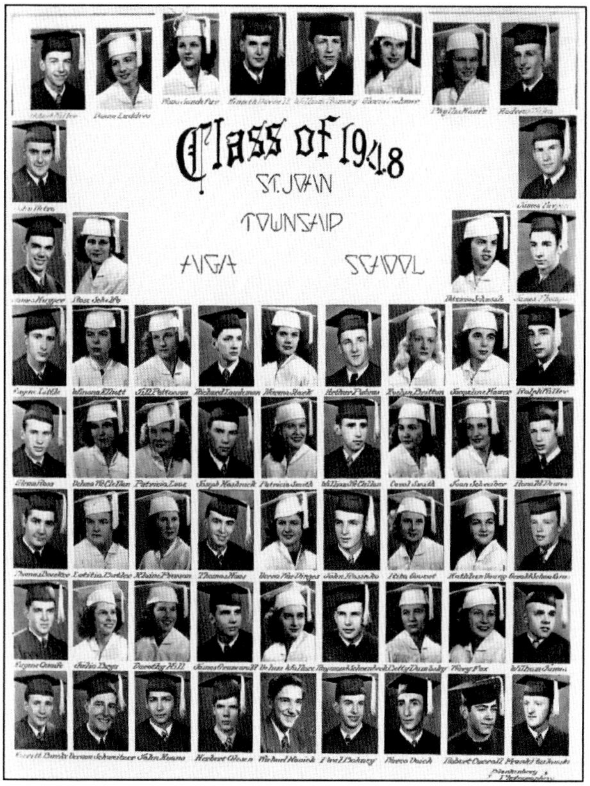

This photograph features the St. John Township High School class of 1948. The name of the school was changed from St. John Township High School to Dyer Central High School. On October 15, 1958, an open house and dedication took place to mark the occasion.

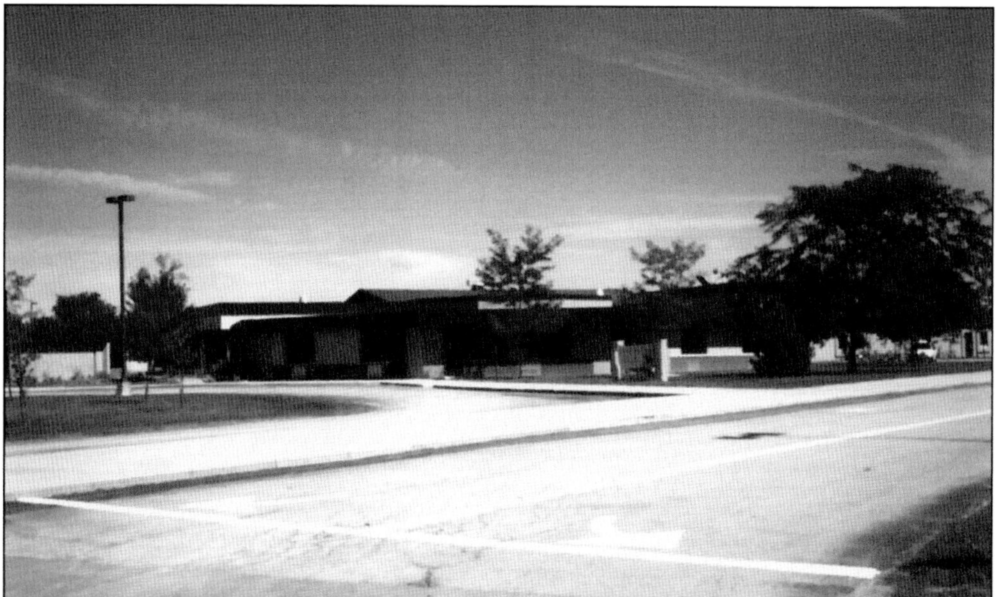

Shown here is the Roscoe E. Protsman Elementary School. It was dedicated January 12, 1963, in honor of Roscoe Protsman, who taught at the St. John Township High School. He and Vada McPherson organized an orchestra in 1926, which was replaced by a band in 1938. Protsman was also involved with the drama club.

Five

The Police Department, Volunteer Fire Department, and Town Hall

Upon establishing Dyer as a town in 1910, Eugene Stech was appointed marshal. Some of the duties of the town marshall go beyond law enforcement. At least they did for Eugene Stech. Not only was he to uphold the law, but act as the town's maintenance man as well. Here are a couple exerpts from the early town board minutes relating to his position and tasks: "Town Marshall be authorized to procure some cinders and fix up the sidewalks . . . hereby authorized [Town Marshall] to order one extension ladder, two 14 or 16 foot ladders, and two 22 foot ladders, also three dozen fire buckets, same to be placed in some suitable place."

As the town grew, so did the need for a larger police force. Others serving as town marshal were Joseph Endres, Henry Batterman, John Moeller, Louis Hartman, Joseph Hoffman, Paul Miller, Frank Gruenwald, and Clifford Geise. Dyer ran under the marshal system until 1971, when it was put under the Metropolitan Police system.

It was not until 1915 that Dyer was under the protection of a volunteer fire department. Before then, fires were extinguished by a bucket brigade where men in town would pass pails of water from a water source along a chain of men to the burning structure. Dyer Water Works was almost completed in 1915 when the men decided to organize the fire department. This, along with a hand drawn hose cart, would assist in fighting fires.

The first men serving on the department were Fire Chief John Burge, Assistant Chief Andrew Peschel, hose captain Leo Hoffman, ladder captain Frank Beiriger, and secretary-treasurer Nicholas Austgen. Other charter member were Nicholas Fagen, Joseph Gettler, Paul Gettler, Matt Herrman, Peter Herrman, William Herrman, Michael Nondorf, Herbert Keilman, Phillip Keilman, Joseph Schaller, George Spanier, and William Zeisenhenne. Their first fire alarm system was the church bell until 1916 when the department bought its own. In 1972, the fire bell was officially dedicated to the firemen of Dyer, past, present, and future.

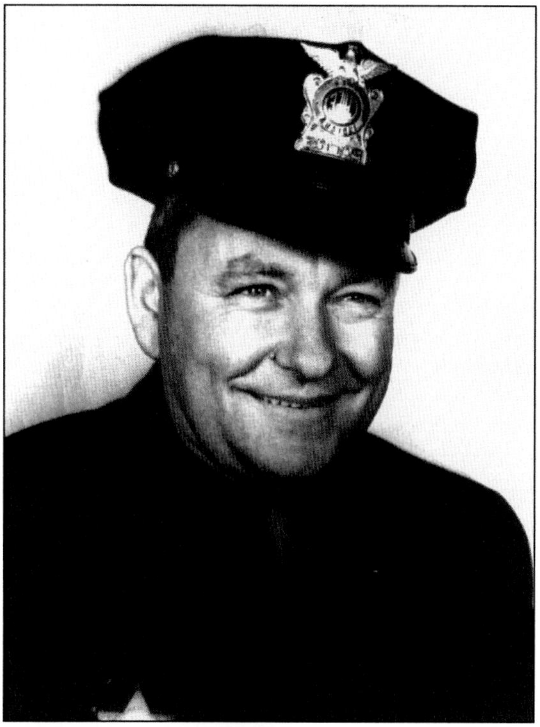

Pictured here is Clifford "Bud" W. Giese. He served as Dyer's town marshal from 1948 to 1961. He was known as the Andy Griffith of Dyer. Giese also served as the town's water department superintendent and street commissioner. He was a World War II veteran, electrician, and businessman.

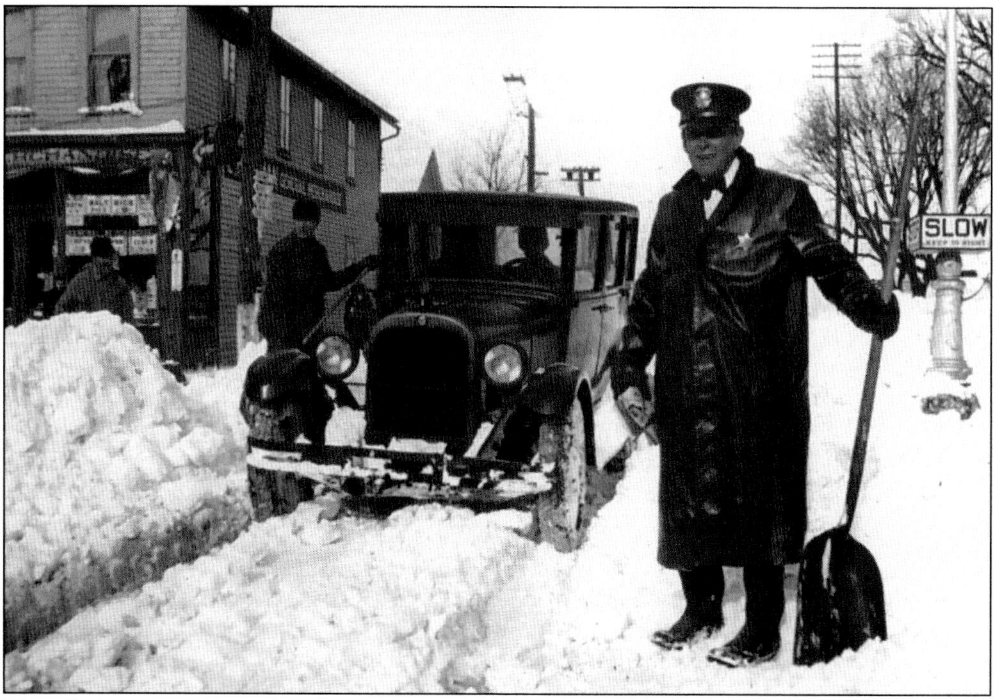

This 1928 picture features Louis Mathias Hartman (front right) who served as the town marshal in Dyer until his death at the age of 97 in 1938. Louis was married to Matilda Hoffman and had four children. Louis also operated Hartman's Saloon, which eventually became the location of the L. Keilman Company.

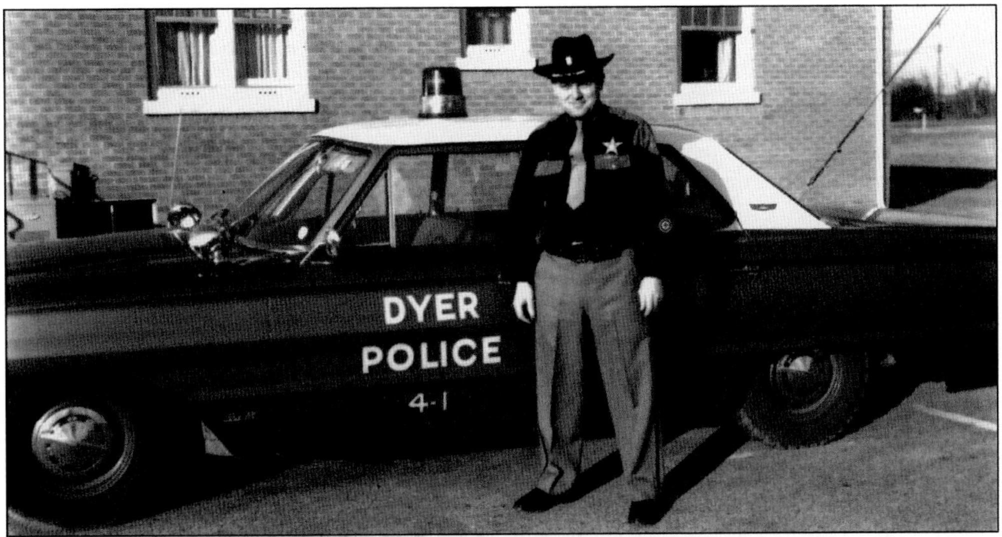

Pictured in this c. 1964 photograph is Dyer police officer Stan Lukasik. Lukasik was the original owner of Stan's Towing and Recovery Service located on Route 41 in Schererville, which is still in operation today. Dyer operated under the marshal system until 1971, when it went under the Metropolitan Police system.

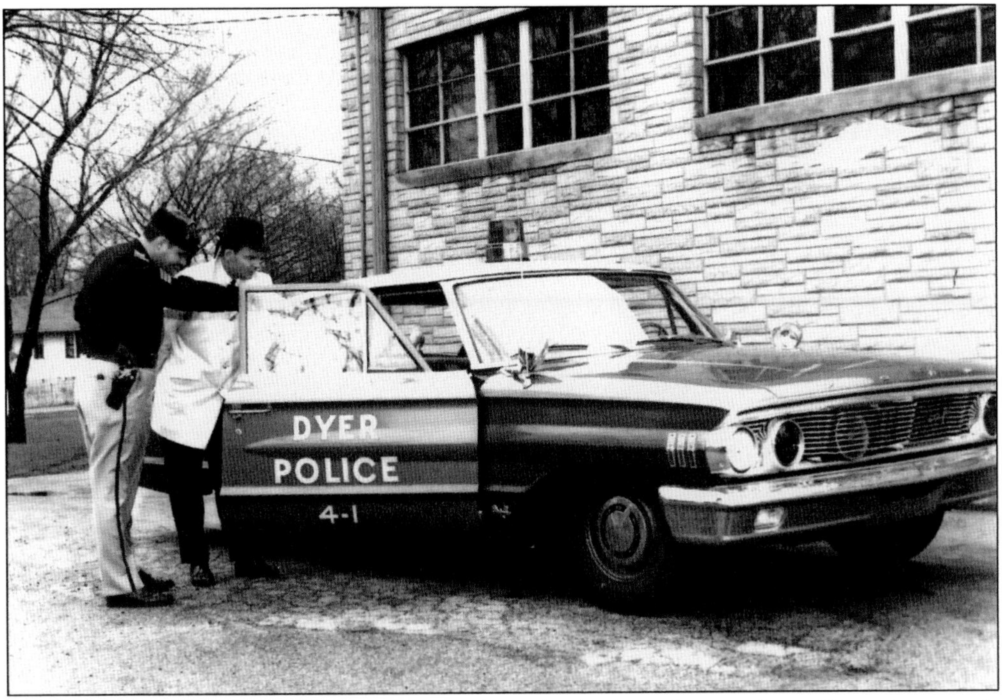

In this picture, Ray Oliver (left) gives Chuck Neil a look in the squad car. This photograph was taken in the early 1970s. In 1975, the first Fraternal Order of Police lodge was established with Tom Hoffman as president, Louis Barnes as vice-president, and David Walker as secretary and treasurer.

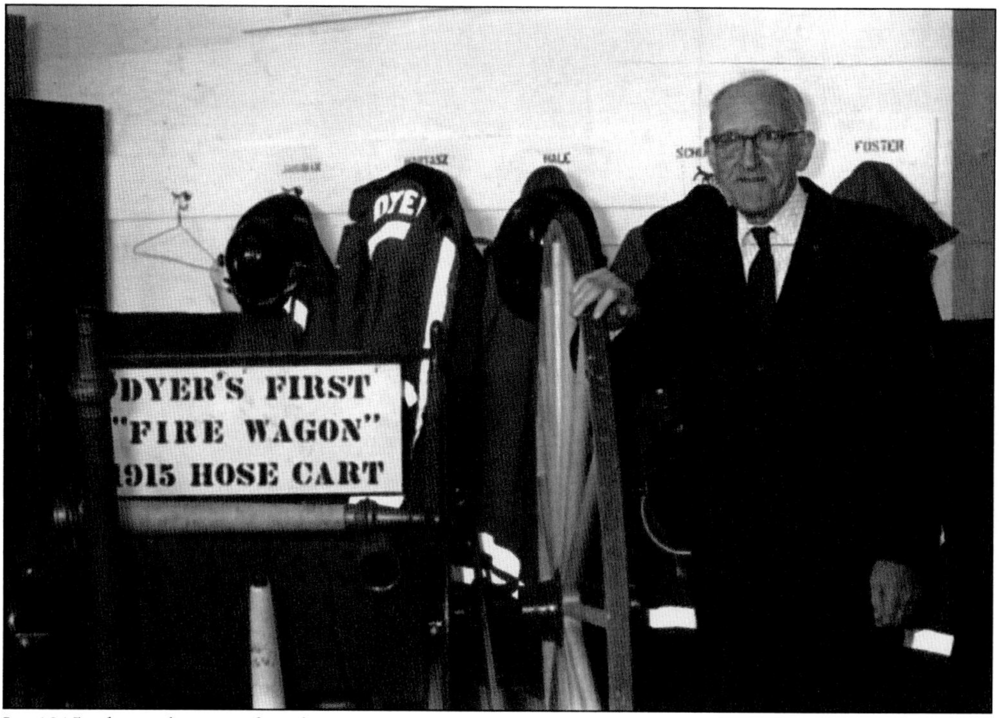

In 1915, the volunteer fire department was established. Up until then, Dyer depended on a bucket brigade to extinguish fires. Pictured is Frank Beiriger, the first ladder captain of the original Dyer Fire Department, with the original hose cart that was drawn by hand unless an available horse was nearby.

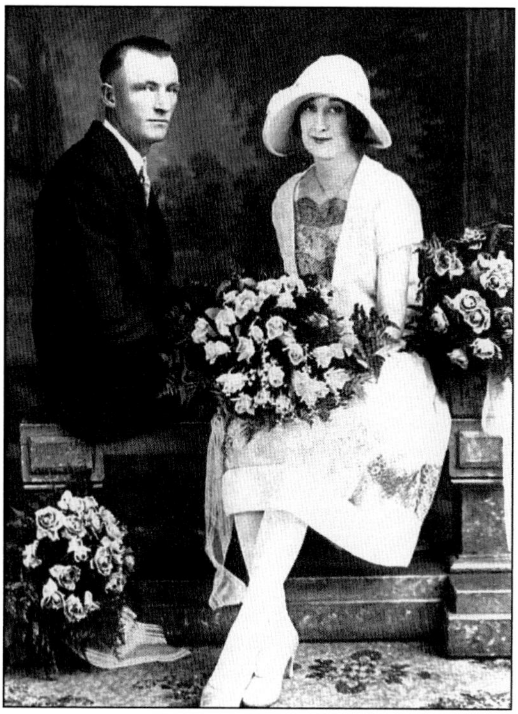

Pictured are Fire Chief John P. and his wife Lucille (Hilbrich) Dumbsky. They had six children: Ronald (who followed in his father's footsteps and became a volunteer fireman and married Emma Pericak), Shirley, Betty, Jacqueline (married to Dyer volunteer fireman Raymond Burke), Eileen (married to Dyer volunteer fireman Ernest "Harvey" Benninghoff), and Carol.

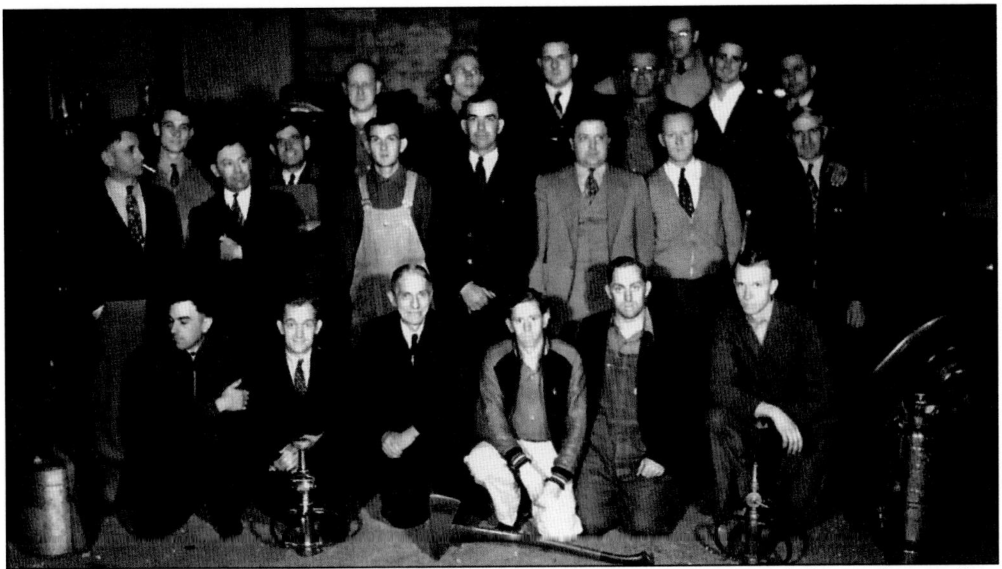

Seen here is a photograph of the Dyer Fire Department, 1937–1938. From left to right are (first row) Maurice Baker, Syl Grothaus, Andrew Peschel, Chuck Grothaus, Ludwig Grothaus, and Wayne Walker; (second row) Leo Hoffman, Roy Jointer, Alois Keilman, Joe Hoffman, Bill Gettler, Earl (Red) Harless, and Dave Miller; (third row) Pete Kremser, Hulmut Schwab, John Thiel, Joe Miklik, Ray Gettler, Joe (Buff) Keilman, A. Erwin Peschel, Clarence Wehmeyer, and Henry Greiving.

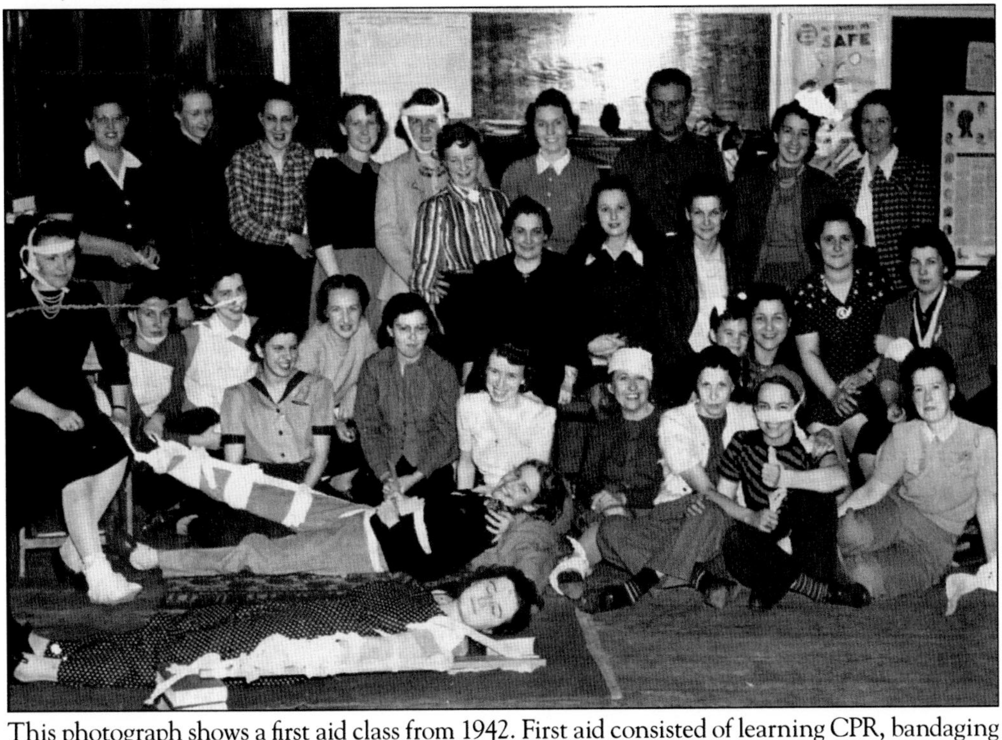

This photograph shows a first aid class from 1942. First aid consisted of learning CPR, bandaging wounds, and applying splints, among other important practices. As this picture shows, many women of Dyer, who saw this as being part of their civic duty, participated in this class.

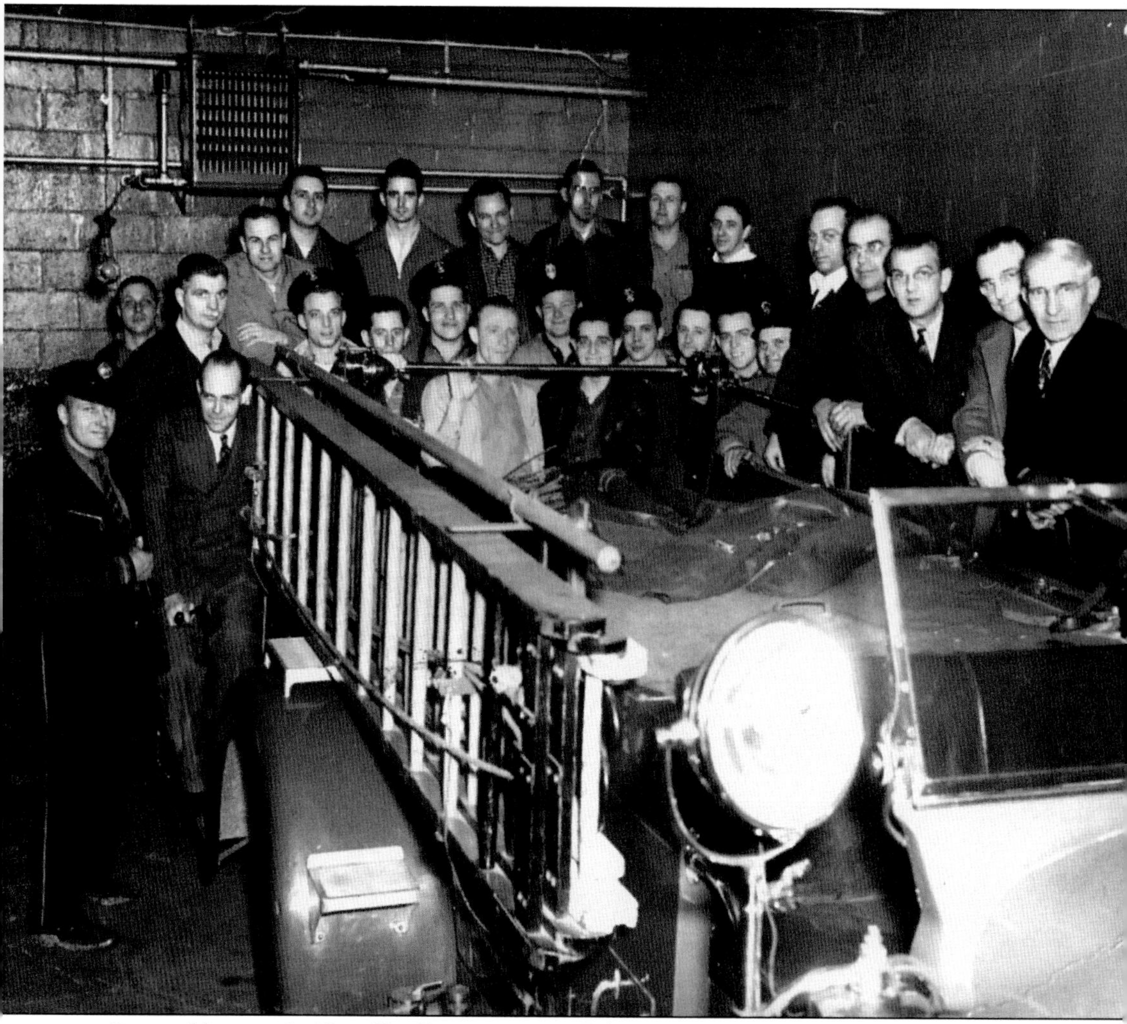

Pictured here is the Dyer Fire Department in February 1947. The fire department was organized in 1915. Before then, fires were extinguished by organizing bucket brigades. The first elected officials were Fire Chief John Burge, Assistant Chief Andrew Peschel, hose captain Leo J. Hoffman, ladder captain Frank Beiriger, and secretary/treasurer Nicholas Austgen. In addition to the elected officials of 1915, the Dyer Volunteer Fire Department roster included Nicholas Fagen, Joseph Gettler, Matt Herrman, William Herrman, Michael Nondorf, Herbert Keilman, Phillip Keilman, Joseph M. Schaller, Peter Schaller, George Spanier, Henry Spanier, and William Zeisenhenne. These men understood the importance of having an organized fire department within the town. Many buildings have been lost to blazes, being that the first structures were made of timber. Before 1915, when the fire department was organized, Dyer saw many of its buildings destroyed. It lost a planing mill, the original St. Joseph Church, the State Line Hotel, a hay and press barn, a door and blind factory, and a furniture store.

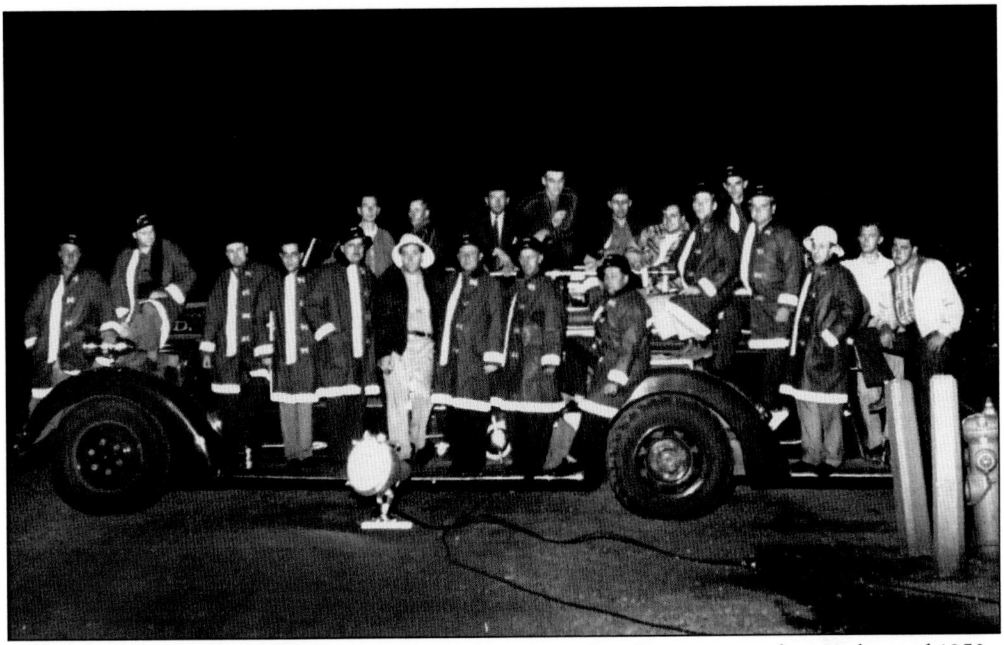

Pictured here are the members of the Dyer Volunteer Fire Department during the mid-1950s. Before the establishment of the fire department, many structures in Dyer were destroyed by fire. Among those that succumbed to fire were a planing mill in 1872, the State Line Hotel in 1880, St. Joseph Church in 1902, and many others.

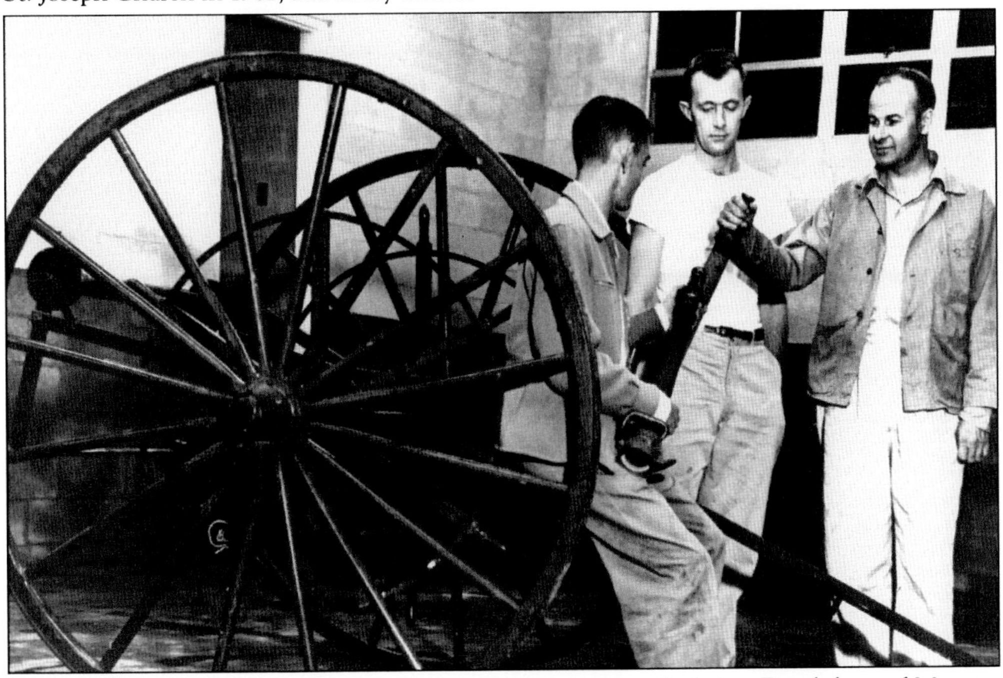

Pictured here, from left to right, are volunteer firemen unidentified, Ron Dumbsky, and Maurice Keilman as they look over the hand-drawn hose cart. At one time the cart was in need of repair. The firemen contacted the Amish community to repair the wagon wheels of the cart. This photograph was taken in the late 1950s or the early 1960s.

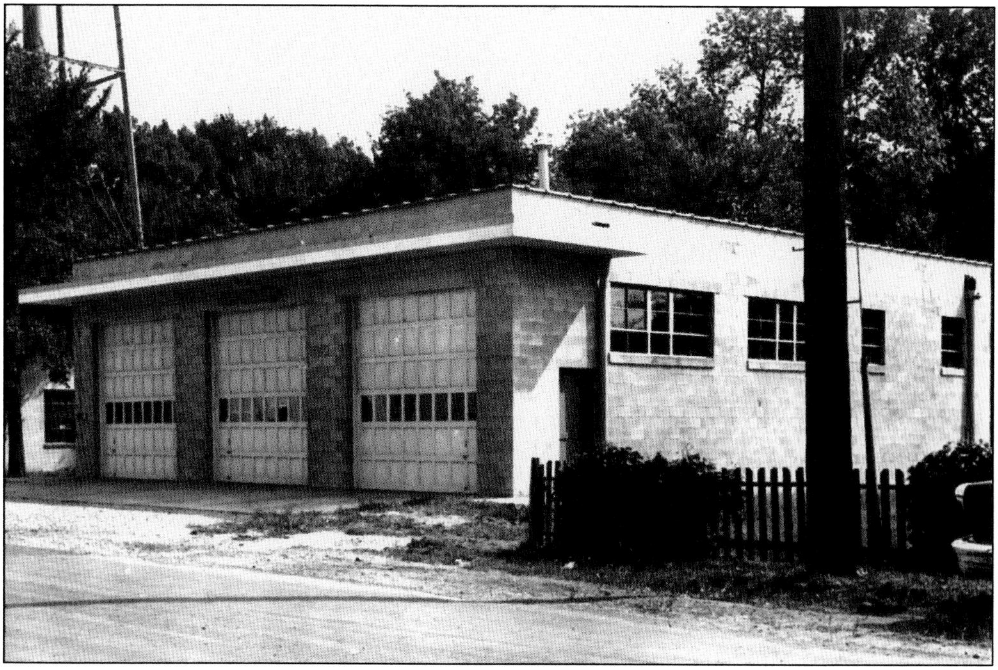

Pictured here is Fire Station No. 1, located on Schulte Street. This was the second station built. The first structure had been demolished. Fire Station No. 2 sits on the north end of Dyer. Fire Station No. 1 functions today as a public works building. The station that replaced it is located on Hart Street.

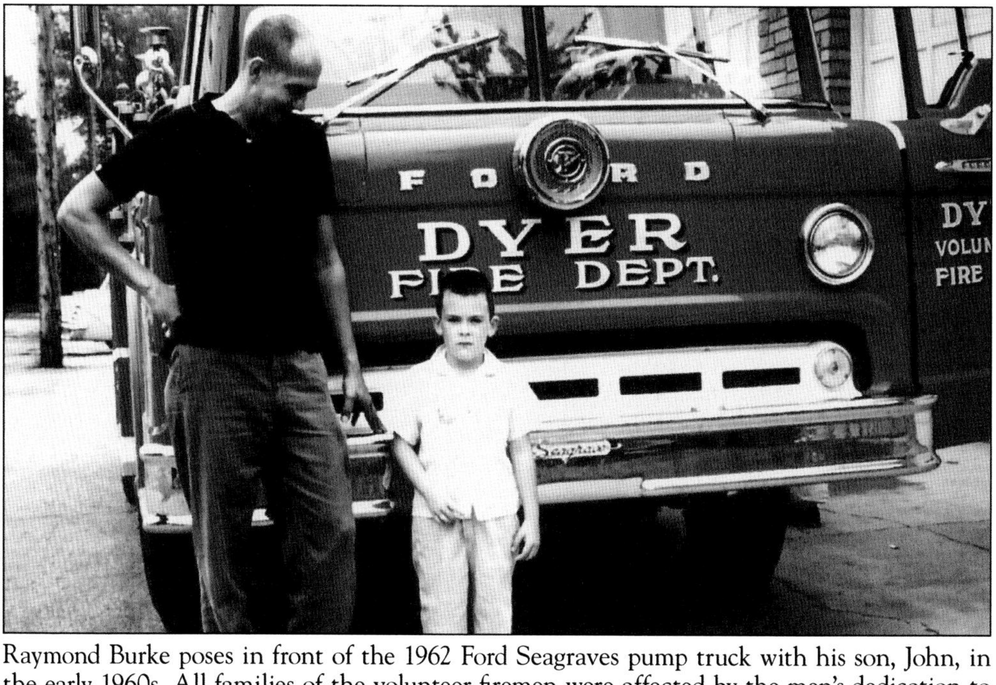

Raymond Burke poses in front of the 1962 Ford Seagraves pump truck with his son, John, in the early 1960s. All families of the volunteer firemen were affected by the men's dedication to the department. When the fire call came the men would leave, whether or not it was during the night, a bad storm, or a holiday celebration.

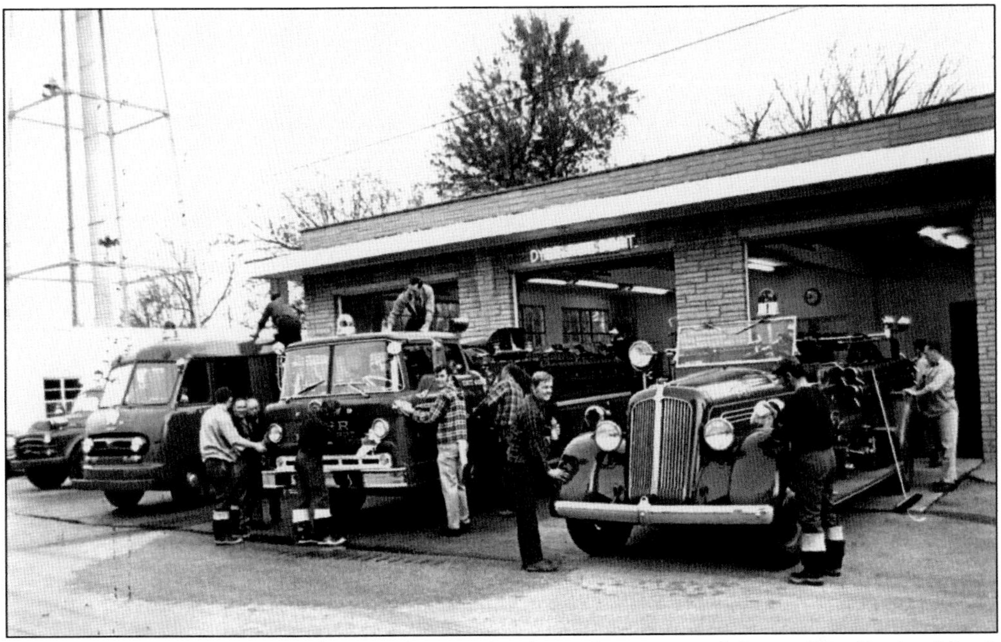

Pictured here are the Dyer volunteer firemen busily working on washday at Fire Station No. 1 sometime in the 1960s. Their duties as firemen were to attend calls, perform maintenance, instruct the public, and wash the equipment. Their diligence ensured that the equipment and tools were in top working order.

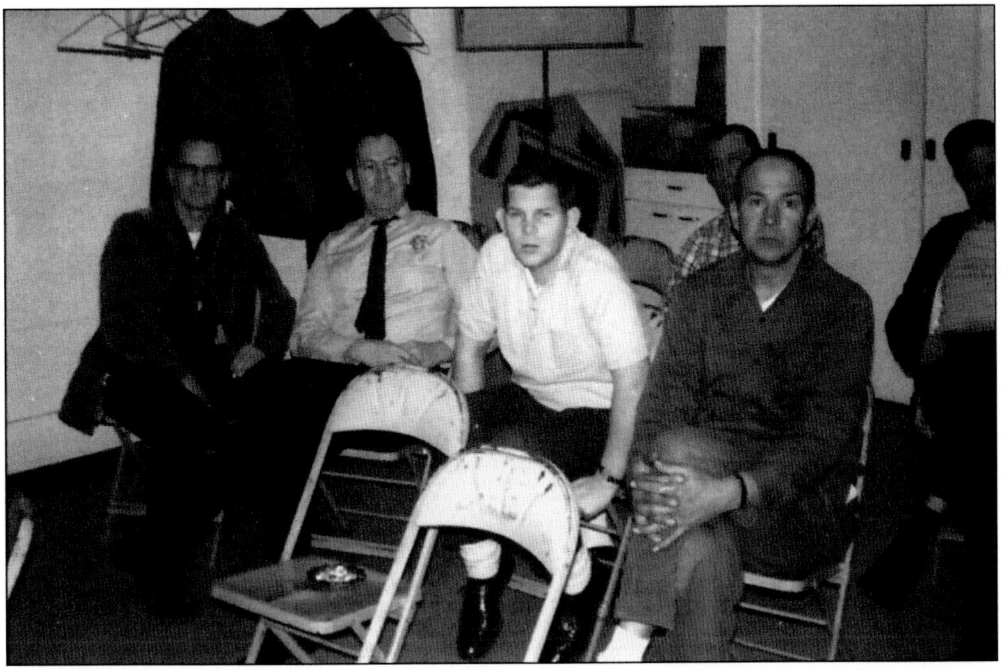

This photograph was taken at a fire department meeting in June 1969. From left to right are unidentified, Archie Herman, Ernie Benninghoff, Ronald Dumbsky, Raymond Burke, and Maurice Keilman, who also served as Dyer's postmaster at that time. Meetings were held regularly with specific agendas: training, maintenance of equipment, or general business.

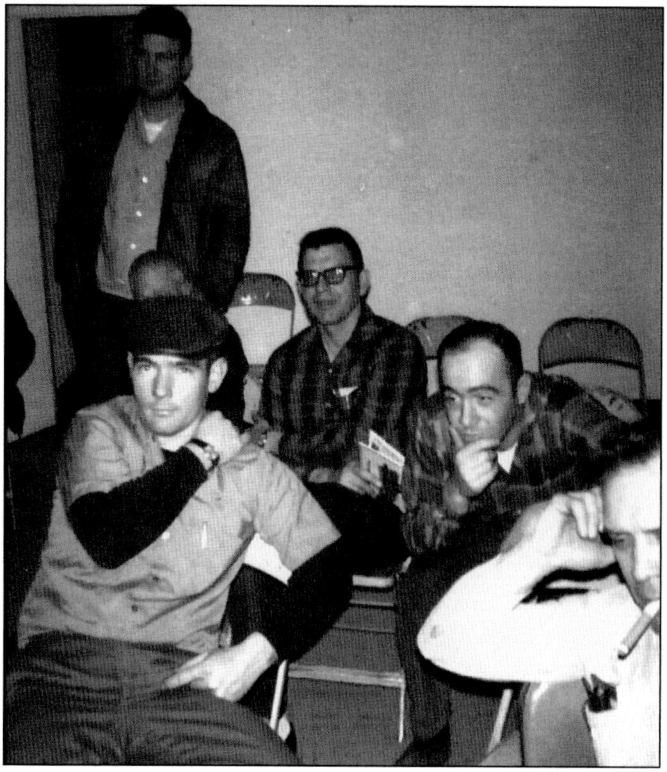

This photograph was taken during a fire department meeting in June 1969. Pictured from left to right are Larry Margraf, Charlie Grothaus, Jimmy Higgins (in front), Roy Henson, John Quinn, and Bill Kaiser. Meetings took place in the office of Fire Station No. 1.

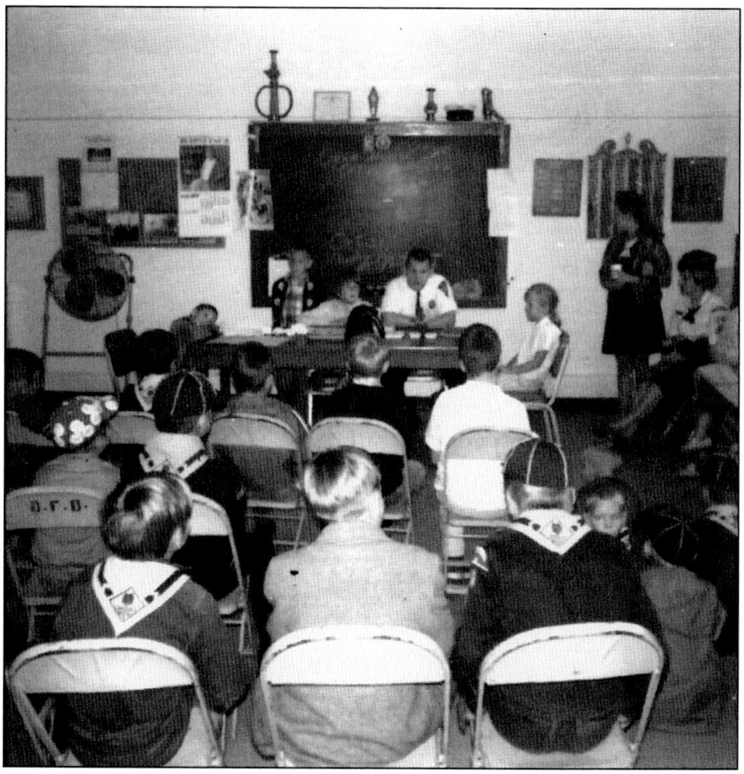

In addition to protecting the town from fire, the firemen of Dyer were dedicated to teaching fire prevention and safety. Pictured here is fireman Ernie Benninghoff instructing Dyer's children on fire safety in the office at Fire Station No. 1 during a December 1969 open house.

In this photograph, children of the Dyer firemen gear up to play Waterball at the 1969–1970 firemen's picnic. This yearly event, which still goes on today, is a great treat for the families of the firemen. It offers good food and fun for all.

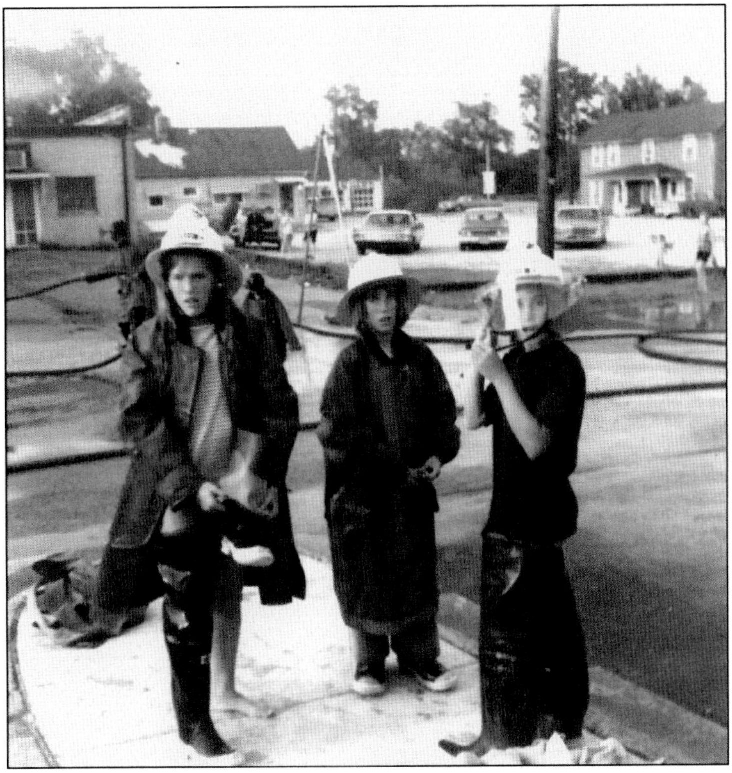

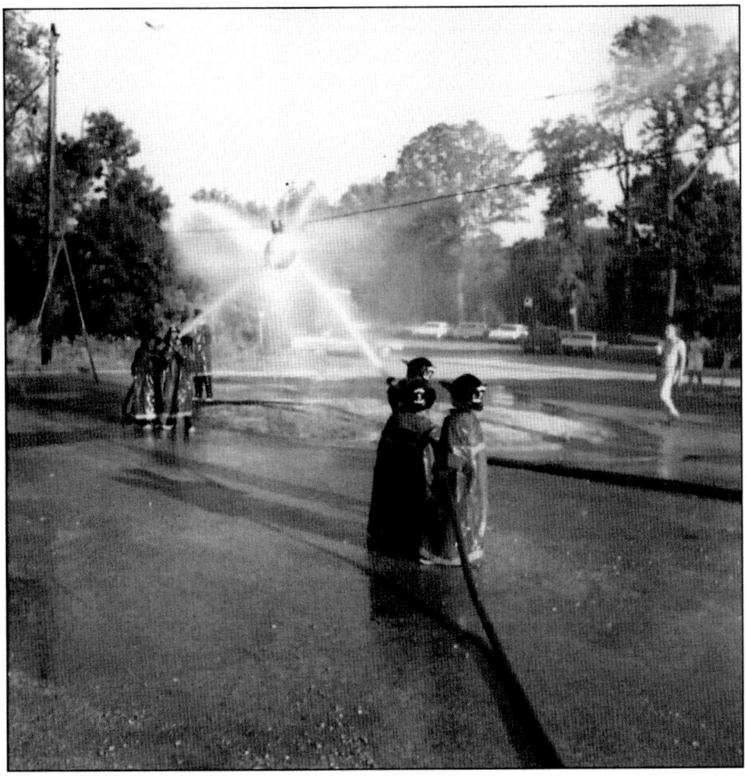

This picture features the children of the Dyer firemen as they play waterball at the 1969–1970 firemen's picnic. It was a refreshing game, especially during a hot summer day. Other games, such as sack and wheelbarrow races took place. There were even horseshoe competitions for the older generations.

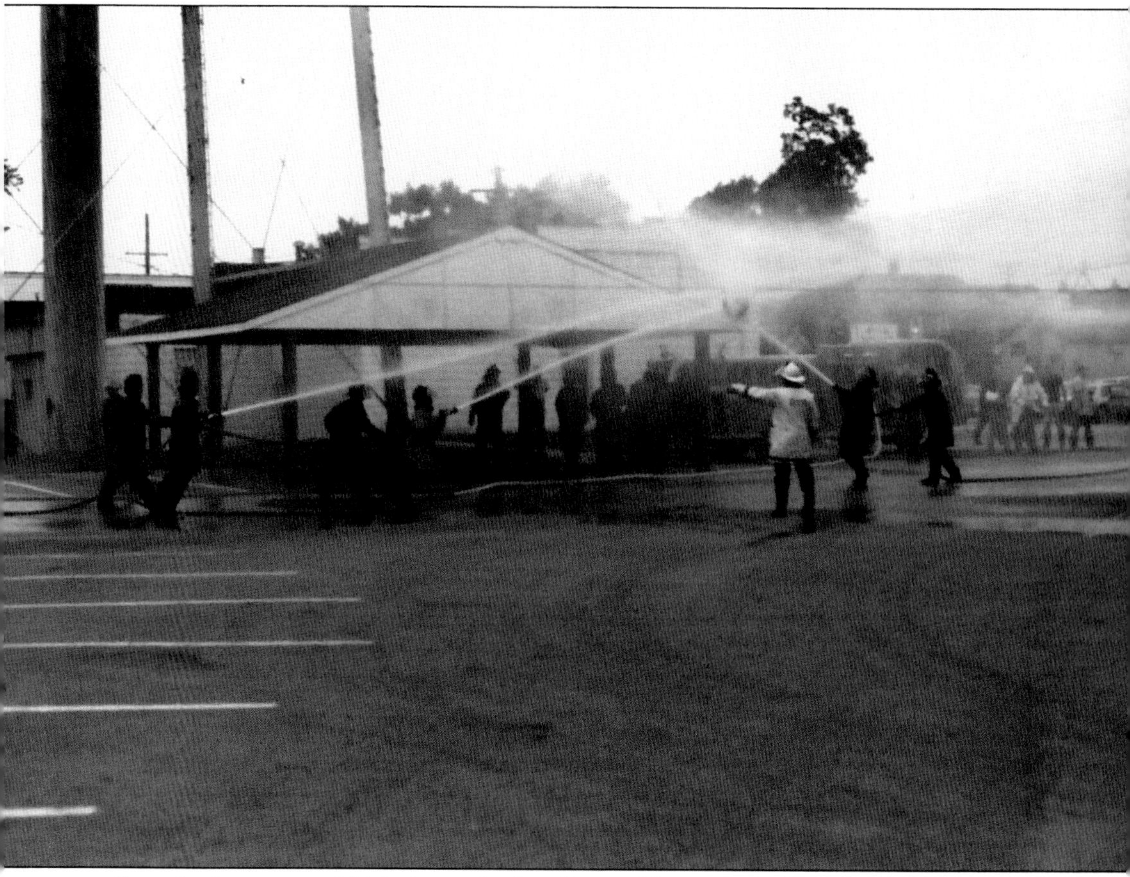

Even the firemen would join in on the fun. Pictured here are the Dyer firemen playing waterball at the 1969–1970 firemen's picnic. The object of the game was to push the ball across the wire to the opponent's side by the powerful stream of water. Participants and spectators alike enjoyed this game. The firemen's picnic is a very family-oriented event. The families of the men who serve on the Dyer Volunteer Fire Department are directly affected by the men's devotion to their duties as firemen. A fire call can come in at any time of the day, taking the fireman away from his family for hours at a time. During these calls mothers remain home to watch over the children. Firemen often miss out on family functions, holiday gatherings, and even sleep. These men work in all kinds of temperamental weather as well, not to mention the personal risks they may take servicing a call. These are just some of the sacrifices these families make to provide protection for the town of Dyer.

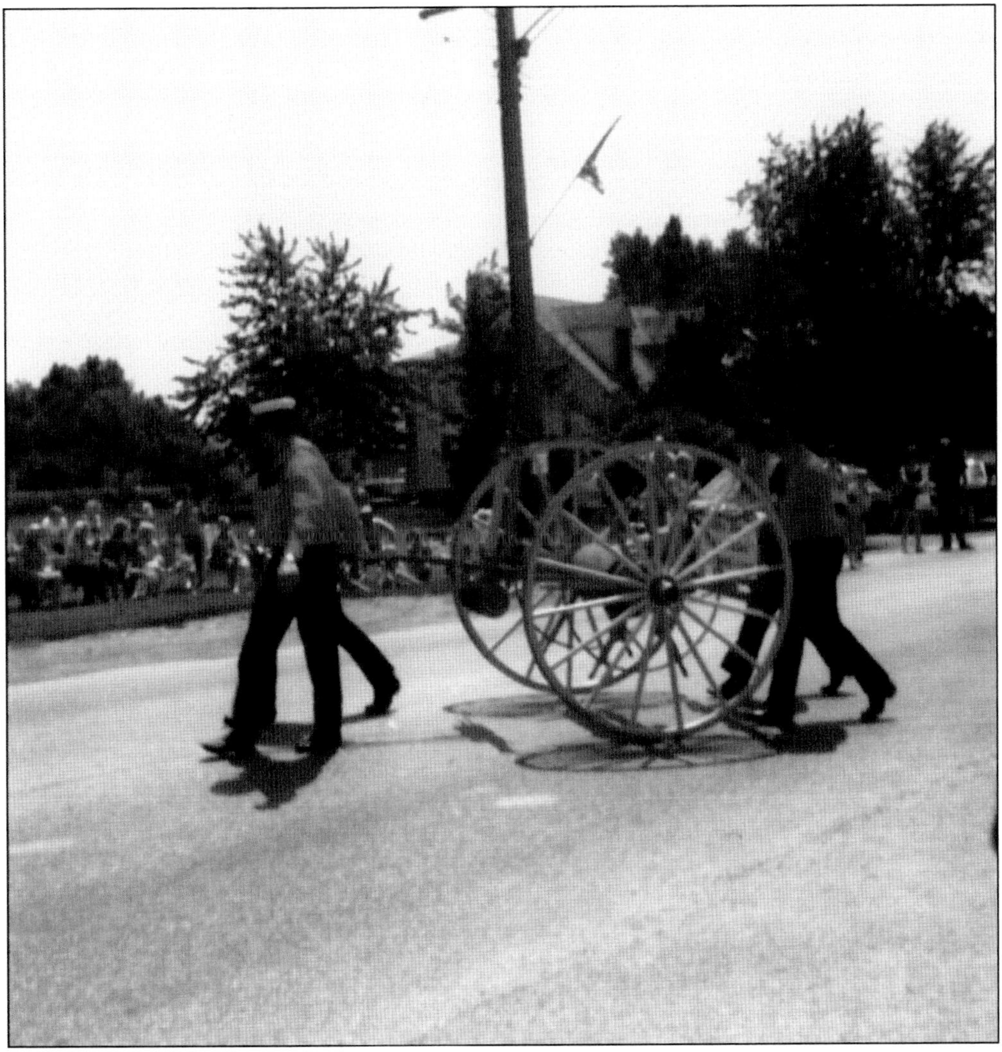

The Dyer firemen pulling the hand drawn hose cart led many Dyer parades. The hose cart was purchased in 1915 for a cost of $55 when the Dyer Volunteer Fire Department was established. They also purchased a ladder wagon for $52.50 that same year. In 1916 a 1,200-pound fire bell and bell tower was purchased and erected for $100 to alarm the firemen of a fire call. That same year, a chemical wagon was purchased. The first fire station built was an 18-foot-by-20-foot-by-16-foot building at a cost of $125. These were all very essential purchases for the protection of the town. Quoting an early town settler, "A fire in those days was a terrifying thing; the pounding at your door, the cry of fire and helplessness in combating a fire with no equipment and no trained men."

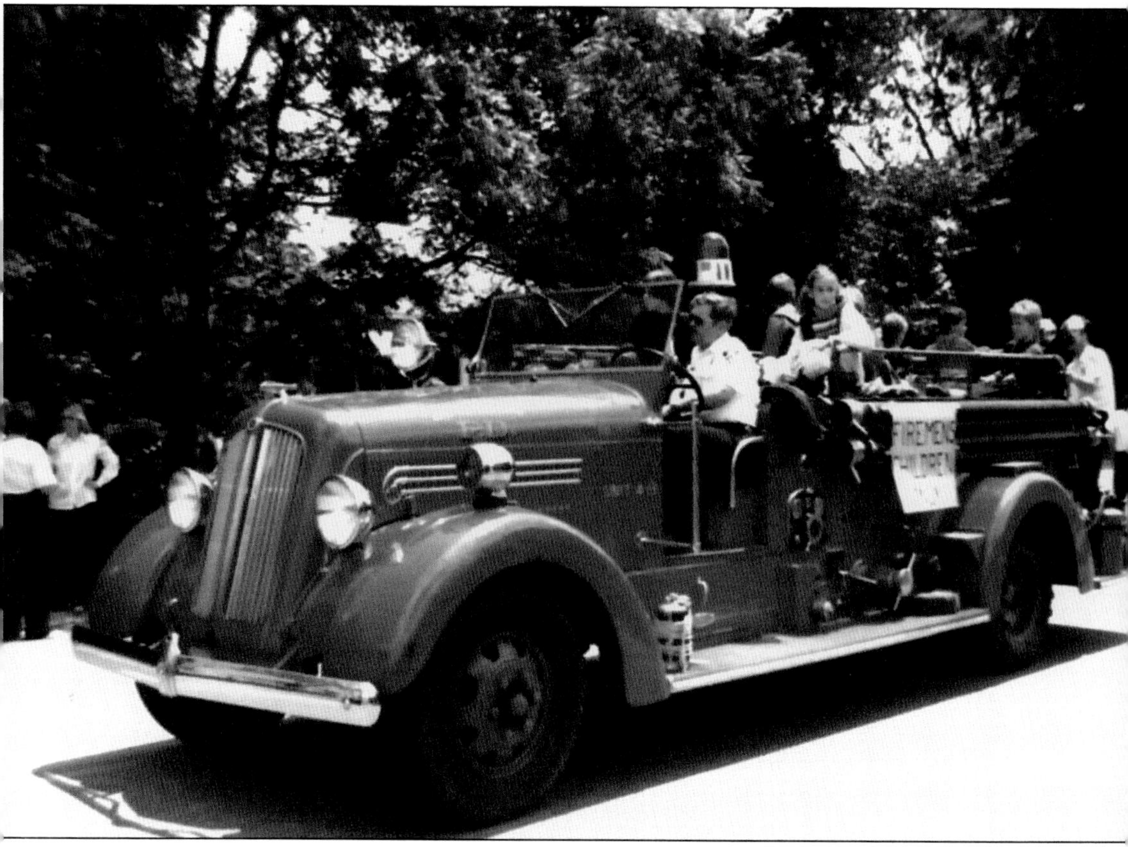

Pictured here is Ernie Benninghoff driving the 1939 Seagraves pumper fire truck in a 1970s Dyer parade. As is traditional, riding on the back during the parade are the children of the firemen. The Seagraves fire truck featured a 250-gallon water tank that could pump 500 gallons per minute. To date, the Dyer Volunteer Fire Department protects 20,000 citizens in a 6.2 square mile area consisting of primarily residential property. The department has two stations that house 11 emergency vehicles. The protection they offer the town of Dyer consists of firefighting, hazardous material response, ALS emergency medical service, vehicle rescue (extrication), and search and rescue. The Dyer Volunteer Fire Department operates on a paid on-call status. During the publication of this book, serving as fire chief is Thad Stutler, and Bob Bonin is assistant fire chief. Thad's father also served as fire chief in previous years.

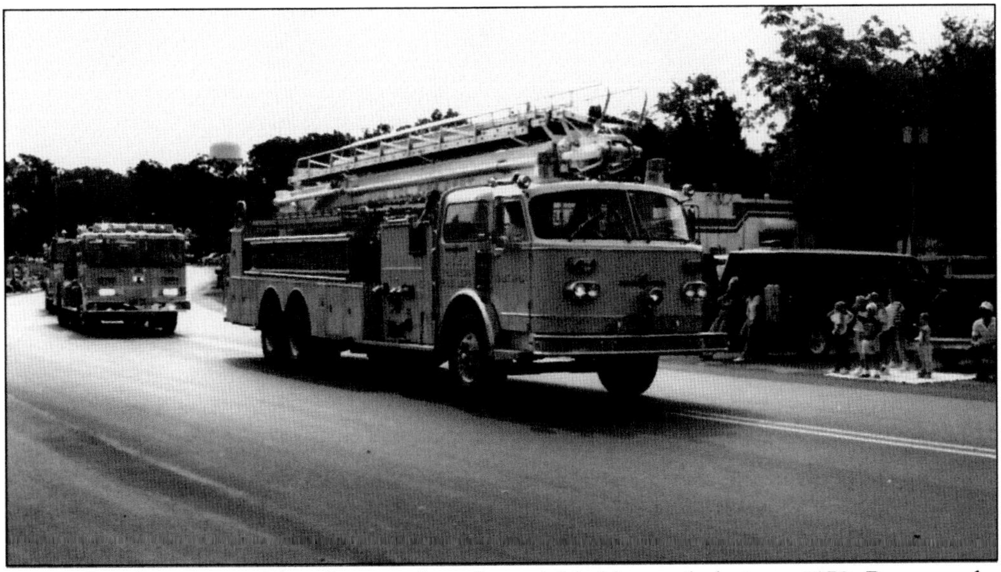

Pictured in the center of this photograph is the aerial ladder truck during a 1970s Dyer parade. As the structures in Dyer grew taller, the demand for a fire truck that could reach such heights needed to be served. At the time, the hospital and church steeple were the tallest constructions in town.

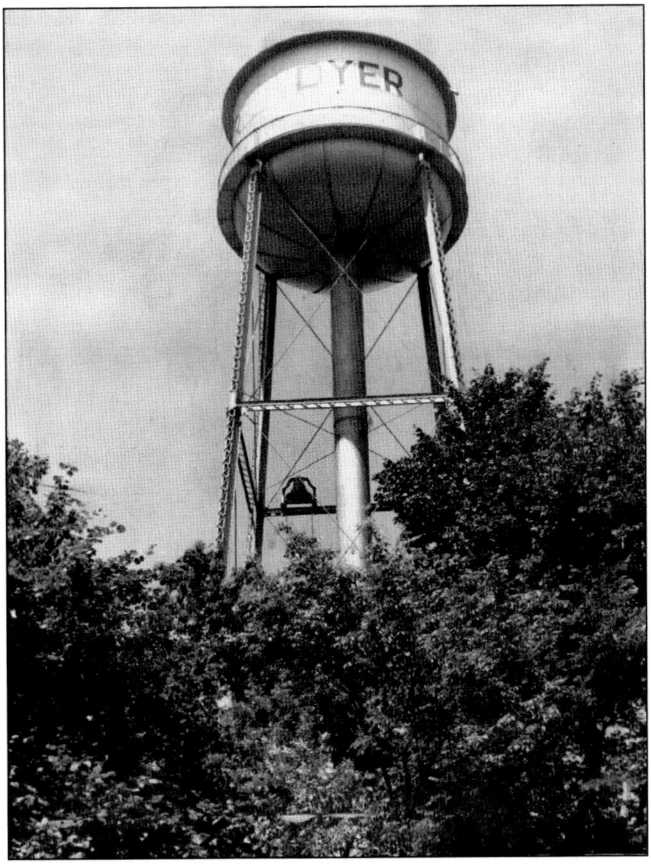

This 1973 photograph features Dyer's water tower with the 1916 fire alarm bell. When the telephone system came to Dyer, the women within earshot of the fire bell would make a call to all the volunteer firemen, alerting them of the alarm. A siren eventually replaced the fire bell.

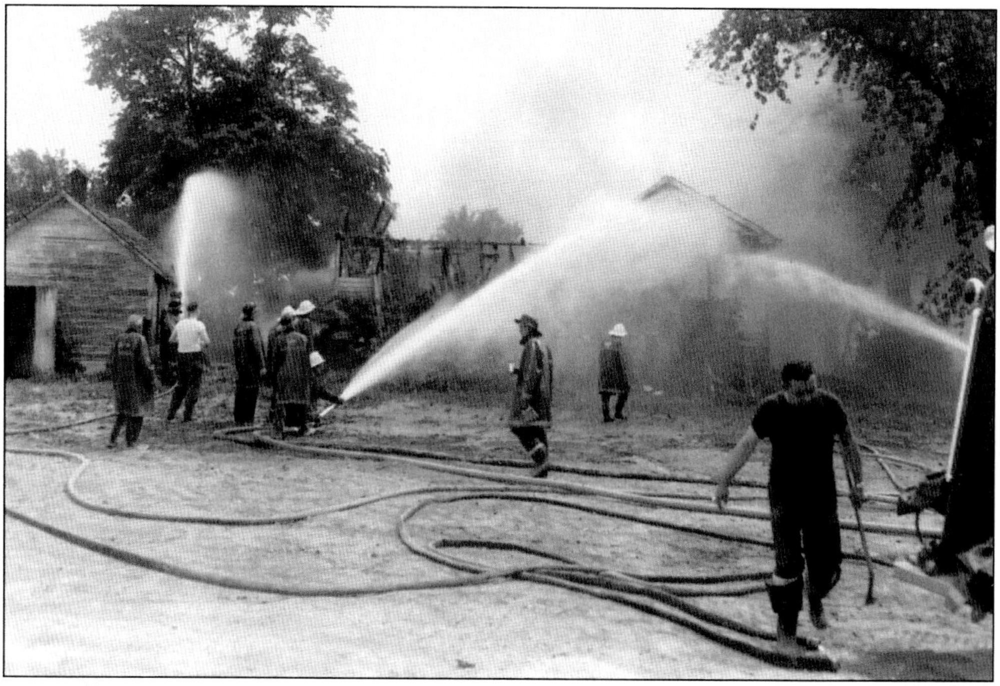

Pictured here are the Dyer firemen servicing a call. At the far right, facing the camera, is fireman Ken Murray. The other firemen are unidentified. The fire call that made the biggest impact on Dyer came on the morning of May 6, 1974, when the grain elevator ignited. This affected farmers throughout the area.

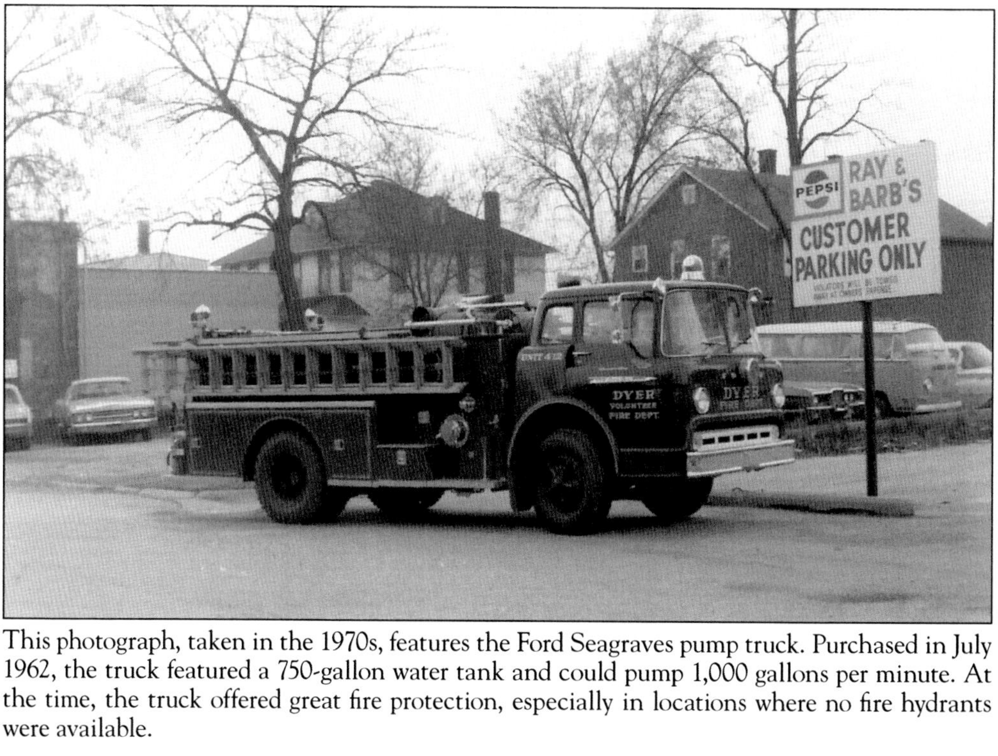

This photograph, taken in the 1970s, features the Ford Seagraves pump truck. Purchased in July 1962, the truck featured a 750-gallon water tank and could pump 1,000 gallons per minute. At the time, the truck offered great fire protection, especially in locations where no fire hydrants were available.

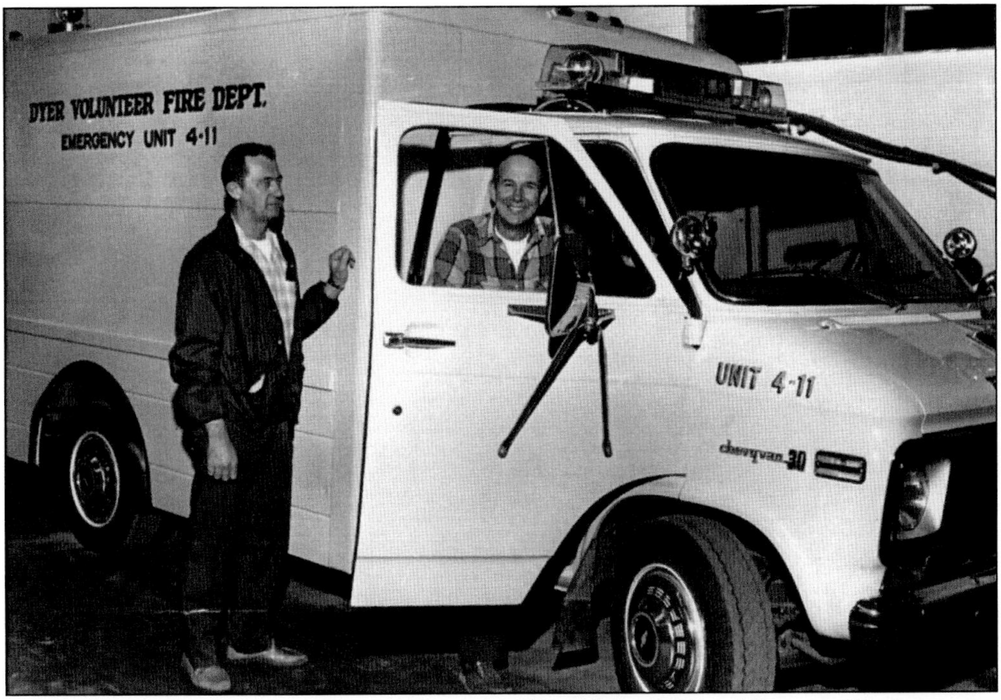

In this photograph, taken on April 8, 1977, Ronald Dumbsky (left) and Raymond Burke pose in front of the Inhalator truck. The Inhalator was a 1974 Chevrolet Suburban. It was purchased by the town in January 1974, and used for first aid and resuscitation calls.

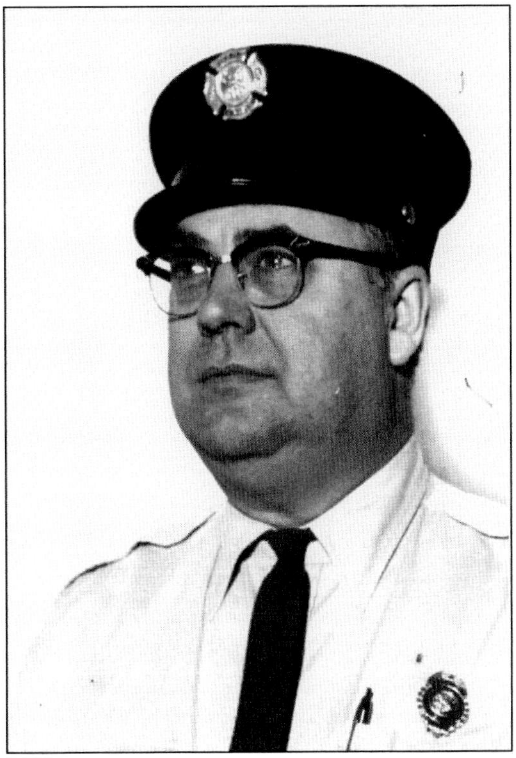

Pictured here is retired Dyer fireman Robert Keilman. As written in the fire department by-laws of 1916, to qualify for an honorary retirement roll, one had to have served for at least 20 years, have reached age 55, or be permanently ill or disabled.

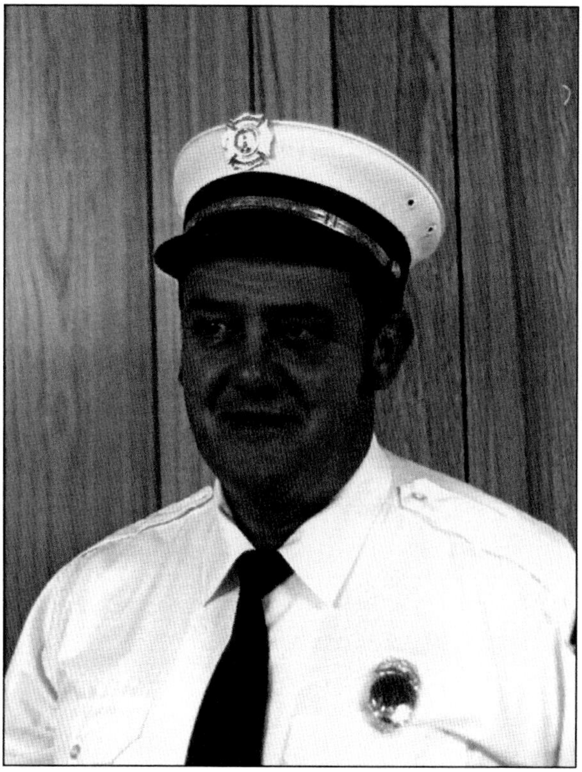

This 1976 picture features Tom Hilbrich, the Dyer Volunteer Fire Department's seventh serving fire chief. Today he is an active member of the Dyer Historical Society, as well as firemen Ronald Dumbsky, Ronald Reichelt, and past member John Ozahanics.

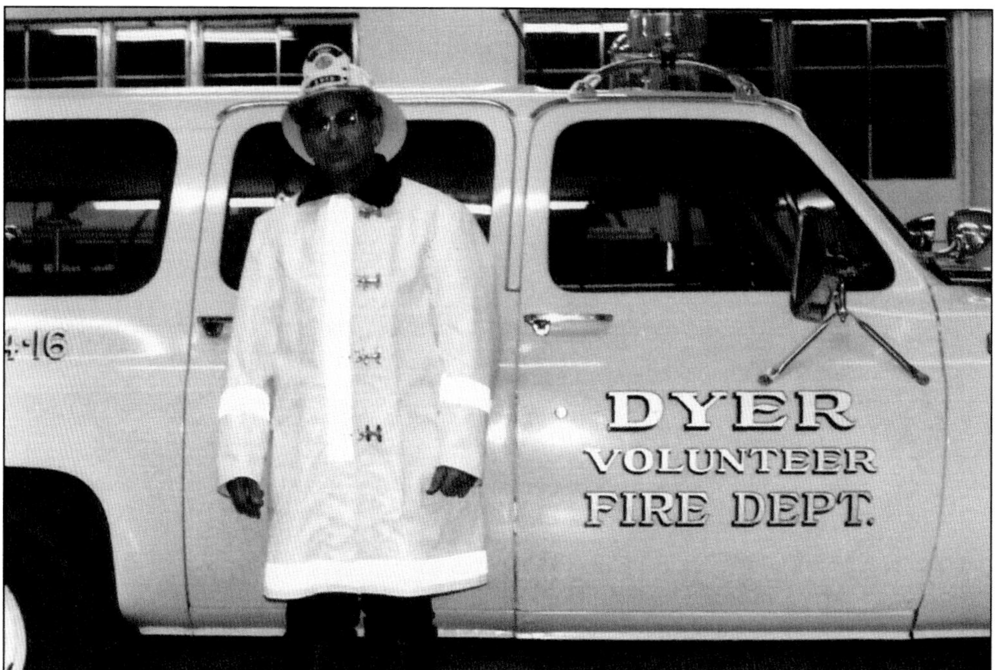

Pictured here is Ewald Rietman, eighth fire chief of the volunteer fire department during the 1980s. It is not uncommon for the fire departments of local towns of the St. John Township to assist one another on fire calls depending on the severity of the fire.

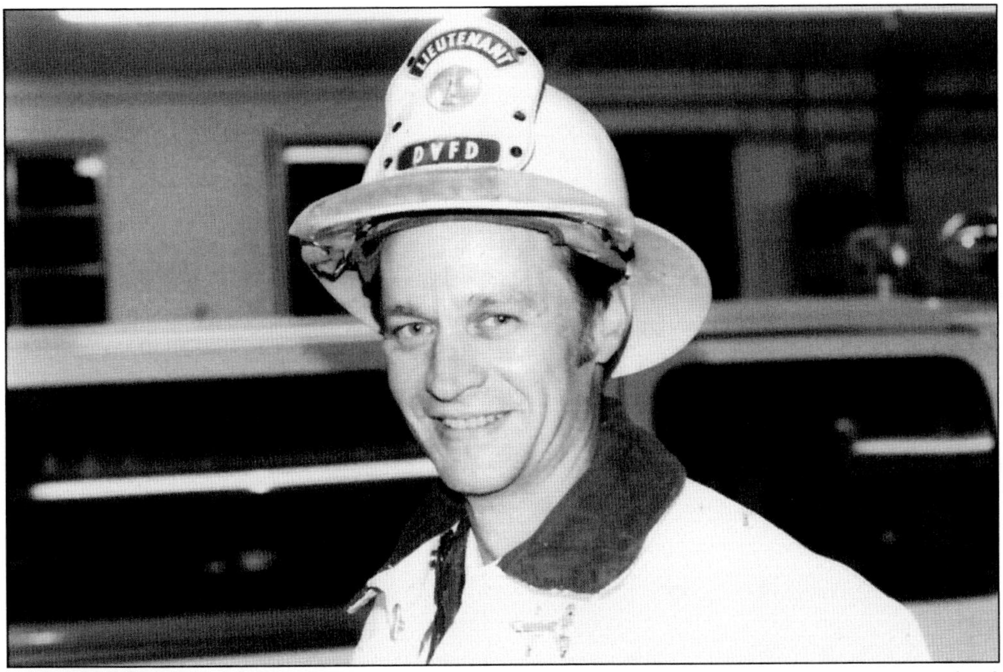

This 1980s photograph features Don Meyer, Dyer Volunteer Fire Department's ninth fire chief. All fire chiefs were nominated and elected into their positions. Great responsibility comes with the position of fire chief, for the lives of the firemen are under the chief's supervision.

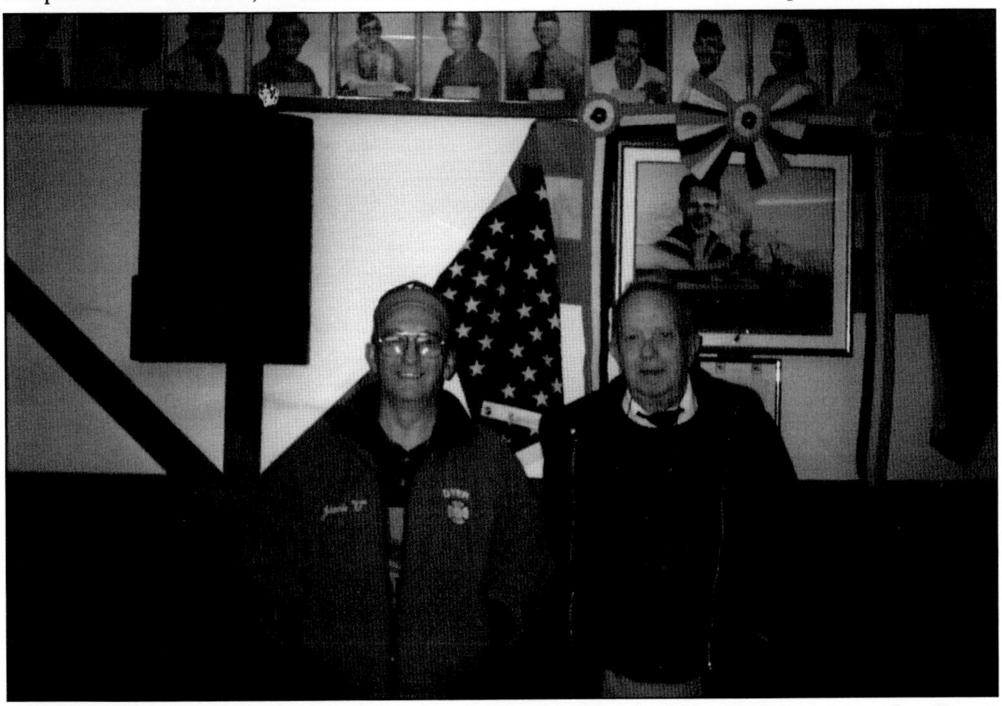

John Ozahanics, pictured on the left, poses with Glen Eberly. John Ozahanics served as Dyer's 12th fire chief. Glen Eberly was a founder of the Dyer Historical Society and served on the town board for many years. This picture was taken in the late 1980s or early 1990s.

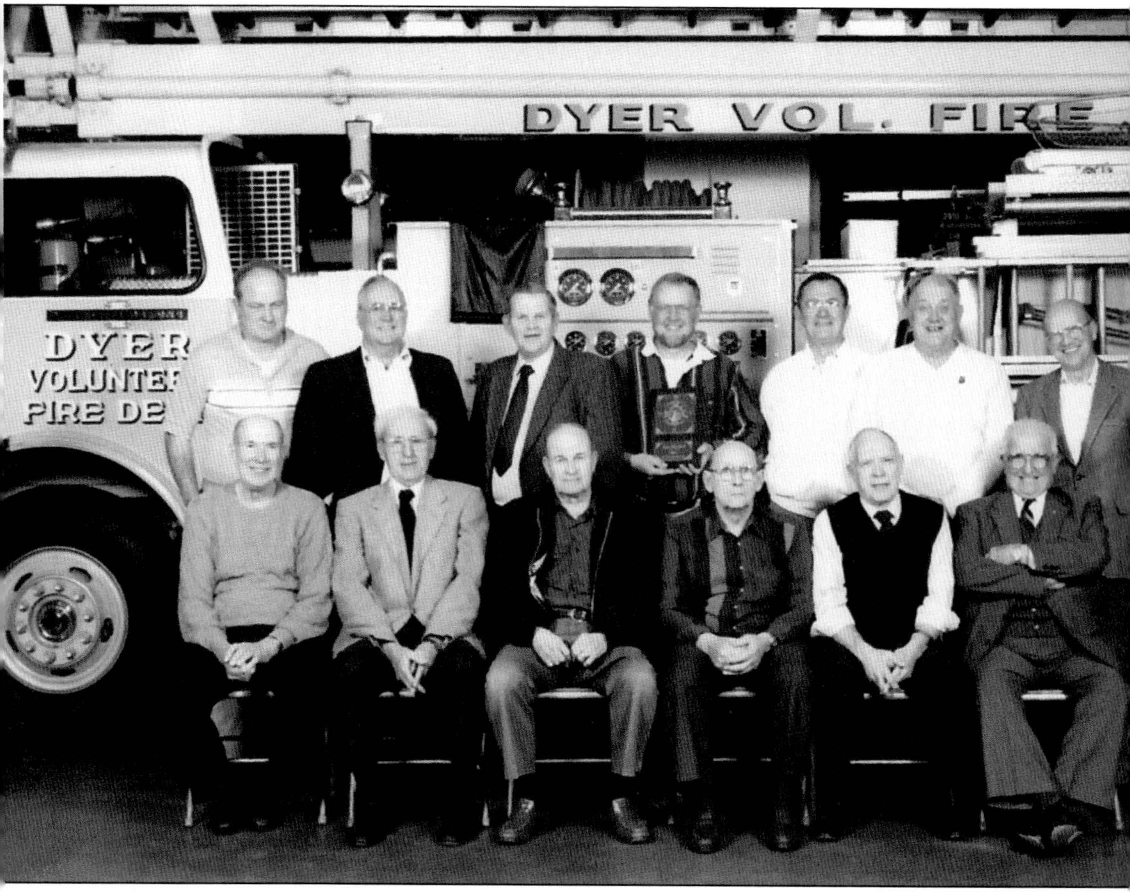

This 1980s photograph features retired firemen posing in front of an aerial ladder truck. From left to right are (first row) Ray Burke, G. Hoffman, M. Keilman, Ewald Reitman, W. Kaiser, and W. Gettler; (second row) L. Margraf, K. Hoffman, Ernie Benninghoff, Ron Reichelt, Ron Dumbsky, Tom Hilbrich, and K. Keilman. From the years 1915 to 1964, it is reported that the Dyer Volunteer Fire Department roll call served the town of Dyer collectively a total of 917 years. In 1964, it is reported that years of service for the individual volunteer ranged from 1 year to 33 years. The following is a list of fire chiefs that served from 1915, the year the Dyer Volunteer Fire Department was organized, to 1975: John Burge, Nicholas Austgen, Paul Miller, John Dumbsky, Joseph Miklik, Robert Austgen, Arthur Herrman, Thomas Hilbrich, and Ewald Rietman.

This photograph, taken in the late 1930s, shows the construction of the water tower that once stood behind the old town hall and police department, next to the fire station. For many years the water tower was a prominent feature in Dyer's skyline, along with the St. Joseph Church's steeple.

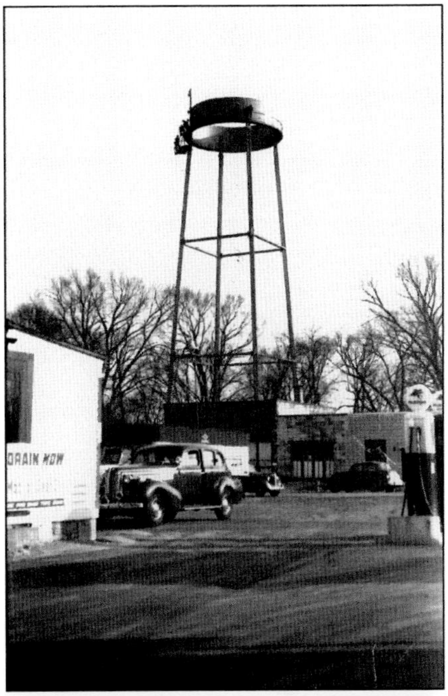

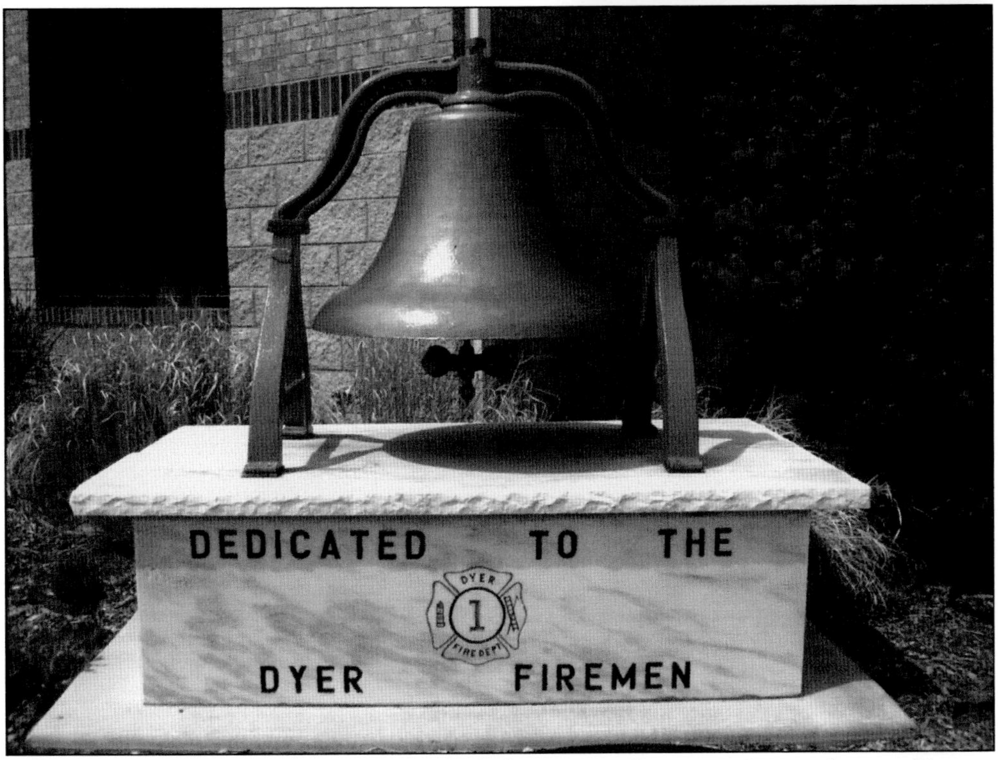

Pictured here is the 1916 fire bell. When the bell was rung, firemen within earshot would come running to the station. When the phone system came to town, the women within the town would make fire calls to all the firemen. In 1972, the fire bell was dedicated to the firemen of Dyer, past, present, and future.

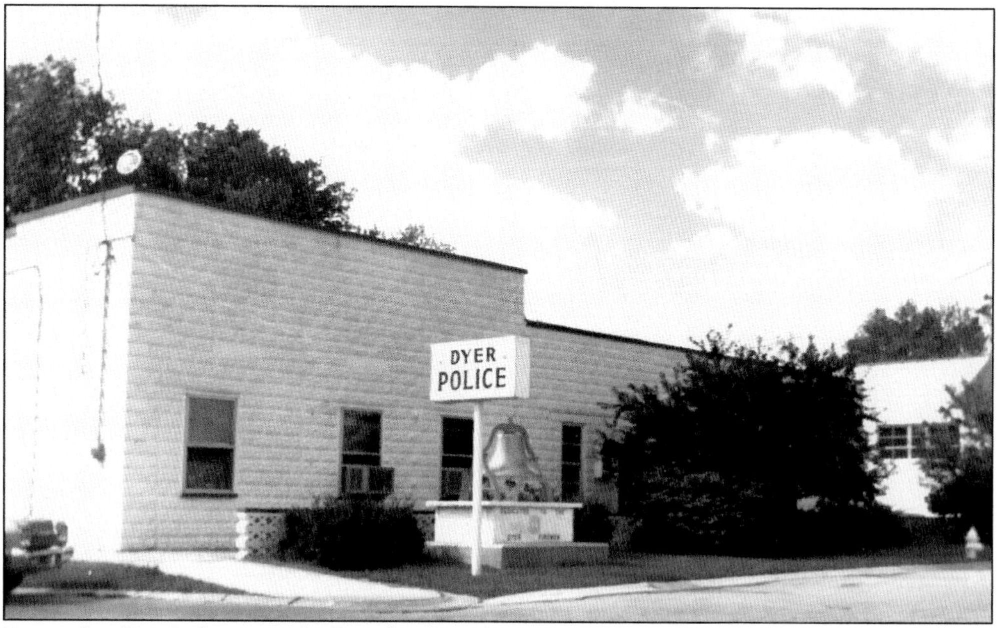

Pictured is Dyer's first town hall and police department. It was built in 1938 and torn down December 1987. Prior to the town hall, town board meetings used to take place at a store building owned by Henry Schulte, who was one of the town's first board members.

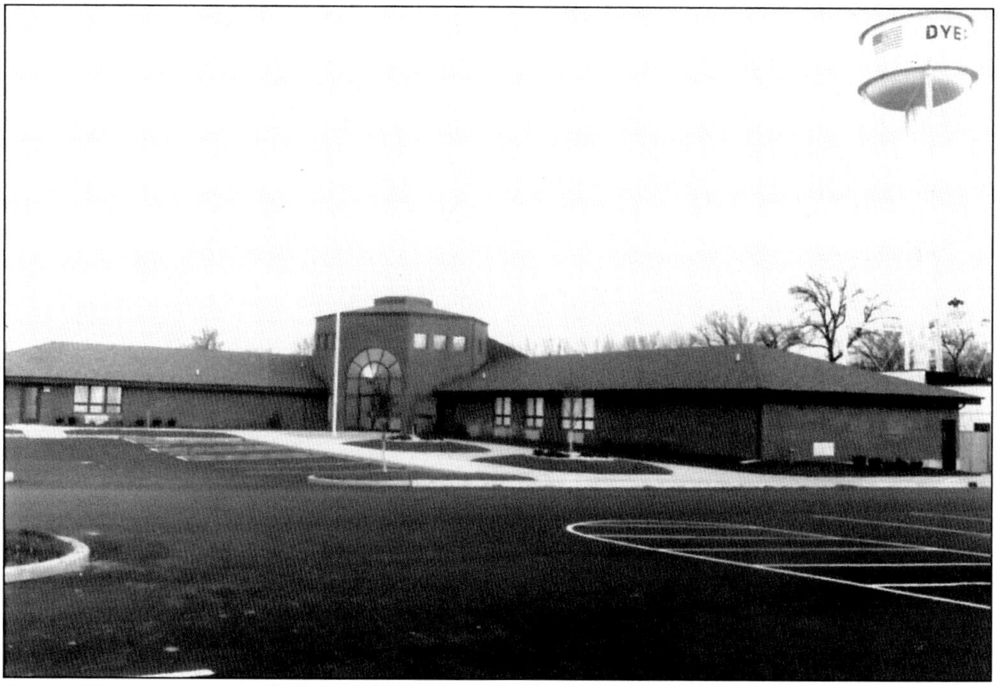

Pictured here is the town hall that Dyer has today. It was dedicated on December 13, 1987. The water tower standing behind the Dyer Town Hall was used to support the old fire bell and, as seen in this photograph, the fire siren.

Six

The Railroads and Grain Elevator

Before railroads, farmers would take their goods by wagon to Chicago. From Chicago the goods would be loaded on barges going west via the canal, or ships going east via Lake Michigan. Getting from Dyer to Chicago could take up to four days, as recalled by Dyer resident Alma Gettler. There were no paved roads to travel on or bridges to cross. If it happened to be a rainy season then one could count on their wagon getting stuck in the mud repeatedly, or traveling miles out of the way to find safe passage across rivers and creeks. Not only did the railroads make transportation of goods easier on the farmers, they also got the harvest to buyers faster, thus providing fresher products with a longer life span.

The heart and hub of any farming community is the grain elevator. Seed is bought for planting and the harvest is brought in for storage and shipping. The elevator in Dyer was originally constructed by the Michigan Central Railroad and operated by J. L. Hart. Hart eventually sold his interest in the grain elevator to J. DuBriell and Leonard Keilman. Soon after, DuBriell sold his share of the business to a man by the name of Lowenburg. In 1858, the business was operating under the name of Keilman and Lowenburg. In 1882, the two businessmen purchased the elevator from the railroad and enlarged and converted it to steam power.

Lowenburg passed away, leaving the business to Keilman, who then renamed it the L. Keilman Company. By this time, the business had expanded to farm machinery, lumber, coal, and feed. Major exports were corn and oats. The corn was shelled at the grain elevator and the cobs were used as fuel for kitchen ranges. The main outlets for the grain were feed stores in Hammond, East Chicago, and Indiana Harbor.

By 1953, the L. Keilman Company expanded and had an office building and store that had display windows. The grain elevator itself fell to fire sometime after 7:00 a.m. on May 6, 1974.

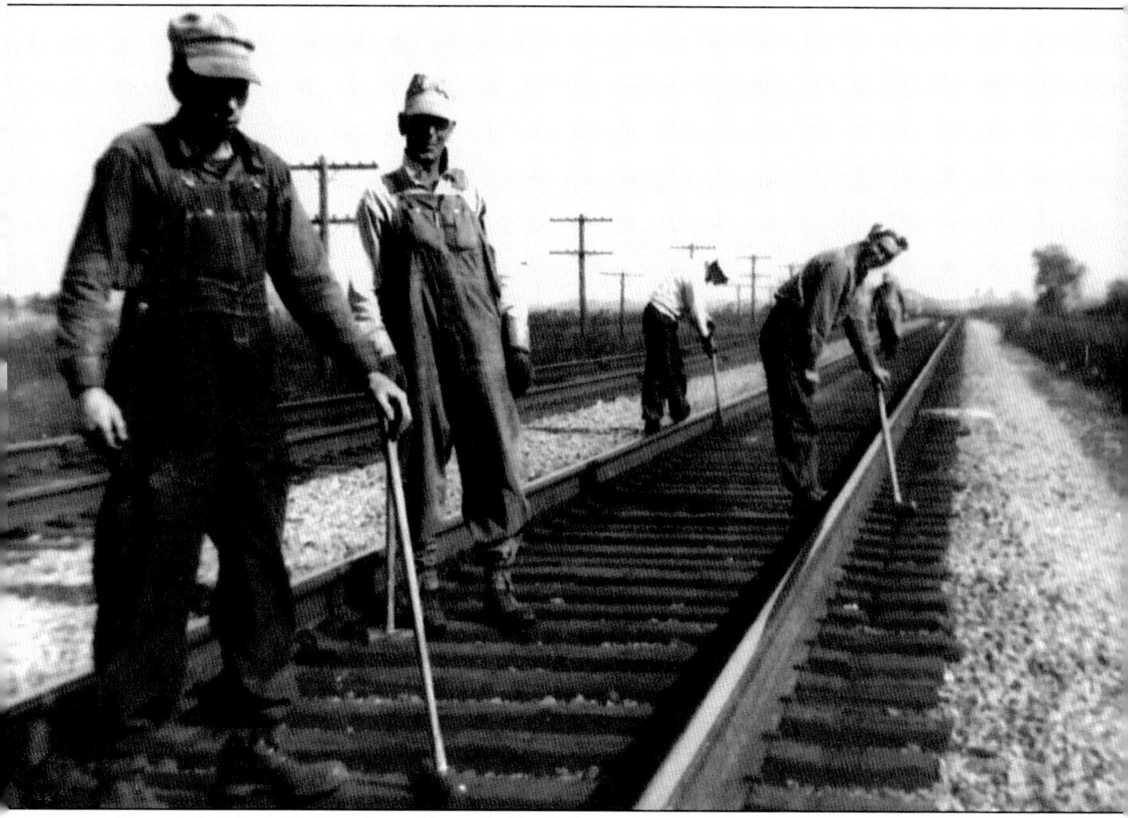

Pictured is Joseph Grothuas (front left) working on the railroad tracks with the section gang. Not only did the railroads make traveling and shipping of goods more efficient, they made jobs available to the people in the region. Not only were jobs available working for the railroad but they also made commuting quicker and easier for employment opportunities in outlying towns and cities such as Hammond and Chicago. Dyer had the Elgin, Joliet and Eastern Railway (EJ&E), Monon Railroad, and Michigan Central Railroad crossing its borders. Not only did the railroads transport goods out of Dyer, they also brought goods in as well. When Aaron Montgomery Ward started his mail-order catalogue in Chicago, many of the farmers took advantage of the opportunity to purchase goods from him, which would be shipped by railroad. The rural communities now had a connection with the outside world.

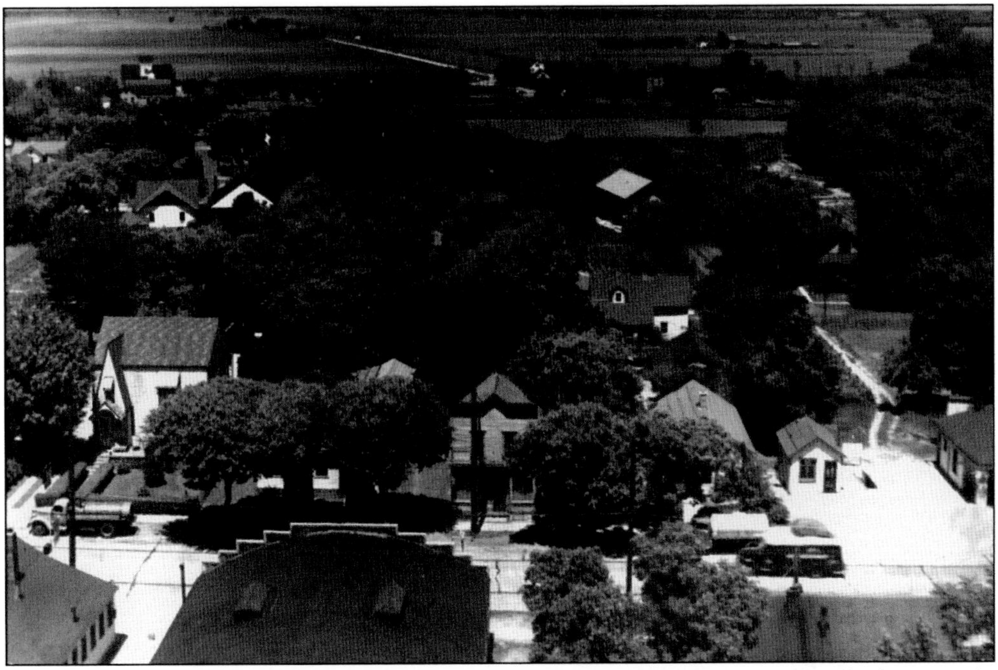

This photograph, taken in the late 1940s to early 1950s, features downtown Dyer looking north. The Lincoln Highway runs east and west on the lower portion of the picture. On the upper left, north of Lincoln Highway, is the L. Keilman Company grain elevator. To the east of the elevator is the switch house, and further still, the train depot.

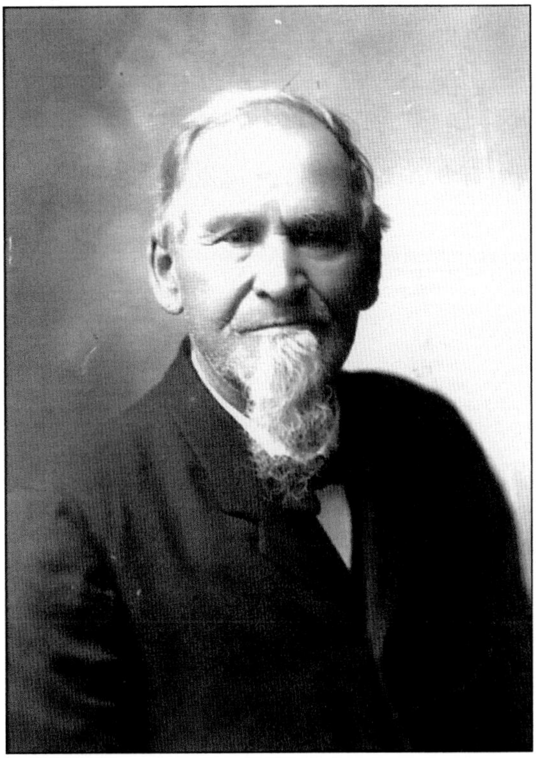

This photograph, taken in 1833, shows Leonard Keilman. In the early 1800s, Keilman was in partnership running the grain elevator. In 1858, the business was operating under the name of Keilman and Lowenburg until 1910, when Lowenburg passed away, leaving the business to Leonard, who then renamed it the L. Keilman Company.

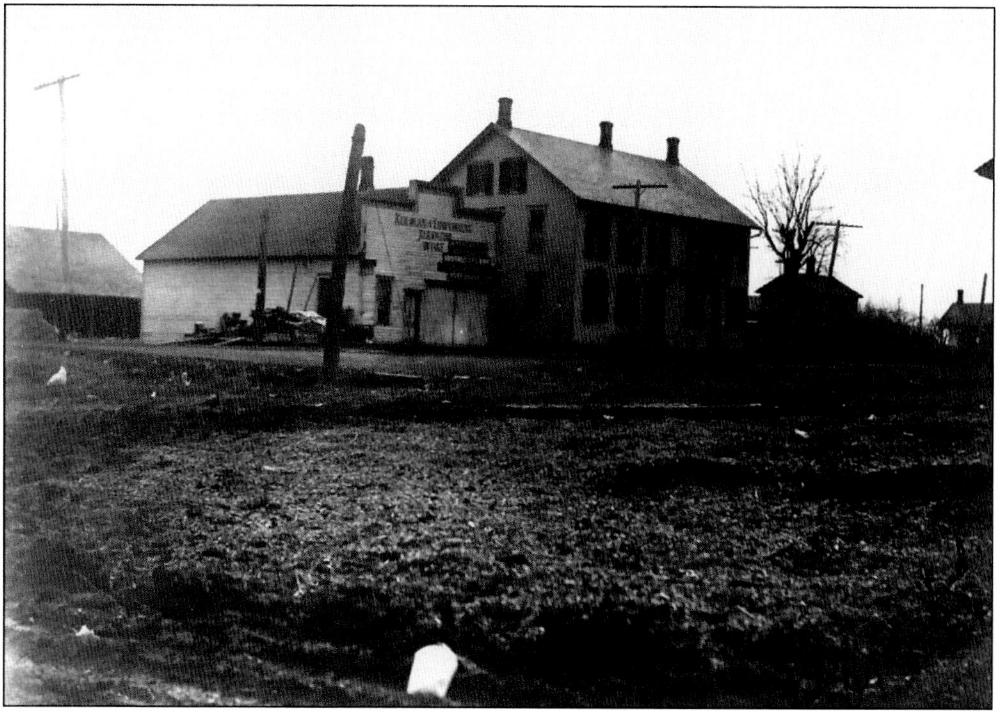

Shown here on the left is the Keilman and Lowenberg elevator office. To the right stands the Hartman Hotel and Saloon. Keilman purchased the Hartman property to expand his business. Other businesses near this location were a sauerkraut and pickle factory and a flourmill, both of which utilized the railroads.

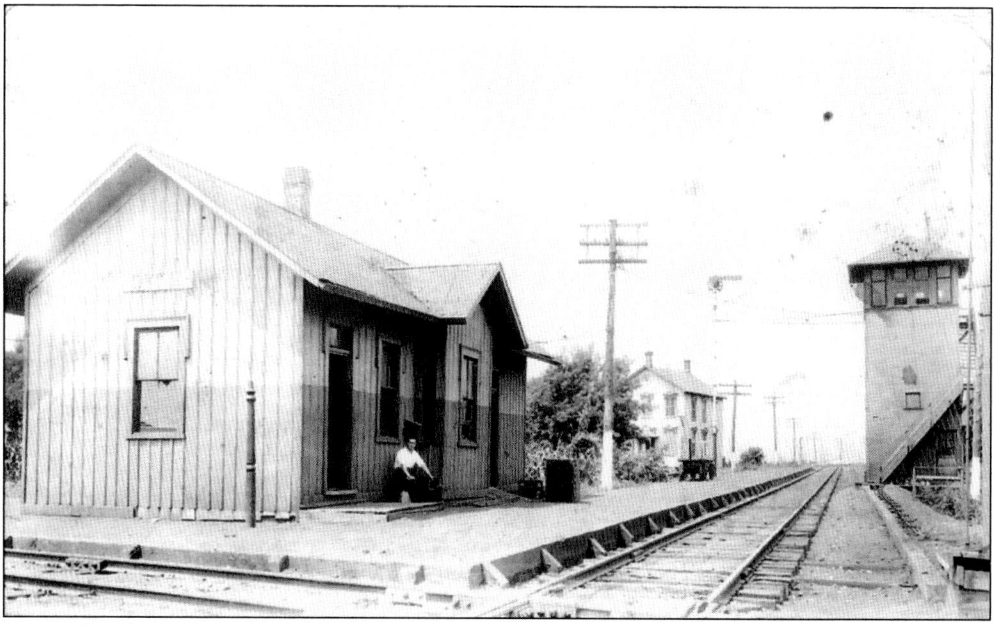

Pictured at the far left is the Monon depot and at far right is the switch control tower around the 1930s. Paul Gettler was the last to operate the switch house. Gettler worked a total of 53 years for the railroad, 45 of which were spent in the tower, which was demolished in 1953.

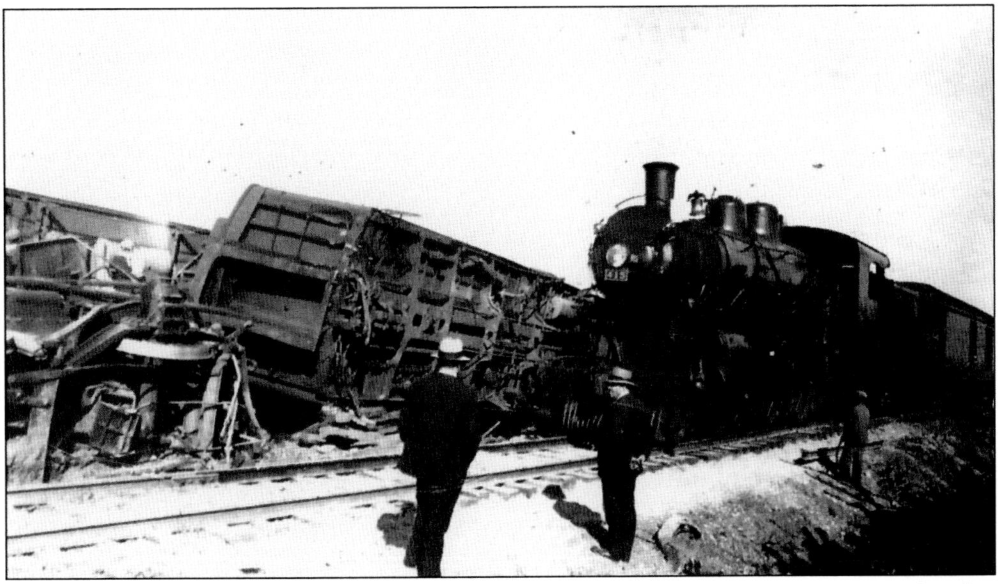

This train wreck took place at the Keilman crossing, near the L. Keilman Company, on October 16, 1922. Although the railway system brought many benefits to town, it also brought along the dangers of road crossings. This train line ran east and west through Dyer. The spectators in this photograph are unidentified.

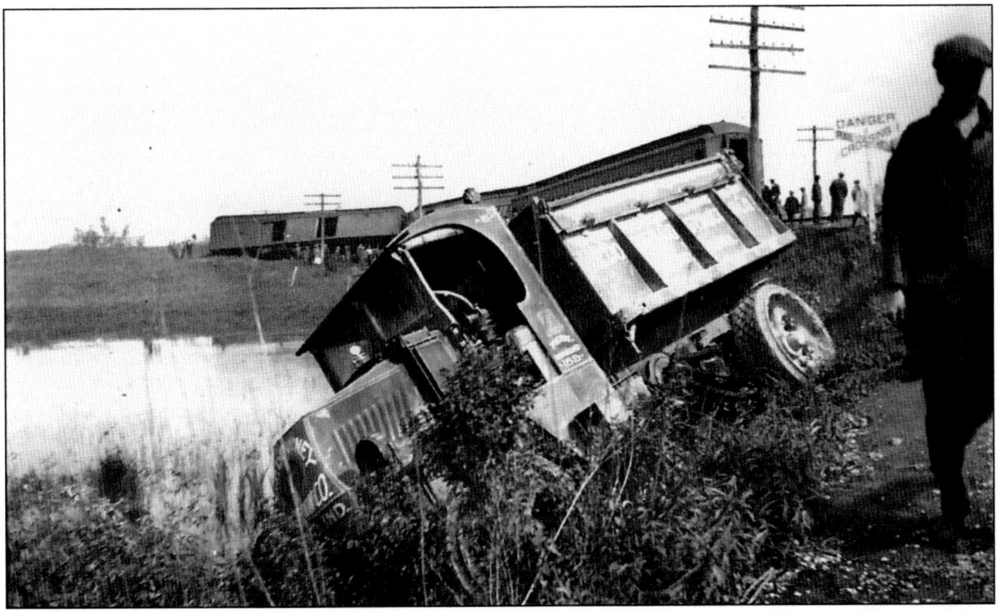

The train wreck at the Keilman crossing on October 16, 1922, was caused by a collision with a truck, shown here. There were three railways running through Dyer at the time. The Michigan Central and the EJ&E ran east and west. The Monon Railroad ran north and south.

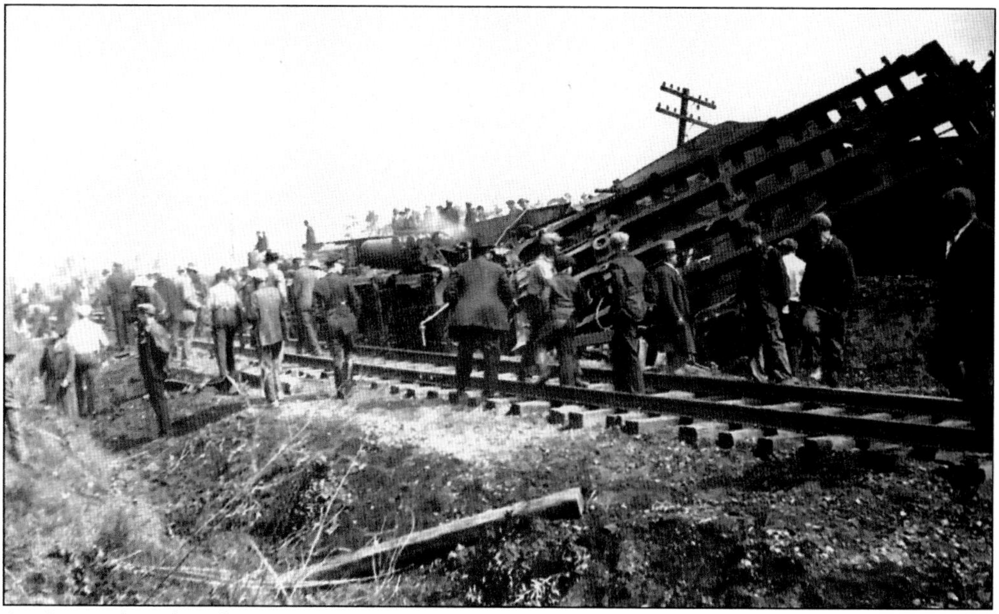

As depicted in this photograph, train wrecks brought many spectators to the scene. This train wreck took place in the Michigan Central Railroad line at the Keilman crossing near the grain elevator. The train involved was a freight train. This picture was taken on October 16, 1922.

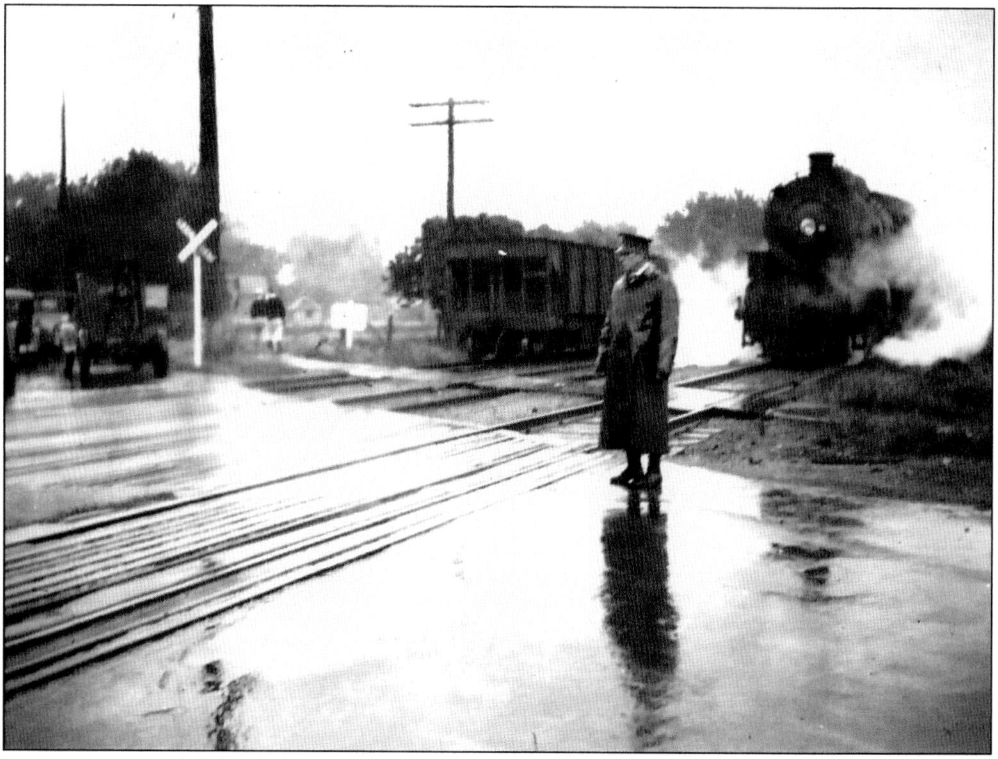

In this photograph, Marshal Louis Hartman directs traffic at the railroad crossing on the Lincoln Highway. This train wreck took place on Joliet Street, previously the Lincoln Highway, on May 14, 1944. The wreck stretched behind the Overhage and Koepl homes.

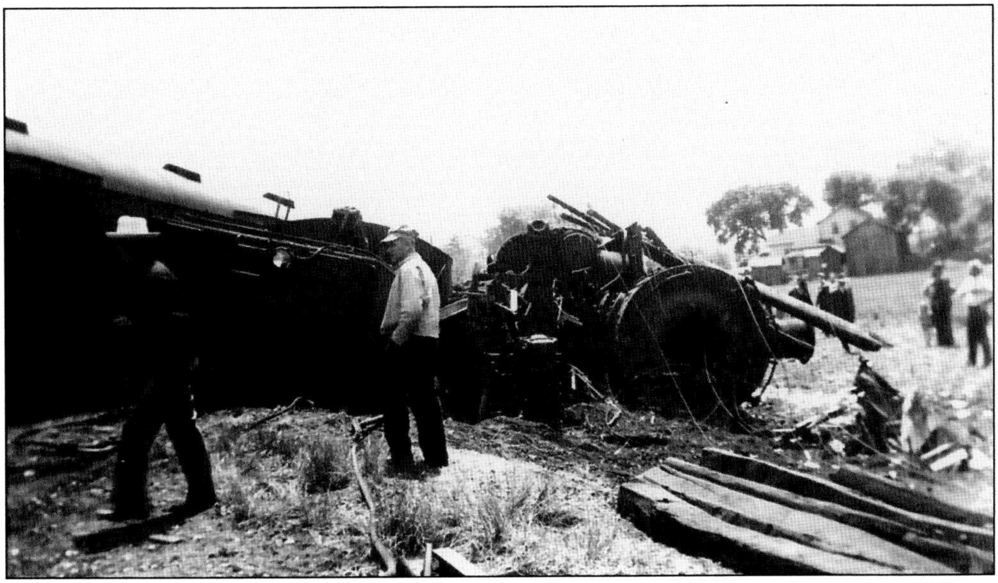

In this photograph of the May 14, 1944, train wreck is the severely damaged steam engine lying on its side. Railroad ties and telegraph poles were torn out of the ground. Such a wreck caused much devastation. This took place on the Monon Railroad line, which ran north and south through Dyer.

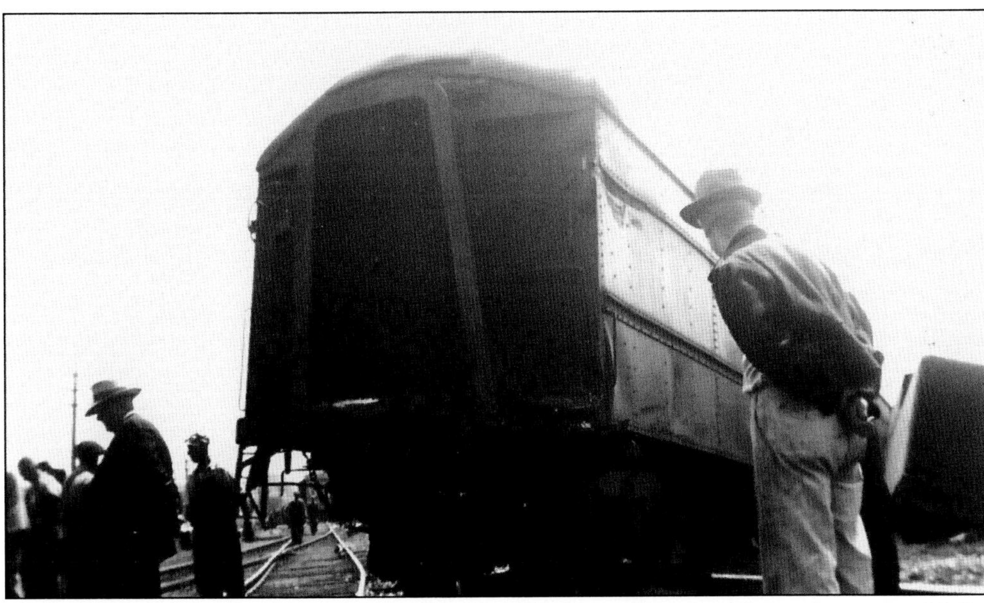

This train wreck involved a passenger train. It took place where the Monon line crossed Joliet Street, also known as the Lincoln Highway. It is unknown if any injuries or deaths were reported. This photograph was taken on May, 14, 1944.

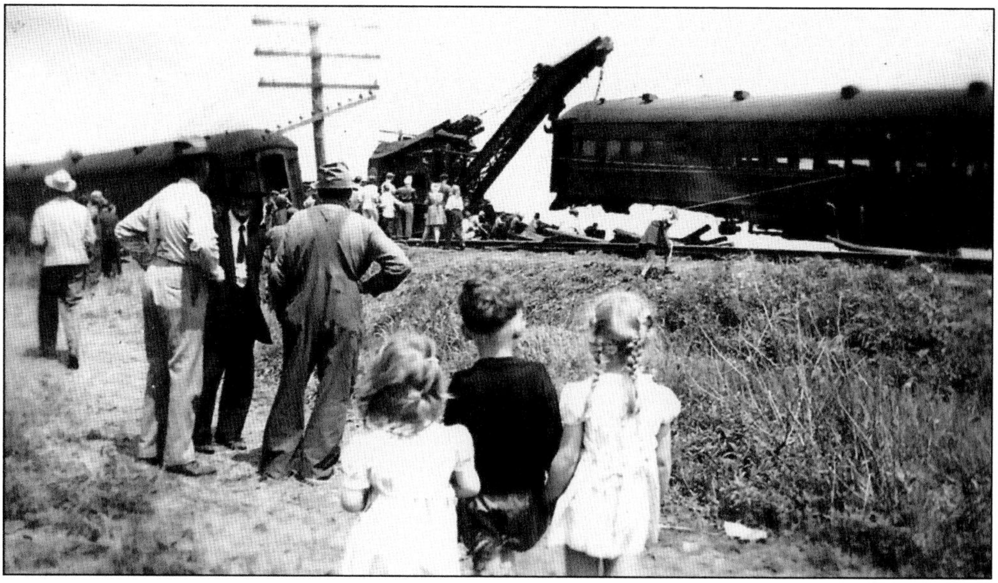

In this photograph, taken on May 14, 1944, spectators watch as a steam crane lifts a derailed passenger car. This wreck took place on the north and south running Monon Railroad system. The Monon line ran passenger trains to and from Chicago and Indianapolis.

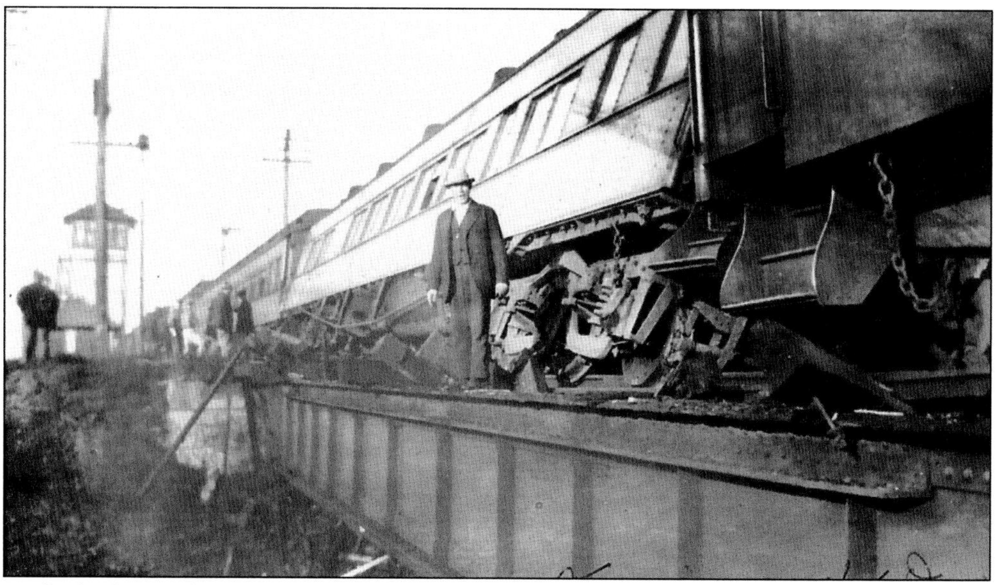

In the background of this photograph is the switch control tower. In 1846, there were 23,000 miles of telegraph lines stretching over the country that the railroad used to communicate from one switch control tower to the next. This made train travel safer by reducing accidents, collisions, and derailments.

Seven

The Lincoln Highway and the Ideal Section

On May 19, 1903, a bet was made. Dr. Horatio Nelson Jackson wagered $50 that he could travel from San Francisco to New York by automobile in less than three months. Keep in mind that in 1903 there were roughly 33,000 cars in the United States and only 150 miles of paved roads. Four days later, Jackson and a mechanic by the name of Sewall K. Crocker left San Francisco, their destination New York. Along the way they picked up a bulldog named Bud for a mascot.

The trip proved difficult, pitted as they were against weather, mud, and breakdowns. Little did they know that word of their odyssey was spreading across the country. People were turning out to see the team and their automobile pass by. On July 17 they entered Chicago, where they received a warm reception from the city officials.

On Sunday, July 26, at 4:30 in the morning, the trio entered Manhattan, winning the wager. In total the trip took them 63 days, 12 hours, and 30 minutes. Distance traveled was over 5,600 miles. Although their journey did not take them through Dyer, they did affect Dyer's history in an indirect way.

Proving that travel across country by automobile was possible encouraged companies to invest in the building of roads and highways. Through Dyer, stretching from Schererville to East Chicago, the section of the Lincoln Highway called the Ideal Section was constructed along part of the old Sauk Trail. Financed by state, federal, and county governments and the United States Rubber Company, this Ideal Section was adorned with fancy street lamps and concrete. This section served as a model for what all roads were to become. It opened in 1921 with great celebration. With the completion of the highway, travel by automobile from coast to coast was greatly reduced to just five days. In 1925, the U.S. Bureau of Public Roads eliminated the names of trails and highways to switch to a numeric system; thus the Lincoln Highway became Route 30.

By the way, Dr. Horatio Jackson never did receive his $50.

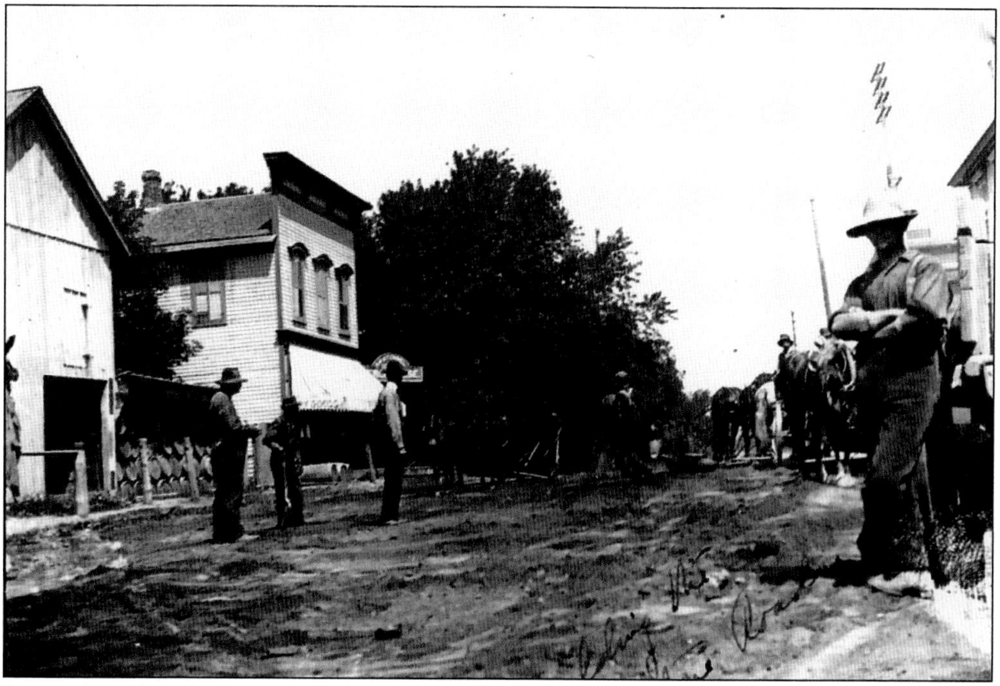

Pictured in this photograph are men building the stone roads on Hart Street and the Sauk Trail during the late 1800s. The building close to center is the Cheap Store, owned by August Stommel, later to become Mathias Hoffman's General Store.

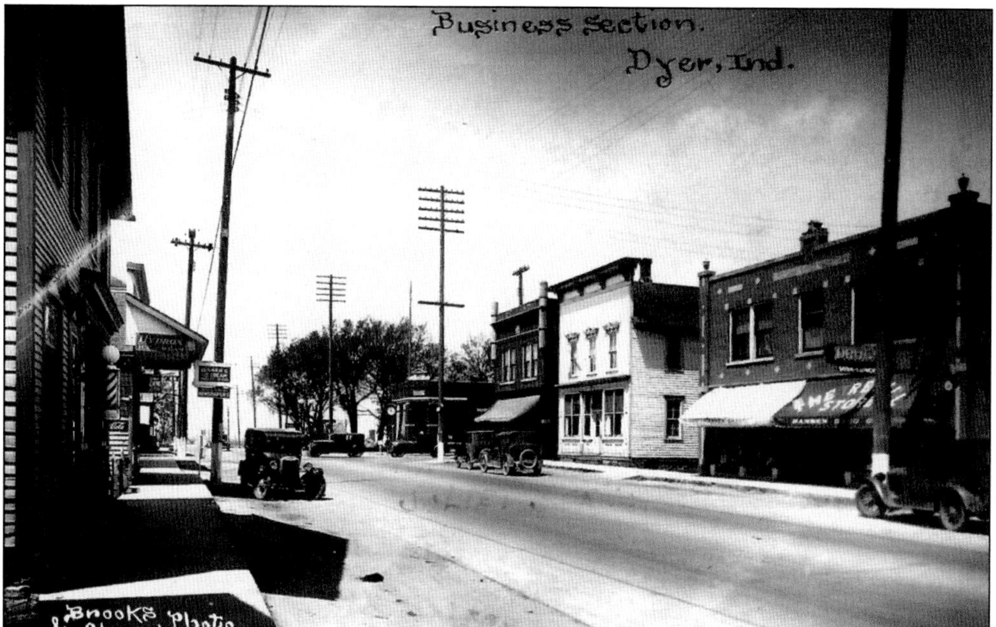

Pictured here is Dyer's business district looking west. The road in the scene was once the Sauk Trail, traveled by many Native Americans. It became the Ideal Section of the Lincoln Highway, later to become Route 30. This thoroughfare is also called Joliet Street. This photograph was taken in the early 1900s.

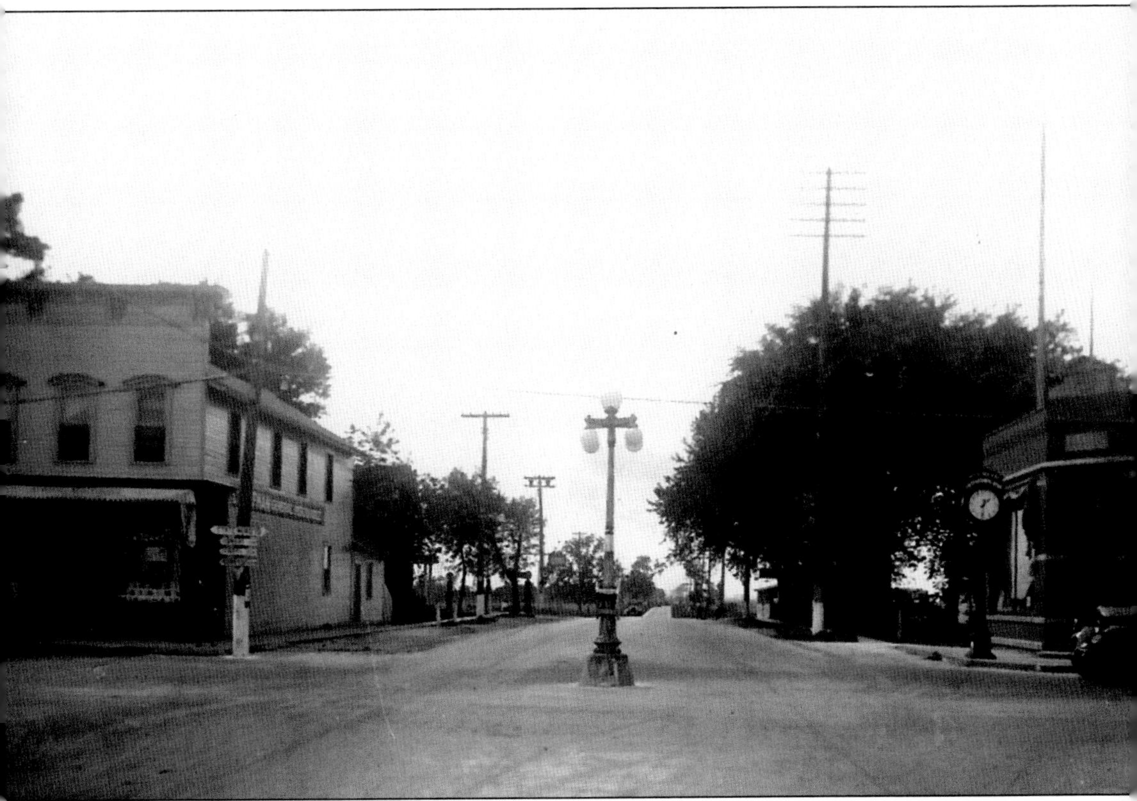

Pictured here is the Sauk Trail looking west, *c.* 1900. The bank is on the right, and directly behind it is where the old Hart family home was located. Aaron and Martha Hart had a second home on their farm at the same time, situated on the northeast side of town. The Hart farm and homestead was known as Hartsdale. They built this house on the Sauk Trail for Martha, who wanted to raise the children closer to town. Most residents lived on the outskirts of town where they farmed. As seen in this photograph, beyond the business district there was open land for miles. This made travel in the wintertime difficult due to snowdrift leaving the fields and crossing the roads. For many farmers, coming to town for necessities during wet or snowy seasons may require a stay overnight in one of the hotels located in the business district of Dyer. Once paved roads were laid, travel became easier and less time consuming.

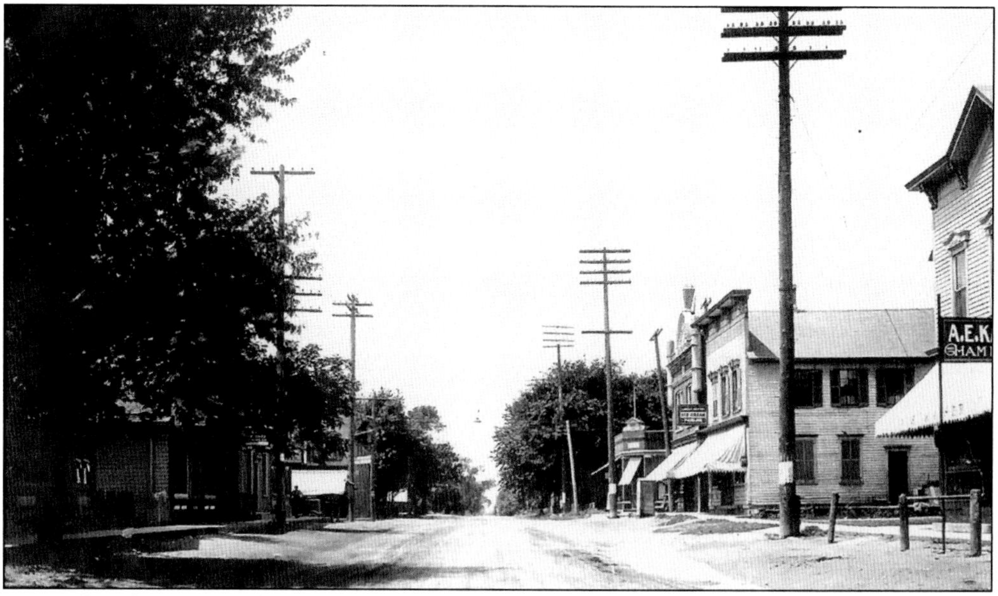

Pictured in this *c.* 1900 photograph is the Dyer business district on Sauk Trail looking west. The white building on the far right was owned by Henry Schulte, one of Dyer's first board members, who let the town use the building for its meetings.

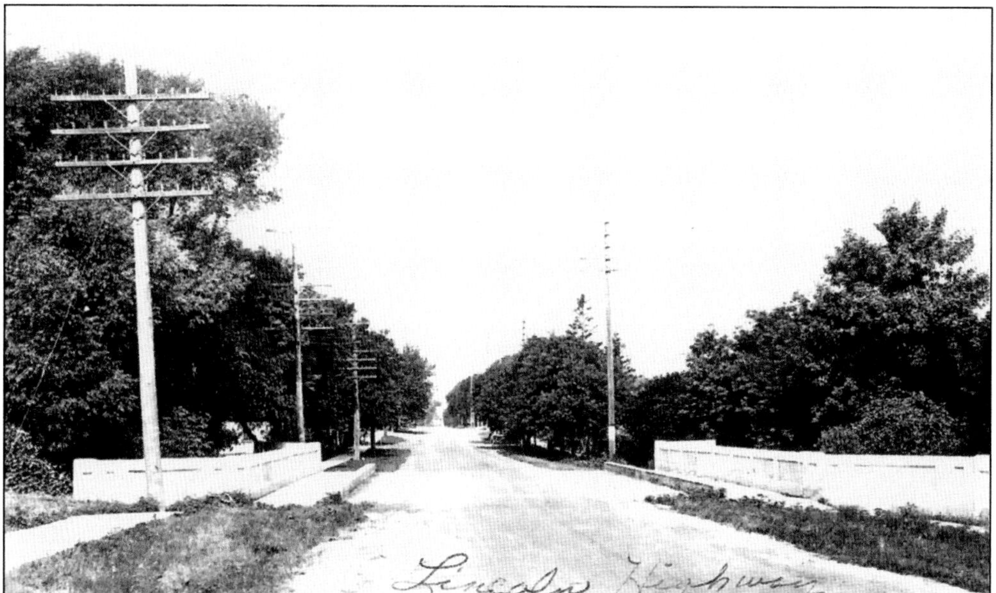

Here is the Sauk Trail crossing Hart's Ditch. This picture was taken in 1900. Along with the swamps being drained away, sand dunes, left behind by Lake Michigan when its shore reached this far south, were excavated and carted away. Only one sand dune remains standing in town today.

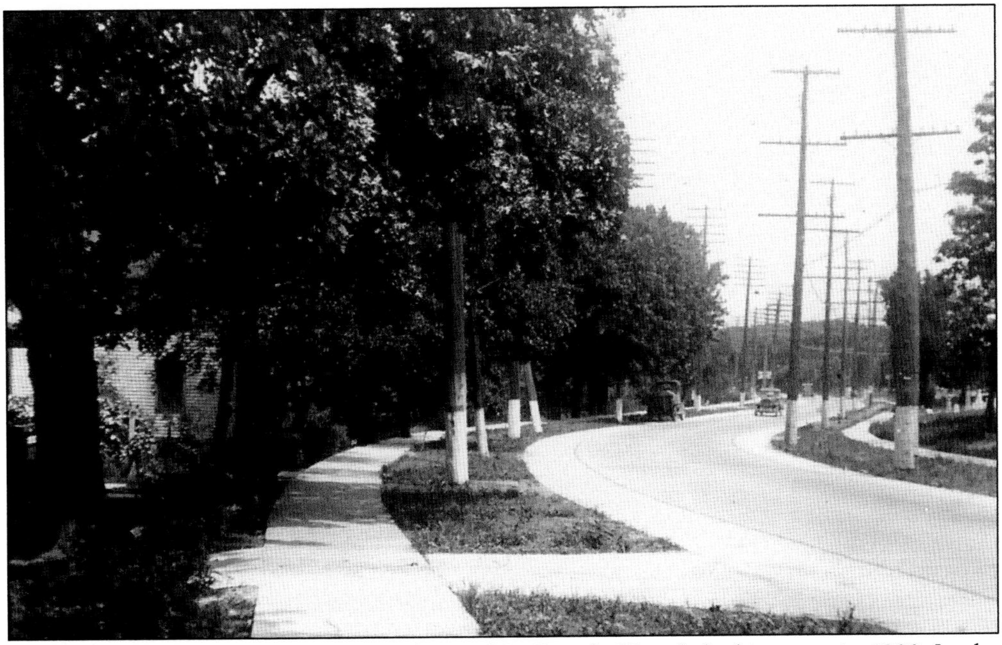

This is a picture of the Sauk Trail in front of St. Joseph Church looking east in 1900. In the distance, rising above the road, a tree-covered sand dune can be seen. To the right is the St. Joseph cemetery.

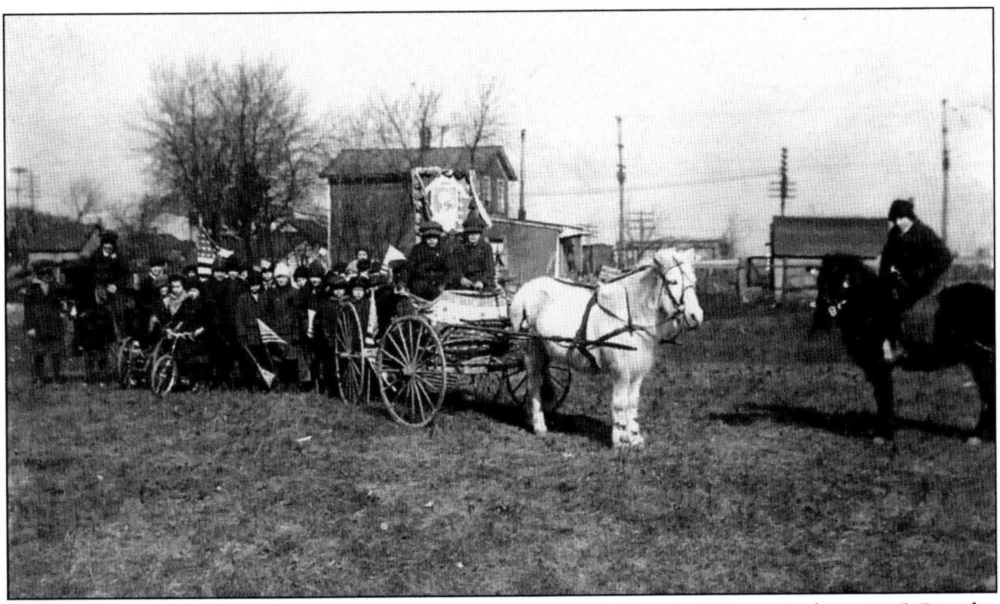

In this photograph, people are preparing for the George Washington Day parade in 1915. Parades often took place along Hart Street or the Lincoln Highway. As in many other towns, parades are a long-standing tradition in Dyer.

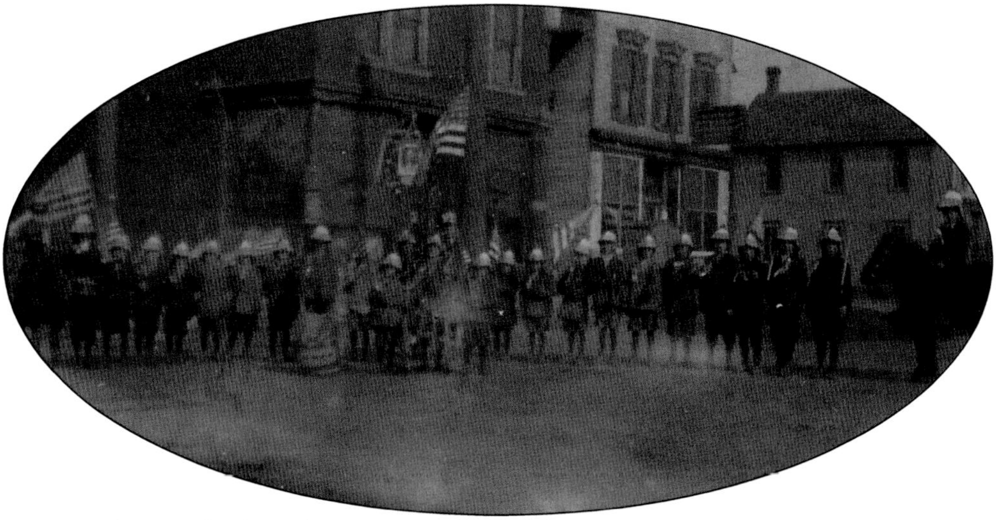

Here is a photograph of marchers participating in the George Washington Day parade in 1915. This picture was taken on the corner of Hart Street and the Sauk Trail. Today, Dyer has a yearly Freedom Festival parade in conjunction with a carnival and fireworks.

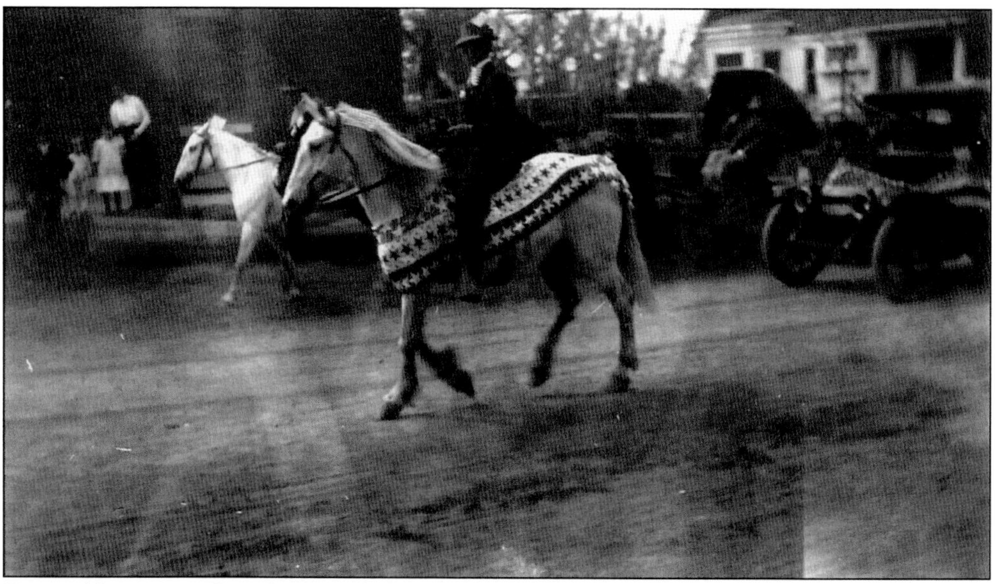

Featured here is another photograph from the George Washington Day parade in 1915. Not long after, the Sauk trail would become part of the Lincoln Highway, where one could travel from New York City to San Francisco in just five days.

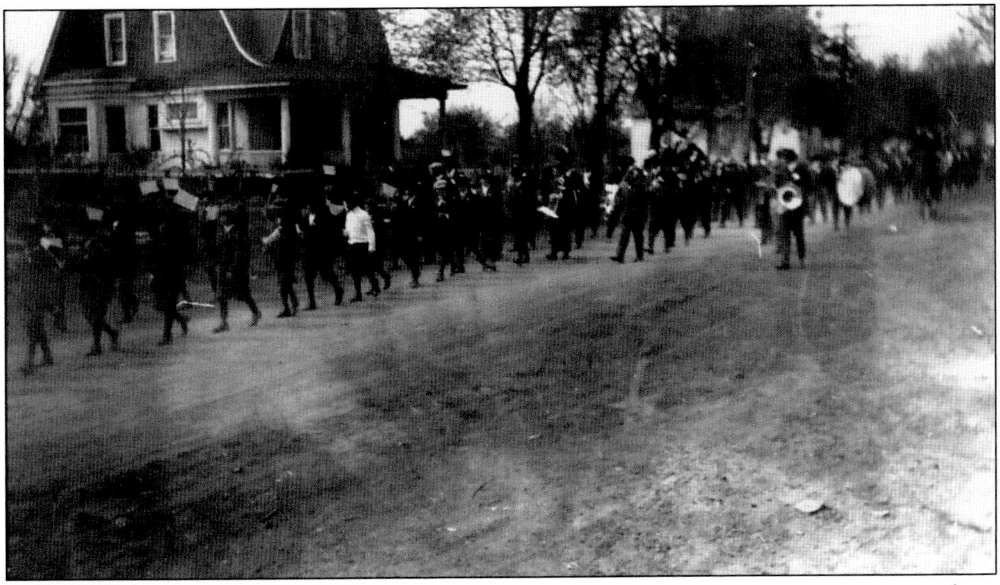

Pictured here is a marching band on the Sauk Trail from the George Washington Day parade in 1915. When the Sauk Trail became part of the Ideal Section, people came from great distances to drive along the lamp-lit road at night with their headlights off.

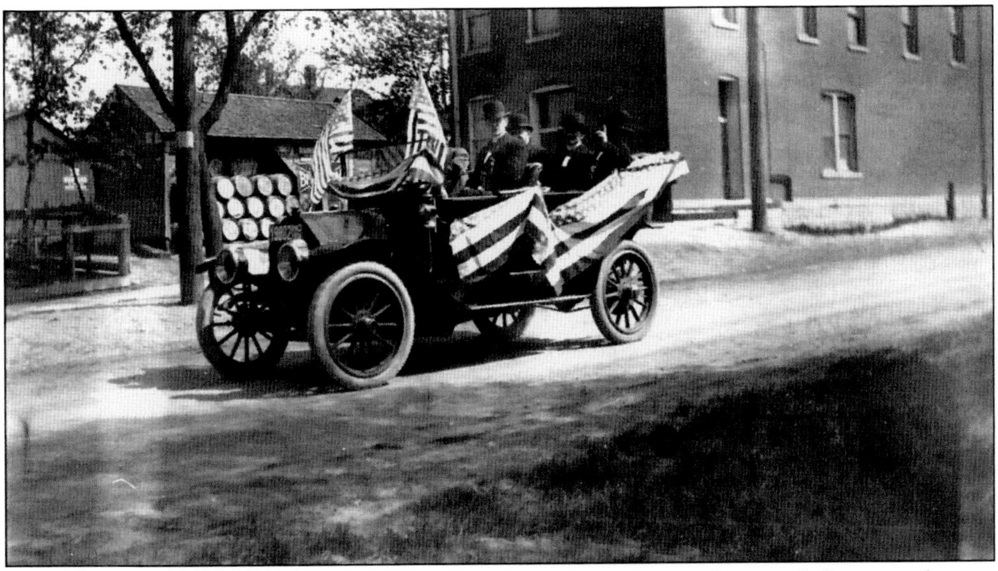

In the George Washington Day parade in 1915, many participants decorated their cars, horses, and wagons for the occasion. Adults and children alike enjoyed participating and bearing witness to such celebrations.

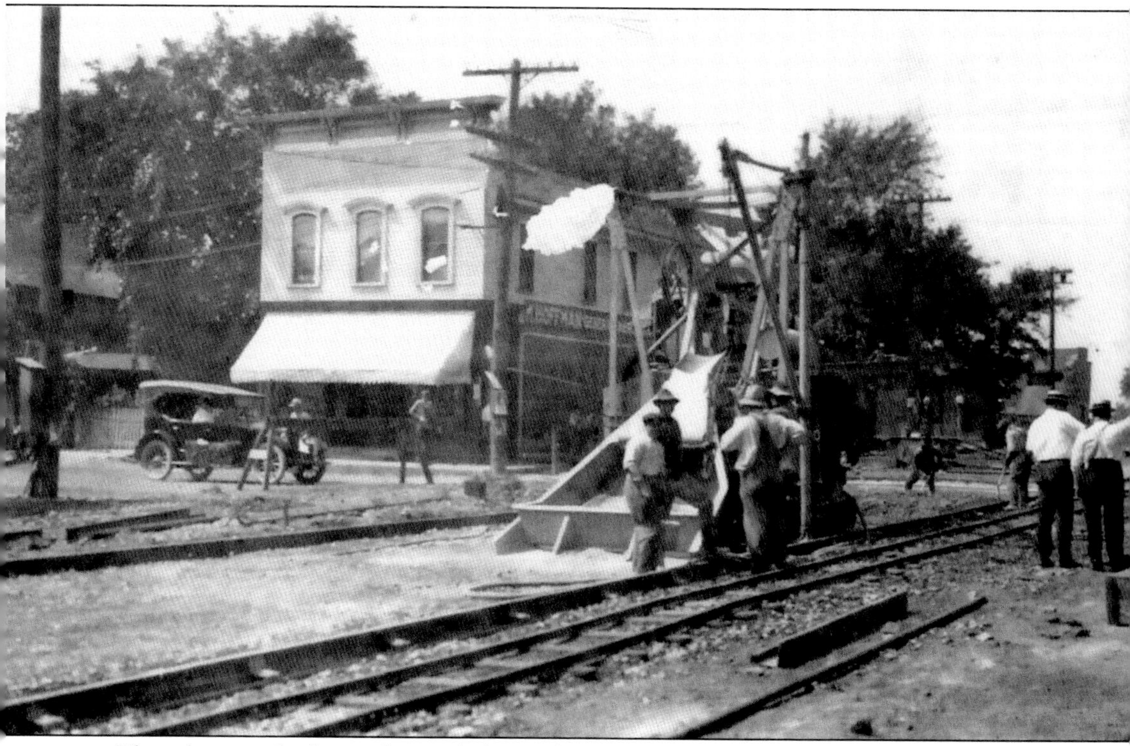

This photograph shows the work being done to complete the Ideal Section of the Lincoln Highway. A rail system was constructed to move equipment and material for the project. The Ideal Section was financed by state, federal, and county governments and the United States Rubber Company. Many local businesses pushed for the construction as well. They were aware that the more traffic the highway brought through the town, the more business revenue would increase. It was a great investment all around. It opened in 1921 with great celebration. The Ideal Section stretched between Dyer and Schererville, and they were the centers of attraction. People came from all around to see the Ideal Section. Never before had they driven on a paved road or driven at night by street light. In the 1950s, many people took to the roads for vacation. Their interest was not the destination but the journey. People were leaving their hometowns to see America. Hotels and motels sprung up along the highways. At one time, Dyer had a campground for the vacationers.

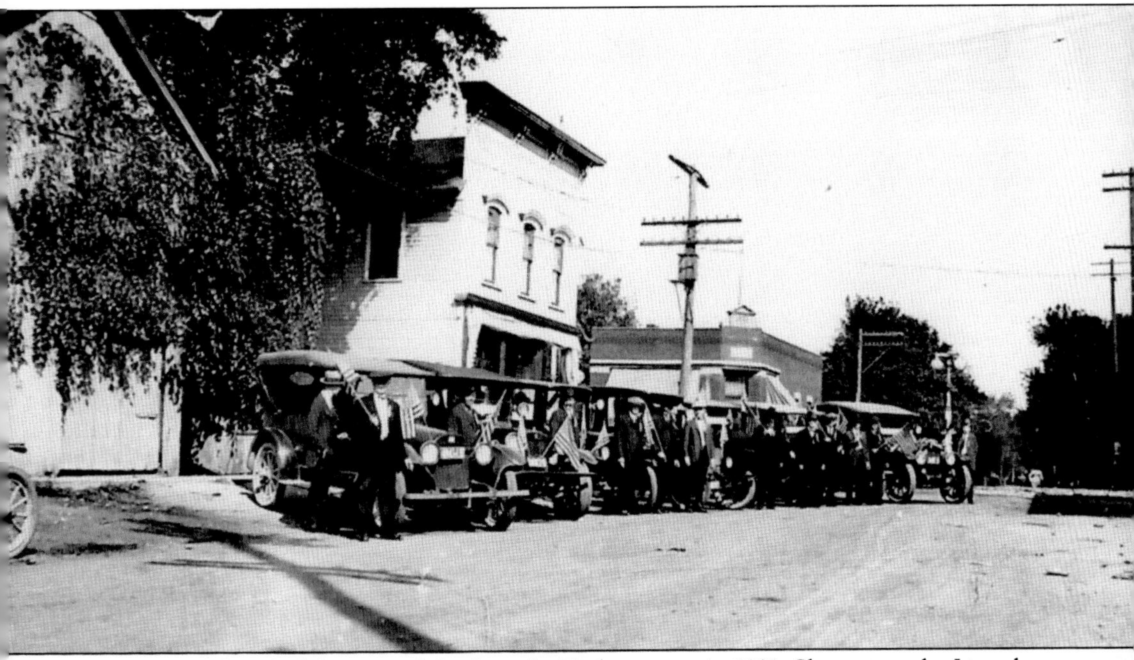

The opening of the Ideal Section of the Lincoln Highway was in 1921. Shown are the Lincoln Highway Association members. From front to back are Nicholas Austgen, Henry Batterman, Michael Fagen, Nicholas Fagen, William N. Gettler, Leo Hoffman, Alois (Grace) Keilman, John L. Keilman, Joseph M. Schaller, William Teutemacher, William Ziesenhenne, and August Stommel. The others remaining in back of the line are unidentified. In 1925, the U.S. Bureau of Public Roads eliminated the names of trails and highways to switch to a numeric system; thus the Lincoln Highway became Route 30. The Lincoln Highway Association dedicated the highway by casting 3,000 markers to be placed along the route. The markers had rectangular heads atop a hexagonal post with the Lincoln Highway logo, bronze medallion, and an arrow pointing out the direction the highway was laid. On September 9, the markers were placed at 9:00 a.m. by Boy Scout troops all over the country. In the end, 2,436 markers were actually placed, laid out by field secretary of the Lincoln Highway Association, Gael Hoag.

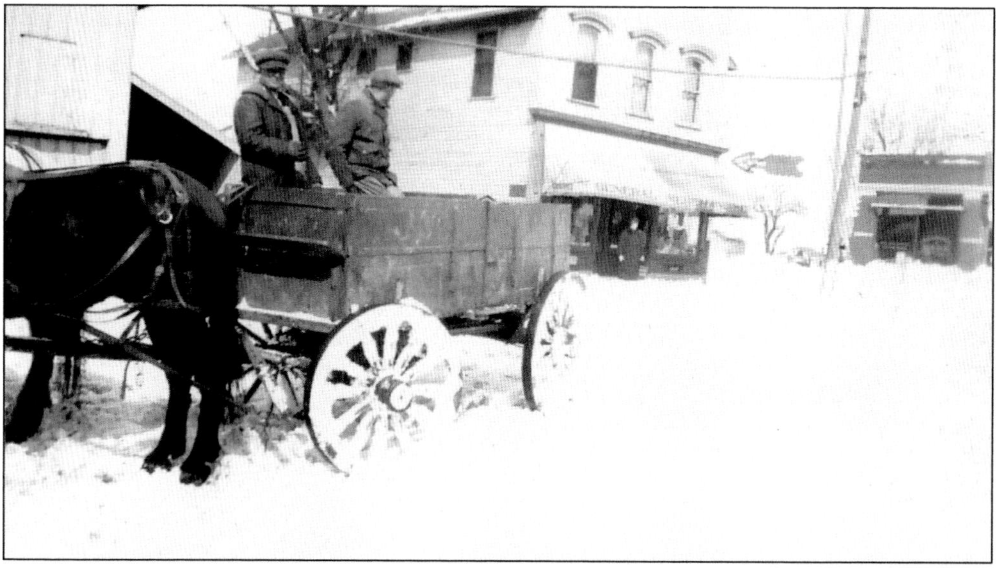

Pictured here is a snowy scene in downtown Dyer in 1923. Snow could make travel very difficult. Due to the open farm fields, large drifts would block the roads. Many times the men in town would assist in clearing the Sauk Trail/Lincoln Highway.

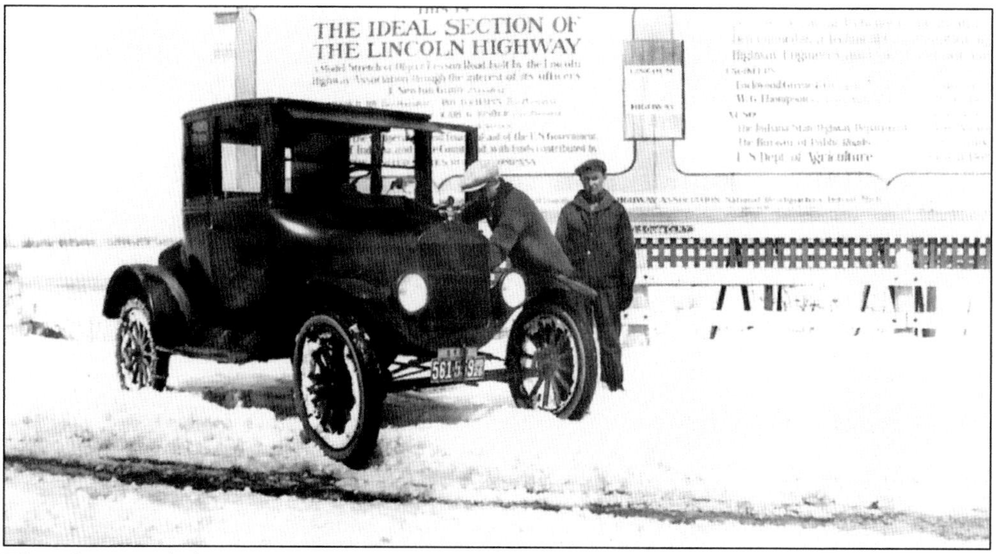

This photograph features travelers in front of an Ideal Section of the Lincoln Highway sign in 1926. The Dyer business owners pushed for the construction of the Ideal Section in hopes of bringing in new business, which it did. Many people came from long distances to see this Ideal Section.

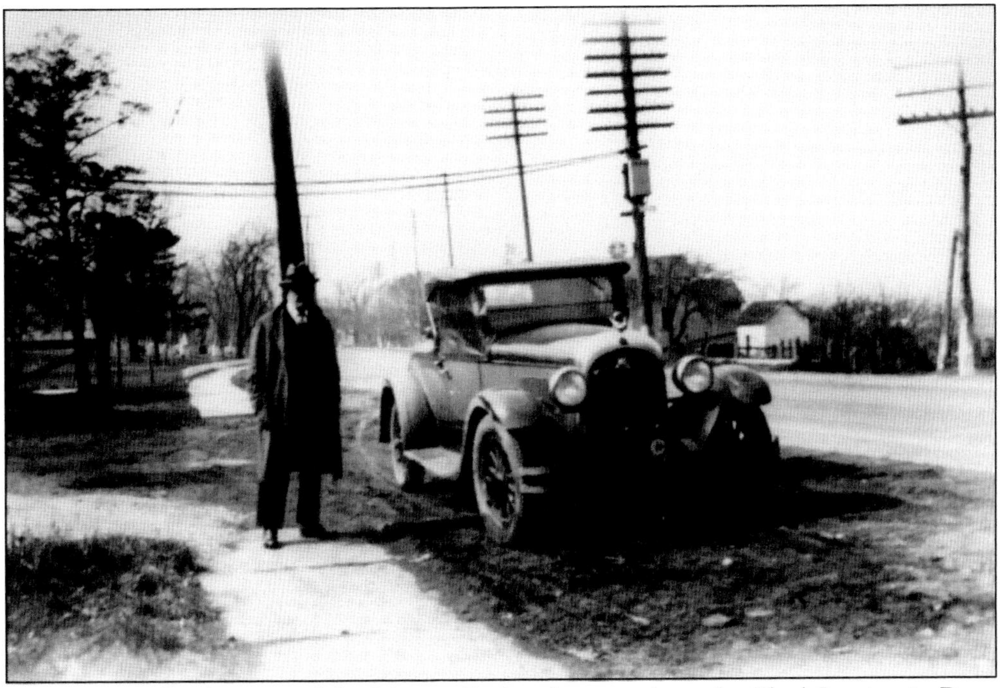

Clarence Depfhuel, agent of the Monon Railroad, poses along the Ideal Section in Dyer, 1928–1929. Not only did the Ideal Section bring new business, it also brought a population boom. People were now able to move out of the cities and commute to work from the outlying rural areas.

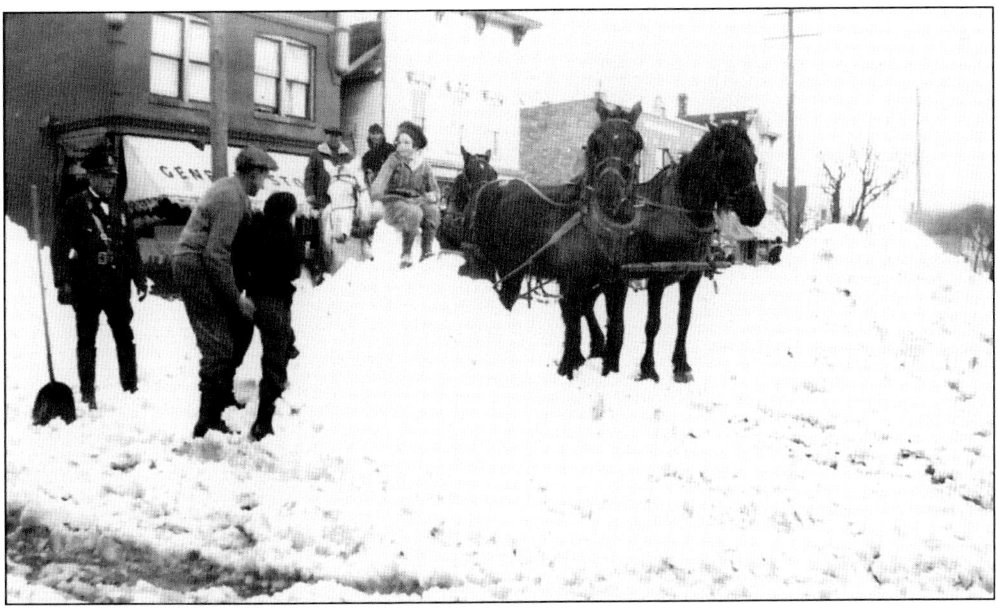

Here is a snow scene from the 1930s. The people in this photograph appear to be having fun, but not all could appreciate the snow. Travelers stranded on the Lincoln Highway were often taken in by friendly Dyer residents until the roads were clear enough to travel.

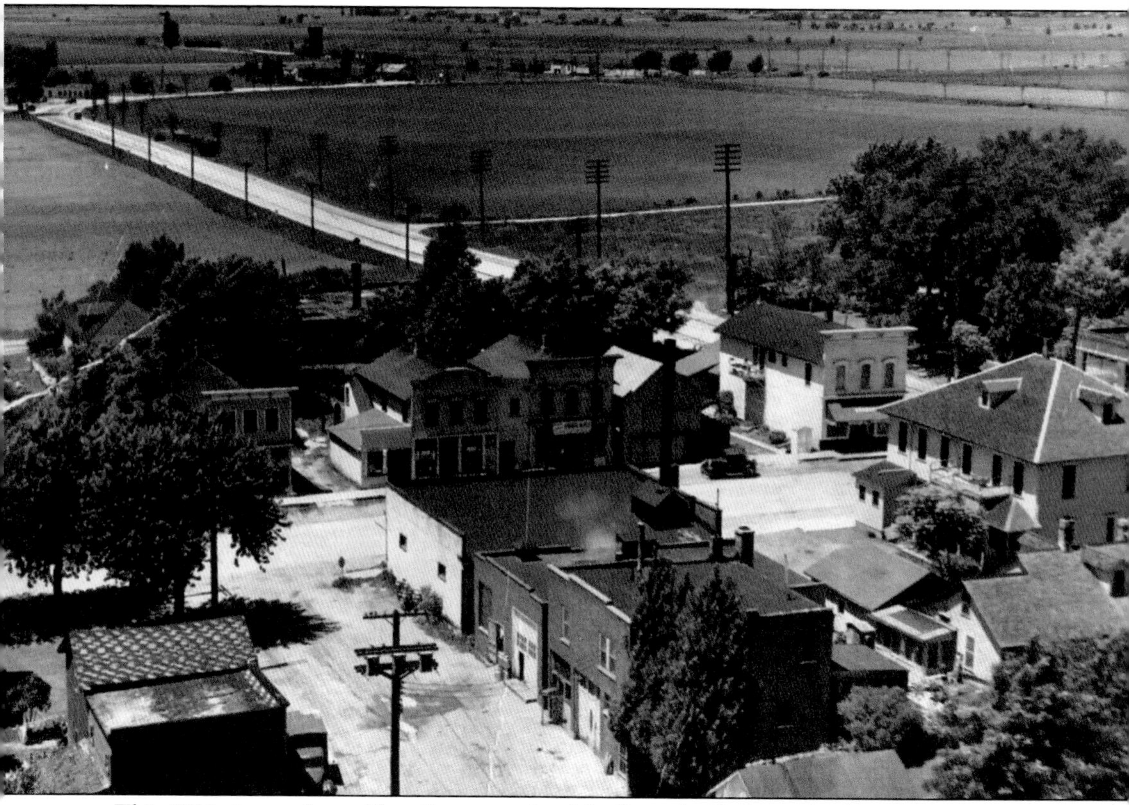

This 1954 picture shows Hart Street south of the Lincoln Highway, looking west. Bottom center is the Dyer Creamery. On the right, going north, is the old State Line Hotel and saloon. Across Hart Street is the Hoffman General Store. Across Lincoln Highway, north of the general store, is the First National Bank of Dyer.

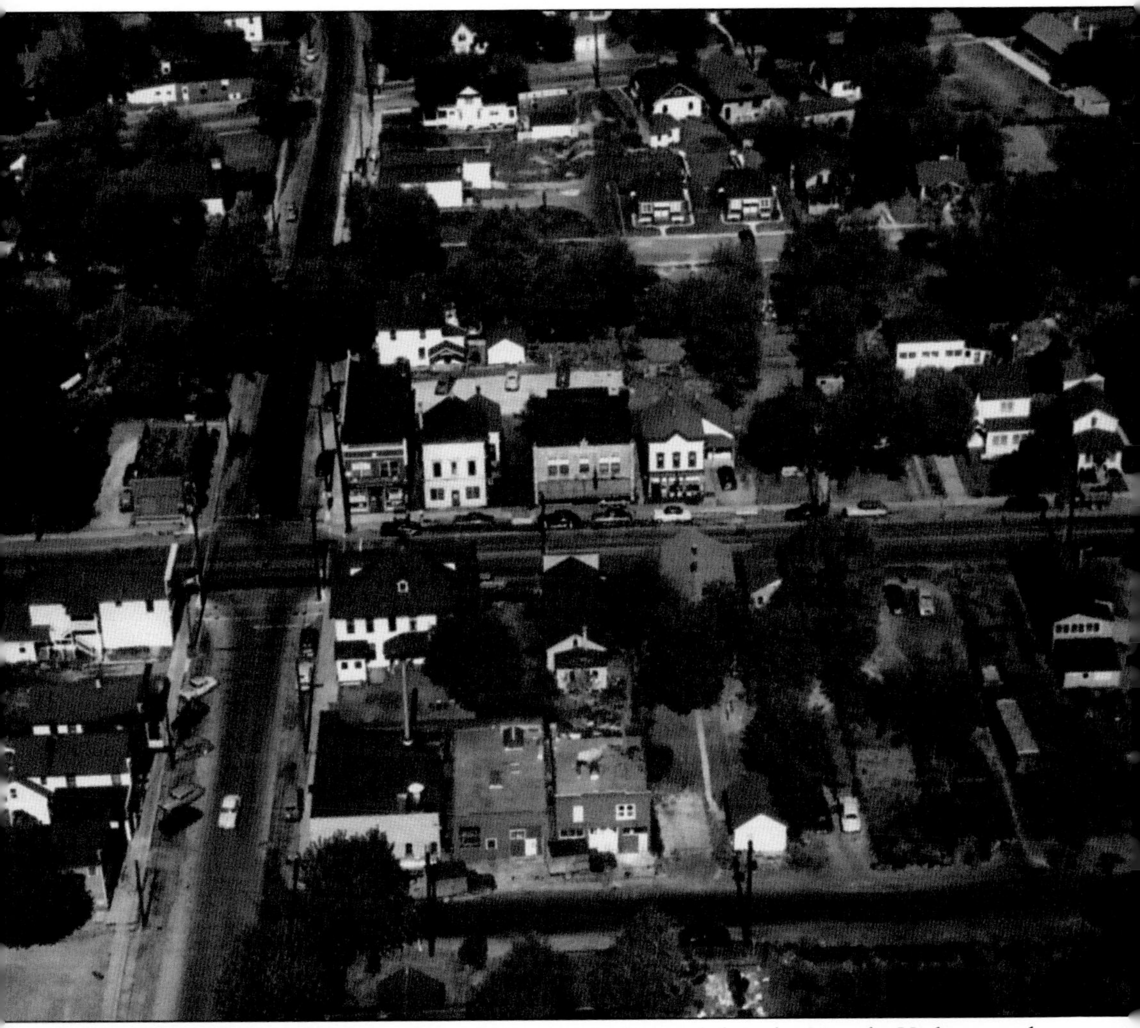

This is a 1954 image of downtown Dyer facing north. Center left is the Lincoln Highway and Hart Street intersection. On the northeast corner is the John L. Keilman building, and three doors to the right is a store once owned by Henry Schulte, who allowed the town board to use it for its first town meetings.

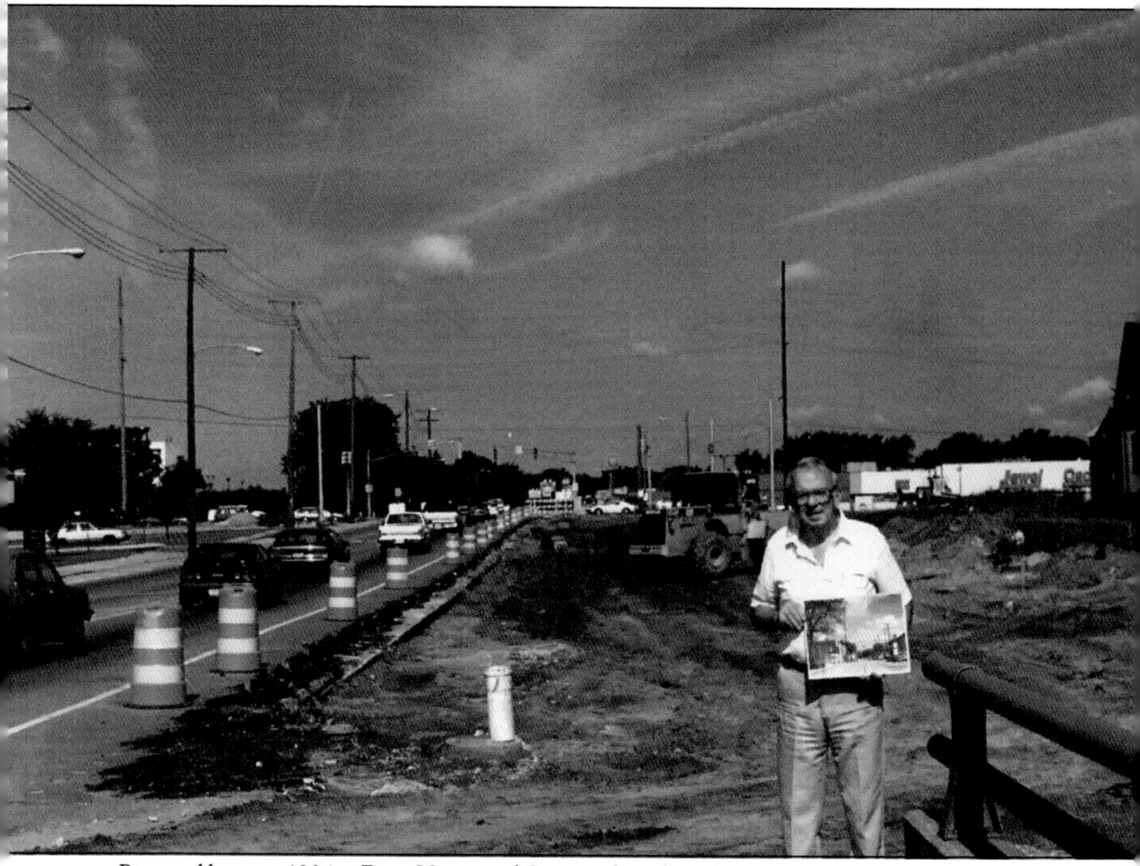

Pictured here in 1994 is Dyer Historical Society founder Glen Eberly standing with a photograph of the old downtown where it once stood. The widening of Route 30, which was once the Sauk Trail, required the removal of the old buildings in the business district. What had once been a footpath followed by the first natives on this continent became a major road connecting New York City to San Francisco. Dyer stood somewhere in-between, located 176 miles from New York and 2,544 miles from San Francisco. Often word got around town of movie stars and other famous individuals passing through the area who stopped at a nearby restaurant. It also changed Dyer by bringing more residents to the area. People were now capable of driving longer distances in shorter amounts of time. They were now commuting to and from Chicago for work. As the population grew, so did the need for larger and wider roads. As Dyer grew, so did the traffic. What put Dyer on the map was now taking its identity of a small farming community away. Farmlands are now subdivisions. The blacksmiths have been replaced by gas stations. General stores have been replaced by convenience stores. Family-owned businesses are now chain stores and restaurants. Dyer is still in the process of rebuilding its downtown and re-creating its image. New construction along the highway is still going on, but Dyer still values its small community feeling. Throughout the year the town holds festivities that bring its residents together. The year 2010 marks Dyer's centennial. Through this celebration, all aspects of Dyer are distinguished, from its beginnings to its changes to its future.

ABOUT THE DYER HISTORICAL SOCIETY

It was in celebration of our nation's bicentennial in 1976 that Dyer's Town Council member Glen Eberly put together a display of antiques and artifacts relating to Dyer. Eberly always had a desire to preserve Dyer's history. In 1984, he, along with other citizens, established the Dyer Historical Society. Today, as in yesteryear, the Dyer Historical Society is very much dedicated to preserving the town's history through obtaining and preserving historic memorabilia in its museum, recording and preserving the life experiences of Dyer's residents, and creating community programs such as presenting guest speakers and hosting field trips. The Dyer Historical Society is always open to new members.

The museum, located on the lower level of Dyer Town Hall, offers artifacts and antiques, video histories, audio interviews, school scrapbooks, albums, newspaper articles, photographs, and genealogical records. The Dyer Historical Society invites everyone to visit its museum whether for pleasure, education, or research. Displays are changed regularly. There is always something new to see and experience in the museum.

www.arcadiapublishing.com

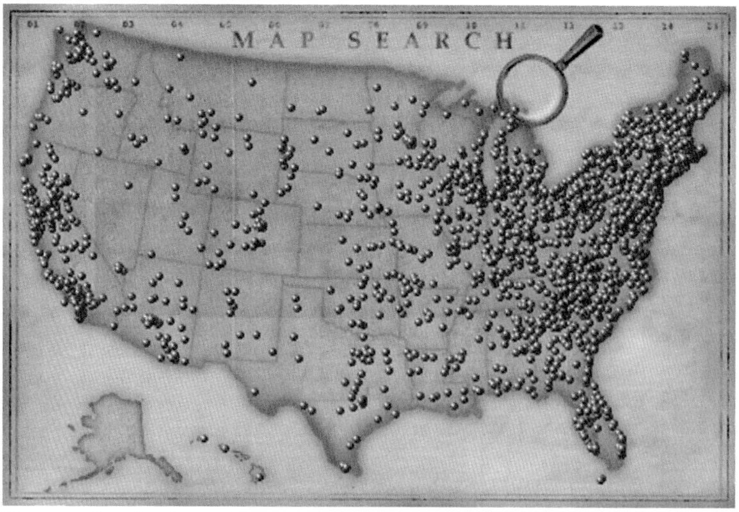

Discover books about the town where you grew up, the cities where your friends and families live, the town where your parents met, or even that retirement spot you've been dreaming about. Our Web site provides history lovers with exclusive deals, advanced notification about new titles, e-mail alerts of author events, and much more.

MADE IN THE USA

Arcadia Publishing, the leading local history publisher in the United States, is committed to making history accessible and meaningful through publishing books that celebrate and preserve the heritage of America's people and places. Consistent with our mission to preserve history on a local level, this book was printed in South Carolina on American-made paper and manufactured entirely in the United States.

This book carries the accredited Forest Stewardship Council (FSC) label and is printed on 100 percent FSC-certified paper. Products carrying the FSC label are independently certified to assure consumers that they come from forests that are managed to meet the social, economic, and ecological needs of present and future generations.

FSC
Mixed Sources
Product group from well-managed forests and other controlled sources

Cert no. SW-COC-001530
www.fsc.org

Find *Your* Place in History.